ANCIENT NEAR EASTERN THEMES IN BIBLICAL THEOLOGY

ANCIENT NEAR EASTERN THEMES IN BIBLICAL THEOLOGY

Jeffrey J. Niehaus

Ancient Near Eastern Themes in Biblical Theology

© 2008 by Jeffrey J. Niehaus

Published by Kregel Publications, a division of Kregel, Inc., P.O. Box 2607, Grand Rapids, MI 49501.

ISBN 978-0-8254-3360-3

Printed in the United States of America

08 09 10 11 12 / 5 4 3 2 1

To my dear son, John,
who is in the world
but not of it

Contents

HELIOPOLIS

Across the courts of Heliopolis
Not far from where palms rattled in the breeze
An orchestra made music to the gods.
Accomplished hands of long instructed slaves
Plucked and strummed and fingered reedy stops:
Lutes, harps, lyres, drums, rattles and tambourines
And flutes and double oboes could be heard
(The very best that Egypt had to offer);
A thousand instruments could sound as one.
Pharaoh had prepared a harp of gold
Inlaid with purest silver for that day
And lapis lazuli and malachite
And it contributed numinous tones
And added to the aura that was there.

Long ago that music graced the air
And celebrated Atum under shade
With pentatonic strange sonorities.
We cannot know, we now can hardly guess
What harmony or what new counterpoint
Or lack of counterpoint informed that music.
We cannot know who the composer was
Or what his stipend was or his reward
As he composed for Pharaoh and the gods
Those harmonies that resonated far
Across the courts of Heliopolis
And penetrated to the royal courts
Of a celestial Anu far above.

Perhaps that music satisfied the gods
Who were all sons of Atum their creator,
And sons of Ptah also; they occupied
Those images on earth that he had formed
Of wood and stone and metal for each one—
Idols that stood in temples of the land
Accessible for human adoration.
A spirit of an incorporeal god
Would come upon an idol made for him
And insinuate himself into it
Because it had been made to look like him.

Perhaps no gods attended to that music,
Or maybe it was only heard by men
And one more god, a God they did not know.
—Jeffrey J. Niehaus

Preface

This book began years ago as a collection of essays on ancient Near Eastern themes presented at regional meetings of the Evangelical Theological Society. Those essays stemmed from research into Assyrian royal tradition, research that opened my eyes to theological concepts and figurative language that resonated with things that I had read in the Bible (e.g., the concept of divine temple abandonment, and the metaphorical portrayal of a monarch as a shepherd). My research into Assyriology, and then into other ancient Near Eastern domains, was first stimulated by a course taught by Dr. Meredith Kline, which I took at Gordon-Conwell Theological Seminary. Dr. Kline's demonstration of the relationship between key concepts in the ancient Near East and the Bible—especially the concept of covenant and the practice of covenant making in the ancient world—awakened my interest in that world and led to many years of further study and discovery. It seems only appropriate, therefore, to mention him in this preface as I give a brief account of the genesis of this book.

Ultimately it is not man who gives insight and understanding but the God who has both of these in abundance and who forms the ground of their possibility in humans. Somehow, in his sovereignty over history and the development of human cultures, he has allowed a variety of parallels to arise between theological concepts and practices in the ancient Near East and their counterparts in the Bible. Scholars and anthropologists have tried for over a hundred years to account for such parallels in different ways. I have written this book with the understanding that there are true and legitimate ways of assessing those parallels—ways that are not my discovery or known uniquely to me—and of presenting those parallels in a way that will be clear and helpful to others, particularly to students who are fairly new to the subject.

One thing that became clear to me as I saw parallels and as I sought to present them clearly is that there is not only a parallelism between certain themes and practices in the Bible and its world, but there is also a structure of thought that is common to them both and that forms the theological backbone of the Bible. I delineate this structure briefly in the first chapter and discuss it more fully in the last chapter of this book, but I reserve full exploration of it for treatment in a forthcoming biblical theology.

The God who is more generous than any of us deserve also has provided generously for me in the completion of this book. I am especially grateful for the help of my wife, Margaret, who read through each chapter carefully, noting typographical errors and points that needed to be made more clearly, and raising helpful and challenging questions. I am also grateful for the help and friendship of Amy Rasmussen Fisch, who did further proofreading and offered helpful suggestions; and I am grateful for the comments of Judith Rasmussen, whose friendship has been a constant encouragement to me. Finally, I am thankful for sabbatical time, granted by the trustees of Gordon-Conwell Theological Seminary, which made the completion of this work possible.

ANCIENT NEAR EASTERN THEMES IN BIBLICAL THEOLOGY

His mother, the goddess Nina, answered the vice-regent: "My shepherd, I will explain your dream to you: the man, whose stature reached up to heaven and down to earth, whose head showed him to be a god . . . at whose feet was a thunderstorm . . . is my brother Ningirsu. He commanded you to build his temple. . . . The second man, who was like a warrior . . . who had a tablet of lapus lazuli in his hand, is Nindub. He gave you the plan of the temple."

—GUDEA, KING OF LAGASH

(SOUTHERN MESOPOTAMIA, 2143–2124 B.C.)

Moses and Aaron, Nadab and Abihu, and the seventy elders of Israel went up and saw the God of Israel. Under his feet was something like a pavement made of sapphire, clear as the sky itself. . . . [Yahweh] called to Moses from within the cloud. . . . "Have them make a sanctuary for me, and I will dwell among them. Make this tabernacle and all its furnishings exactly like the pattern I will show you."

(EXOD. 24:9–10, 16; 25:8–9)

I

Approaching Biblical Parallels
in the Ancient Near East

The gods of Gudea, king of Lagash, commanded him to build a temple according to a particular pattern. His account dates more than seven hundred years before God commanded Moses to build a sanctuary with a plan to follow. The contrast between the polytheism of the one account and the monotheism of the other does not obscure the parallelism between them.

This parallel is one of many that we will explore in the following chapters. In almost two hundred years of patient archaeological research, many such parallels between the Old Testament and the ancient Near East have come to light. Archaeology has in fact altered the whole climate of Old Testament studies. No study of biblical material can now be complete without some understanding of its ancient background.[1] Comparative studies have

---

1. Unfortunately, this does not mean that all scholars give the ancient world its due. But they fail to do so at their own risk. For a good example of a recent work that ignores the ancient Near East—in particular the second millennium international treaty form—with disastrous results, see Polzin, *Moses and the Deuteronomist*. Polzin posits alternating positive and negative voices in Deuteronomy (with an increasing emphasis on the negative) and attributes this to a Deuteronomist who is preparing his readers to accept his later negative theological evaluation of Israel in the historical books of the Old Testament. The increase in negativity in Deuteronomy, however, is actually explained by the fact that the book includes a large body of curses at the end for those who would break God's covenant; and the presence of the curses is

become virtually mandatory for a proper understanding of the Old Testament. But a foundational question to comparative study is this: What is the proper comparative method that will assure true results?

Truth

Most scholarly endeavor assumes that truth exists, and the present work is no exception. It is, I hope, founded on truth, and more precisely, on biblical truth, because God's revelation of himself in the Bible is the standard of truth par excellence. We ought to affirm at the outset, however, that truth also exists in myth, only figuratively. Yet no mythology can ultimately satisfy our desire for truth. Only God can do that. As Augustine once remarked, "You [God] have made us for yourself, and our heart is unquiet until it rests in you." For the same reason, what we have said about myth also applies to science. Any scientific *Weltanschauung* is actually poetic because it is a human fabrication, a *poema* (a thing made).[2] Because only God can satisfy ultimately, natural science as a human creation cannot. As Frazer shrewdly observed,

> In the last analysis magic, religion, and science are nothing but theories of thought; and as science has supplanted its predecessors, so it may hereafter be itself superseded by some more perfect hypothesis, perhaps by some totally different way of looking at the phenomena—of registering the shadows on the screen—of which we in this generation can form no idea.[3]

---

explained by the fact that Deuteronomy follows the form of a second millennium Hittite suzerain-vassal treaty, which ends with curses for covenant breaking. Likewise, the positive "voice" at the beginning is actually a historical prologue, as in the Hittite treaties. Such a prologue tells the good things the suzerain (in Deuteronomy, God) has done for the vassal (in Deuteronomy, Israel). Such positive and negative "voices" thus can be found in any Hittite treaty. They are hardly evidence of Deuteronomistic manipulation. For the treaty form, see Kitchen, *Ancient Orient and Old Testament*, 90–102; and idem, *The Bible in Its World*, 79–85.

2. The English word *poem* derives from the Greek *poema*, "anything made or done . . . a poetical work, poem" (Liddell and Scott, *A Greek-English Lexicon*, 5–68).

3. Frazer, *The Golden Bough*, part 7: *Balder the Beautiful*, 1:306. I do not agree that science has supplanted religion or ever can. I do agree with Frazer's inclusion of "religion" in this triad, but only in the sense that "religion" is understood as a human attempt to understand and serve the divine. In contradistinction, biblical Christianity is God's actual revelation to humans, not human guesses about him. I freely admit, of course, that Frazer did not intend the term *religion* to exclude Christianity.

Only God's way of "looking at the phenomena" is objectively true and perfect. But science does aim to understand truth, insofar as it seeks to understand God's created order.

Science has ways of establishing truth. One is the experimental method, which is generally taught in schools. Another is the comparative method, which descends from Aristotle. By this approach, the unknown is compared with the known. If parallels are found, the unknown can be understood and classified accordingly. Sir James George Frazer employed this method of comparison and classification in his major work *The Golden Bough*.[4] The method has become a component of modern anthropology and also of biblical studies today.

Two uses of the comparative method are possible in biblical studies: one may use it to classify biblical material into categories of myth and legend, or one may use it to understand pagan myths and legends according to biblical truth. The first approach cannot be correct, according to the attitude of the New Testament to the Old Testament. The New Testament actors and writers affirm the historicity of such "legendary" figures as Adam and Eve, Abraham, and Moses; Jesus affirms that Jonah spent three days in the belly of a great fish, and so on. A use of the comparative method that places biblical narratives among the mythological or legendary donations of the world is flawed, because it assumes that biblical data are capable of such classification. It ignores (or rejects) the Bible's claims about its own historicity. Once we accept those claims, however, the same comparative method can be turned around and produce valuable results. We can then understand legends and myths by comparison with what God and people actually did according to the biblical accounts.

Those who choose the first approach mentioned above (that is, those who use a comparative method to classify biblical material as myth and legend) fall largely into two categories. Some take a universal approach. They posit some universal aspect of human nature to account for parallel mythologies the world over. Frazer, Freud, and Jung fall into this category. Others compare pagan and biblical data, and conclude that the latter are derived from the former via cultural influence. Gunkel, Delitzsch, and others fall into this category.

---

4.   Sir James George Frazer, *The Golden Bough*, which appeared in three editions: 1890, 1900, and 1910. See also his subsequent *Folk-lore in the Old Testament*.

We wish to understand pagan data from a biblical perspective, because we believe that such a perspective offers a true hermeneutic. Before we do so, however, it is important to consider the approaches just mentioned.

The Universal Approach

Sir James George Frazer

I have spoken of a scientific, comparative method, and Mr. Casaubon, George Eliot's fictional character, employed just such a method. He sought a hermeneutic by which he could understand and categorize all mythology, a task that "had been attempted before, but not with that thoroughness, justice of comparison, and effectiveness of arrangement at which Mr. Casaubon aimed."[5] By 1910, Sir James George Frazer appeared to have accomplished Casaubon's ambition: to discover such a key and to compare and categorize myths accordingly. George Eliot's character had hoped to condense his "voluminous still-accumulating results . . . and bring them . . . to fit a little shelf."[6] Now Frazer's thirteen-volume study, *The Golden Bough*, appeared to do just that. It was global in scope, a monumental work that has influenced generations of anthropologists and remains a classic in its field.

Frazer modestly concluded: "My contribution to the history of the human mind consists of little more than a rough and purely provisional classification of facts gathered almost entirely from printed sources."[7] Today most students of the ancient world would agree with that evaluation. Still, Frazer believed he had made some contribution to the "history of the human mind" (by which he meant the "gradual evolution of human thought from savagery to civilization").[8] Frazer detected a pattern in the evolution of human thought: from belief in magic through belief in religion to belief in science. He thought the pattern was universal.

> If then we consider, on the one hand, the essential similarity of man's chief wants everywhere and at all times, and on the other hand, the wide difference between the means he has adopted to satisfy them in different ages, we shall perhaps be disposed to conclude that the movement of

---

5. Eliot, *Middlemarch*, 26.
6. Ibid., 26.
7. Frazer, *Balder the Beautiful*, 1:vi.
8. Ibid.

the higher thought, so far as we can trace it, has on the whole been from magic through religion to science.[9]

According to Frazer, man's foremost concern has always been to satisfy his wants, and that has preoccupied his "higher thought." Magic, religion, and science are the means man has evolved to satisfy those wants: first magic, which seemed to give him control over nature; then religion, which projected gods in man's image who might be appeased and enlisted to control or affect nature or events on man's behalf; and finally science, which appeared "to revert in a measure to the older standpoint of magic by postulating explicitly what in magic had only been implicitly assumed, to wit, an inflexible regularity in the order of natural events, which if carefully observed, enables us to foresee their course with certainty and to act accordingly."[10]

The evolution of human worldviews from magic through religion to science was a universal process. And because it was rooted in human nature and human needs, it was also an inevitable process. For Frazer, the ideas that characterize the early stages of this evolution are parallel. They are so, not because of any mutual influence of cultures, but because of a universality in the human constitution.

> If there is one general conclusion which seems to emerge from the mass of particulars, I venture to think that it is the essential similarity in the working of the less developed human mind among all races, which corresponds to the essential similarity in their bodily frame revealed by comparative anatomy.[11]

That is to say, the magical and mythological thought of different cultures may be expected to develop along parallel structural lines simply because of a universal "similarity in the working of the less developed human mind" worldwide. As Frankfort notes, Frazer applied this similarity "not only to the processes of mythopoeic thought but to its concrete manifestations in beliefs and institutions."[12] In other words, such institutions as "divine

---

9.   Ibid., 2:304.
10. Ibid., 2:305.
11. Ibid., 1:vi.
12. Frankfort, *Problem of Similarity*, 5.

kingship," the "scapegoat," and the "dying god"—all key figures in the
Frazerian analysis—could be found in all cultures because they arose from
universal mythopoeic processes of the primitive mind.[13] Those processes,
again, sought to deal with the problem presented to primitive human beings
by their wants.

Frazer, Freud, and Jung

It is important to recall at this point that Frazer's work arose out of a
climate of evolutionary thought that had not begun with Darwin but had
received a major impetus from his work. Frazer proposed in effect a phy-
logenesis of culture, which found a ready acceptance because it suited the
contemporary spirit.[14]

Moreover, as Frankfort notes, Frazer's thought also bore a "family re-
semblance" to that of Freud.

> Freud was born two years after Frazer. And if I stress the contemporaneity
> of these two men who have influenced Western thought so profoundly, it
> is because their discoveries show a certain family likeness. Frazer saw the
> whole host conjured up in *The Golden Bough* as sprung from a universal
> preoccupation with food and fertility; Freud found an equally univer-
> sal one in the *libido*, the sexual appetite. . . . Both Freud and Frazer re-
> duced the complexities of civilization to something essentially natural,
> simple—and, we may add, trivial.[15]

Frazer and Freud each found a supposed basis for "the complexities of
civilization" in some universal aspect of human nature.

---

13. Cf. Frazer, *Folk-lore in the Old Testament*, 1:5, where he compares the account of the
creation of man from the dust (Gen. 2) with other such accounts universally: "It offers . . . points of comparison with the childlike stories by which men in many ages
and countries have sought to explain the great mystery of the beginning of life on
earth." Frazer recounts many such stories, some of which arose in various cultures
as a result of missionary or at least European influence, but others of which offer
many parallels yet arose spontaneously in separate cultures.

14. Frankfort, *Problem of Similarity*. "It was Frazer's generation which claimed to discover 'the dying god' behind the figure of Christ, a totemic feast behind the Last
Supper, [and] a corn demon behind Oedipus" (5).

15. Ibid., 19.

Carl Jung, an early advocate of Freud, did likewise.[16] Jung, however, posited a universal "collective unconscious" for humanity, out of which parallel mythologies arose.

> The collective unconscious seems to be the storehouse of latent memory traces inherited from man's ancestral past, a past that includes not only the racial history of man as a separate species but his prehuman or animal ancestry as well. The collective unconscious is the psychic residue of man's evolutionary development, a residue that accumulates as a consequence of repeated experiences over many generations. It is almost detached from anything personal in the life of an individual and it is seemingly universal. All human beings have more or less the same collective unconscious. Jung attributes the universality of the collective unconscious to the similarity of the structure of the brain in all races of men, and this similarity in turn is due to a common evolution.[17]

Frazer speculated that parallels of religious thought were rooted in evolution, specifically in "the essential similarity in the working of the less developed human mind among all races, which corresponds to the essential similarity in their bodily frame revealed by comparative anatomy." Jung postulated a source of mythopoeic thought (a collective unconscious) rooted in "the similarity of the structure of the brain in all races of men . . . due to a common evolution." A "family likeness" is apparent here also, against a background of evolutionary thought.

For Jung, myths and even behavior patterns constitute the collective unconscious:

> The structural components of the collective unconscious are called by various names: *archetypes . . . mythological images,* and *behavior patterns.* . . . There are presumed to be numerous archetypes in the collective unconscious. Some of the ones that have been identified are archetypes of birth, rebirth, death, magic, unity, the hero, the child, God, the demon, the old wise man, the earth mother.[18]

---

16. For Freud and Jung, see Hall and Lindzey, *Theories of Personality,* 29–113.
17. Ibid., 80.
18. Ibid., 82–83.

The archetypes, latent in the unconscious, condition the way humans respond to or understand the world. Because the archetypes are universal, mythopoeic parallels have occurred the world over.

Parallels between the results of scholars (or scientists) who are working independently sometimes illustrate their debt to culture. Frazer, Freud, and Jung were heirs to a background of evolutionary speculation. They gave naturalistic accounts of human nature and culture at a time when natural sciences enjoyed an increasing influence on Western culture. A steady erosion of Christianity's hold upon culture from the Enlightenment onward also helped prepare the ground for such developments. When the Bible was removed as a hermeneutical key for culture and human nature, a substitute was naturally wanted. But the substitute had to provide a universal account for those things in order to prove satisfactory, and that is just what evolution, anthropology, and psychoanalytic theory, taken separately or together, sought to do.

Our goal is not to critique the development of Western culture. Rather, we want to understand the parallels between ancient Near Eastern thought and biblical thought. What we have called a universal approach constitutes one way of accounting for such parallels. Frazer, Freud, and Jung each, in his own way, took a universal approach. However, as a folklorist who also wrote about the Old Testament, Frazer is the most important practitioner of such an approach for our purposes.

One more word about cultural backgrounds is necessary at this point. Frazer's study of folklore must be seen against another element of his own cultural background, in particular the fascination with folklore that increased through the late eighteenth and into the nineteenth century. An interest in oriental tales, and especially medieval European legends and sagas, played a large role in the Romantic Movement that colored European culture even into the twentieth century. Indeed, even Hitler was in some senses a romantic figure, appealing to medieval ideals and to romantic nationalism with such concepts as the *Volk* (ethnic national "Folk") and "*Blut und Boden*" ("Blood and Land").[19]

Germany was the source of much of this fascination. The German philosopher Herder gave a major impetus to scholarly and popular interest in

---

19. See Mosse, *Crisis of German Ideology*. More recently, Köhler, *Wagner's Hitler*, documents the ways in which Hitler developed and fulfilled the romantic ideals and anti-Semitic ideology of the great German composer.

the folk heritage of German and other peoples, as did the brothers Grimm with their collections of fairy tales and stories from the Middle Ages and later. Against such a background, especially in Germany, Old Testament scholarship began to show an interest in folkloristic categories. The name of Hermann Gunkel stands out in this regard.

Gunkel compared the mythologies of Mesopotamian, Egyptian, and Hittite religion to determine to what extent the Hebrew religion had been influenced by the cultures of the ancient Near East. On the basis of such folkloristic comparisons, he concluded that Genesis was itself basically folklore (legends and sagas). Moreover, he argued that accounts of major significance in Genesis, such as the Creation and Flood accounts, were derived from Babylonian sources.[20]

Gunkel was not alone in his approach, and he has had many followers. The assumption that some Old Testament accounts were borrowed from other, pagan sources (especially Babylonian) is normal among Old Testament scholars today.

The Derivative Approach

Babylonian Scholars: Gunkel, Delitzsch, and Company

For over one hundred years, Babylon has been a major source for those who want to explore ancient parallels to the Old Testament. Two major parts of Genesis, the Creation account of Genesis 1:1–2:3 and the Flood account of Genesis 7–9, have parallel Babylonian poetical narratives: the *Enuma Elish* for the Creation, and the *Gilgamesh Epic* for the Flood. Naturally the discovery of such parallels raised important questions regarding provenance. It was possible to imagine three ways of explaining the parallels: the Babylonian accounts depended on the Hebrew; the Hebrew depended on the Babylonian; or both the Babylonian and the Hebrew derived from a common source.

The first view, that the Babylonian accounts depend on the Hebrew, is hardly tenable. The Babylonian accounts are too old for this to be possible. Hebrew did not even exist as a language when the Babylonian poems were inscribed in stone. Heidel notes the unlikelihood of this proposal for the Creation account, since the Babylonian *Enuma Elish* dates from between

---

20. See Harrison, *Introduction to the Old Testament*, 35ff., for a good introductory discussion of Gunkel's work.

1894 and 1595 B.C., and "certain strands of this myth undoubtedly go back far into Sumerian times."[21] Likewise, "We shall probably be safe in placing the date of the earliest written Babylonian account of the flood at the end of the third or the very beginning of the second millennium B.C."[22] Such early dates preclude the notion that the Babylonian versions depend upon the Hebrew accounts.

For over a century most scholars have argued or assumed that the age of the Babylonian accounts must mean the biblical narratives are dependent on the Babylonian (with theological modifications appropriate to the biblical authors' points of view). Those who argue this position highlight the similarities between the accounts as part of the argument for dependence. But after a careful study of the two, Alexander Heidel has concluded that "no incontrovertible evidence can for the present be produced" in favor of biblical dependence on the Babylonian materials.[23] His conclusion regarding the Flood accounts is similar.[24] From the standpoint of divine providence, it is true that God could have provided Babylonian sources for the biblical Creation and Flood narratives. But there is a better way of accounting for the parallels.

Professor Ira M. Price of the University of Chicago traced the parallel Creation accounts to "a time when the human race occupied a common home and held a common faith."[25] Heidel also notes that such an explana-

21. Heidel, *Babylonian Genesis*, 131.

22. Heidel, *Gilgamesh Epic*, 261. Heidel adds, "However, since priority of publication does not necessarily imply priority of existence, the argument derived from the age of the Babylonian account to disprove the originality of the Hebrew cannot be regarded as conclusive; the deluge version which we now call the Hebrew account of the flood may well have existed in some form or other many centuries before it assumed its present form" (261). Note a similar observation regarding the creation narratives in Heidel, *Babylonian Genesis*, 130.

23. Heidel, *Babylonian Genesis*, 139. He adds, "Whatever the true facts of the case may be, whether the biblical account is or is not dependent on the Babylonian material, there is no reason . . . why anyone should be disturbed in his mind and lose his reverence for the opening chapter of the Bible." This is so because, "If certain features of the biblical account *were* derived from the Babylonian, this was done in conformity with the will of Him who according to Heb. 1:1 revealed Himself 'in divers manners.'" Moreover, the "exalted conceptions in the biblical account of creation give it a depth and dignity unparalleled in any cosmogony known to us from Babylonia or Assyria" (140). See his discussion on pages 82–140.

24. "Arguments . . . that the biblical account [of the flood] rests on Babylonian material are quite indecisive" (Heidel, *Gilgamesh Epic*, 267).

25. Price, *Monuments and the Old Testament*, 129.

tion for the different Flood accounts is "a very distinct possibility."[26] This explanation accords perfectly well with the ancient Near Eastern data. It also fits the biblical portrayal of human degradation after the Fall, as portrayed by the apostle Paul (Rom. 1:21–23). Those who forgot God and "exchanged" his "glory . . . for images made to look like mortal man and birds and animals and reptiles" also "exchanged" the truth about Creation and the Flood for polytheistic accounts that suited a fallen understanding. One may object that such a viewpoint is theologically informed, but in fact all points of view are theologically informed or imply a theology. Even science as we know it is no exception. Whitehead has demonstrated how the rise of modern science has depended upon faith in the revealed character of God, although many scientists would now disavow such a faith for themselves.[27] Moreover, no point of view exists without implying God, or at least the question of his existence. Even atheism is predicated on a denial of the same, and agnosticism concludes that God's existence is unknown or unknowable.

The evidence indicates that the Old Testament Creation and Flood accounts did not derive from Babylon. But not all scholars would agree with this statement.

Hermann Gunkel

The study of the Old Testament in light of parallels from the ancient Near East (and especially Babylon) took a giant step with the work of Hermann Gunkel. Gunkel's *Schöpfung und Chaos in Urzeit und Endzeit* appeared in 1895. It is a major effort to understand the biblical Creation account as a fabrication based upon the Babylonian creation myth.[28] Gunkel states that "this narrative [i.e., Genesis 1] is only the Jewish elaboration of far older

---

26. Heidel, *Gilgamesh Epic*, 267.

27. Whitehead, *Science and the Modern World*, 18. Cf. the brief discussion in Niehaus, *God at Sinai*, 44–45.

28. Gunkel, *Schöpfung und Chaos in Urzeit und Endzeit*. I use the term "fabrication" in a neutral sense. Gunkel makes this remarkable statement: "So I present this work to the public. Whatever is error therein, may the wind drive it away. If, however, there is anything true in it, so may it not be entirely unworthy, to assist in its modest way to expedite recognition of God's ways, and thereby to help build his kingdom." The German text reads: "So übergebe ich dies Werk der Öffentlichkeit. Was darin Irrtum ist, möge der Wind verwehen. Ist aber darin etwas Wahres, so möge es nicht ganz unwert sein, an seinem bescheidenen Teile mitzuhelfen, die Erkenntnis der Wege Gottes zu fördern und dadurch an seinem Reiche zu bauen" (x).

material, which must have been originally much more mythological."[29] He adds, "This conjecture is now completely confirmed by a comparison of Genesis 1 with the Babylonian myth."[30]

Gunkel's evidence for a Babylonian origin of the Genesis 1 account includes the virtual equivalence of the Hebrew word *tehôm* ("the deep," Gen. 1:2), with Babylonian *Tiamat* (the sea-dragon goddess in *Enuma Elish*); and the creative word of God paralleling the creative word of Marduk in the Babylonian poem, among others.[31] We list these items, not to demonstrate all the problems with Gunkel's use of the data, but to give some important examples.[32] His major methodological error is an erroneous equation of the Old Testament and Babylonian data, clearly a problem with the parallels we have noted. For example, the analogy between *tehôm* and *Tiamat* is false. The true analogy is between Hebrew *tehôm* and Babylonian *tamtu*, the general term for "the deep" in Babylonian. The gender of the words supports this obvious parallel: *tehôm* and *tamtu* are masculine common nouns, whereas *Tiamat* is a feminine proper noun, not the better match for *tehôm* from a linguistic point of view. Likewise, the comparison of God's creative word with that of Marduk is facile. When God speaks in Genesis 1, a major feature of the known universe comes into being. When Marduk speaks in the *Enuma Elish*, he makes a set of images appear; when he speaks again, they disappear. What is common to both is not the creation of the world but the theological concept of creation by fiat. That idea is not unique to Genesis, and its occurrence in Babylon does not ipso facto indicate dependence. For example, the same idea occurs in the Egyptian Pyramid Texts, where the sun god Atum creates all things visible and invisible by the word of his mouth and that word is itself a god, Ptah![33] Such an example of creation

---

29.   Ibid., 114. The German text reads: "diese Erzählung nur die jüdische Bearbeitung eines bei weitem älteren Stoffes ist, der ursprünglich viel mythologischer gewesen sein muss."

30.   Ibid., 115. The German text reads: "Diese Vermutung wird nun durch einem Vergleich von Gen 1 zunächst mit dem Babylonischen Mythus vollauf bestätigt."

31.   Ibid. For detail see the discussion, 114–17; cf. 4–29. Two other examples are the twofold division of the waters in Genesis 1 and the Babylonian myth, and the presence of darkness and water in both Babylonian and Old Testament narratives. But the former could be explained by descent from a common original, as could the latter, which also appears in Egyptian creation narrative.

32.   Heidel already has presented a reasonable and adequate discussion of the flaws in Gunkel's reconstruction.

33.   See Breasted, *Development of Religion*, 44–45.

by fiat most likely predates the Mesopotamian tradition. But that does not make Genesis 1 dependent on the Pyramid Texts.

The Egyptian example of word cosmogony obviously resembles the Hellenistic concept of the *logos* and the *logos* doctrine of John 1. It suggests another way of accounting for some parallels between the Bible and the ancient Near East. Both biblical and extrabiblical exemplars may enshrine recollections or revelations of truth, whether recollections of God's original self-revelation, as noted above (in the Creation and Flood parallels), or revelations in the realm of common grace, as I shall argue below. In any case, the mere existence of a conceptual parallel (or even a set of conceptual parallels) between two documents does not necessarily indicate dependence of one upon the other.[34]

Friedrich Delitzsch

At the start of the last century, the German Assyriologist Friedrich Delitzsch, building upon the work of Gunkel, produced his famous *Babel and Bible*. This volume comprises two lectures given in 1902 and 1903 before the German Oriental Society in the presence of the "German Kaiser." Delitzsch argues, as Gunkel had done, that significant Old Testament accounts and ideas derived from Babylonia. His presentation is lucid and informed, yet we must disagree with it.

One error that Delitzsch would avoid is the argument—developed for instance by Frazer—that religion is a product of evolution from a more savage state. He rejects out of hand the "popular modern view which would see, both in the Yahwè-religion and in our Christian belief in God, something evolved out of such fetishism and animism as is characteristic of the South Sea cannibals or the Patagonians."[35] By contrast, Delitzsch argues that the earliest Semitic idea of God was a unity, but that it "quickly succumbed before the polytheism which for centuries had been current among the older, and oldest, dwellers in the land."[36] He implies that the original idea of God as a unity may have been the brainchild of Abraham. The Quran, he notes, portrays Abraham as pondering what God might be. The patriarch first discards the worship of a star, then of the moon, and finally of the sun in favor of "him who made heaven and earth."[37] God has not revealed himself

---

34. Cf. Price, *Monuments and the Old Testament*, 129.
35. Friedrich Delitzsch, "Lecture 1," in *Babel and Bible*, 68.
36. Ibid., 72.
37. Ibid., 68–69.

to Abraham. Abraham has selected what seems to him a reasonable idea of God. Abraham's choice is for Delitzsch a mark of progress in religious thought, a step in religious evolution. And Delitzsch does after all see evolution as the means by which religious thought improves. It is not an evolution from magic to religion (as posited by Frazer). Rather, it is an ongoing modification of human thought about God, as humans understand more about him. So, according to Delitzsch, God does not reveal truth; man discovers it.

Delitzsch not only argues that some Old Testament accounts and ideas were borrowed from Babylon, but he also extols Babylon as an older and superior culture.

> Trade and commerce, cattle-breeding and agriculture, were at their prime, and the sciences, e.g., geometry, mathematics, and, above all, astronomy, had reached a degree of development which again and again moves even the astronomers of today to admiration and astonishment. Not Paris, at the outside Rome, can compete with Babylon in respect of the influence which it exercised upon the world throughout two thousand years. The Prophets of the Old Testament attest in terms full of displeasure to the overpowering grandeur and overwhelming might of the Babylon of Nebuchadnezzar . . . "A golden cup," exclaims Jeremiah (li. 7), "was Babylon in the hand of Yahwè, which hath made the whole earth drunken"; and even down to the time of the Apocalypse of John, words are found which quiver with the hateful memory of the great Babel, the luxurious, gay city, the wealth-abounding centre of trade and art, the mother of harlots and of every abomination upon earth. And this focus of culture and science and literature, the "brain" of the Nearer East, and the all-ruling power, was the city of Babylon.[38]

Methodologically Delitzsch follows Gunkel, who took the derivative approach in *Schöpfung und Chaos*. But his preference for Babylonian culture informs his work. For Delitzsch, the simplicity of the Babylonian original often suffers when it is transported into the Bible. The Babylonian flood account, for example, tells how a sea storm drove the Babylonian Noah upon a spur of the mountain range of Armenia and Media. Then the whole story

---

38. Ibid., 36–38.

traveled to Canaan. There, authors posited by the Documentary Hypothesis produced the Flood story as we have it today.

> But owing to the new and entirely different local conditions, it was forgotten that the sea was the chief factor, and so we find in the Bible two accounts of the Deluge, which are not only scientifically impossible, but, furthermore, mutually contradictory.[39]

By contrast with the Old Testament, "the simple narrative of Xisuthros" (the Babylonian Noah) "bears the stamp of convincing truth."[40] Moreover, the Old Testament story is morally deficient compared to the Babylonian. Xisuthros "shrieks aloud, because every human being had perished" in the flood, whereas "of any feeling of compassion on the part of Noah we read nothing."[41]

As with the Flood story, the Creation narrative of the Bible also derives from Babylon. According to the Babylonian creation epic, the sky god, Marduk, defeats Tiamat, a sea-dragon goddess with a host of demon subordinates who seeks to overthrow the gods. Delitzsch remarks,

> As Marduk was the tutelary deity of the city of Babel, we can readily believe that this narrative in particular became very widely diffused in Canaan.... The priestly scholar who composed Gen. chap. i endeavoured, of course, to remove all possible mythological features of this creation story. But the dark, watery chaos is presupposed, and that, too, with the name Tehôm (i.e., Tiâmat).[42]

Many scholars follow Delitzsch to this day in his view of the Creation account.[43]

As with the Creation and Flood traditions, Delitzsch regularly assumes

---

39. Ibid., 45–46. He adds, "Science is indebted to Jean Astruc, that strictly orthodox Catholic physician of Louis XIV, for recognising that two fundamentally different accounts of a deluge have been worked up into a single story in the Bible."

40. Delitzsch, "Lecture 2," in *Babel and Bible*, 201.

41. Ibid.

42. Delitzsch, "Lecture 1," 49–50.

43. It is ironic that such is the case, since Heidel has dealt so thoroughly with the problems attendant upon it (in particular the false etymological equivalency between *tehôm* and Tiamat). After a thorough discussion of the parallels between the Babylonian and Genesis material, Heidel concludes, "I personally fail to see why it should be

that parallels between Babylon and the Old Testament indicate a derivation of the latter from the former. So the Babylonian *sabattu* is the source of the Hebrew Sabbath.[44] Such key biblical figures and concepts as the serpent,[45] paradise and hell,[46] and angels and demons[47] derive simply from Babylon, and are among the Babylonian features that have attached themselves "to our religious ideas through the medium of the Bible."[48]

Although he exalts Babylonian culture and argues that Old Testament authors who borrowed from it produced inferior results, Delitzsch also believes it is time to cleanse the Bible of its Babylonian influence.

> When we have removed those conceptions, which, though derived, it is true, from highly-gifted peoples, are nevertheless purely human, and when we have freed our minds of firmly-rooted prejudice of every kind, religion itself, as extolled by the prophets and poets of the Old Testament, and as taught in its most sublime sense by Jesus, as also the religious feeling of our own hearts, is so little affected, that it may rather be said to emerge from the cleansing process in a truer and more sympathetic form.[49]

Such "purely human" ideas (as, e.g., hell, angels, and demons) Delitzsch will expunge and so purify our religion.[50]

Parting Company

Gunkel and Delitzsch chose to see parallels between the Old Testament and the ancient Near East as evidence that Old Testament accounts and ideas were derived from extrabiblical sources. Accordingly they dismissed the

---

incompatible with the doctrine of inspiration to assume that Gen. 1:1–2:3 might in a measure be dependent on *Enuma elish*. But I reject the idea that the biblical account gradually *evolved* out of the Babylonian; for that the differences are far too great and the similarities too insignificant. In the light of the differences, the resemblances fade away almost like the stars before the sun" (Heidel, *Babylonian Genesis*, 138–39).

44. Delitzsch, "Lecture 1," 40–41. Delitzsch further remarks, "It is scarcely possible for us to doubt that we owe the blessings decreed in the Sabbath or Sunday day of rest in the last resort to that ancient and civilized race on the Euphrates and Tigris."

45. Ibid., 47–56.

46. Ibid., 56–62.

47. Ibid., 62–66.

48. Ibid., 67.

49. Ibid.

50. Ibid.

doctrine of special revelation and the historicity of the Old Testament. Many scholars have followed their lead, and I will not discuss their work (which is itself somewhat derivative) here. But I do part company with them.

There are better ways of accounting for parallels than those proposed by Frazer (or Jung) on the one hand, and Old Testament parallelists such as Gunkel and Delitzsch on the other.

First, the Old Testament preserves true and accurate accounts of major events (Creation, the Flood). Extrabiblical sources around the world also preserve the memory of such events in distorted forms.

Second, the Old Testament uses literary and legal forms long current in the ancient Near East as vehicles of God's special revelation. Poetic parallelism and the use of stock word pairs in poetry are examples of the former. Use of the second millennium international treaty form in the Pentateuch, and especially Deuteronomy, and of the ancient Near Eastern covenant lawsuit form in the Prophets are examples of the latter.[51]

Third, parallels between the supposed acts of pagan gods and the acts of God appear in the Old Testament and ancient Near East because God allowed concepts that are true of him and his ways to appear in the realm of common grace. The parallel between the temple-pattern revelation to Gudea of Lagash and the similar revelation to Moses, mentioned at the beginning of this chapter, is an example.[52] The purpose was to make such ideas somewhat

---

51. For poetic parallelism and the use of stock word pairs, see Fischer, *Ras Shamra Parallels*; and Cassuto, *Biblical and Oriental Studies*, 2:60–68. Cassuto, a Jewish scholar of the ancient Near East, puts the basic principle quite well: "It is clear why biblical literature is already at a stage of artistic completeness when it first originates. Its rules of literary expression and its path among the Canaanite dialects were already firmly established in the past. Therefore our ancestors, when they first came to express their thoughts in literary form, did not have to fashion techniques of expression; these were quite ready to hand, and it was easy to use them in order to create a new literature, a literature new in truth, in its content and spirit, but a continuation of the old in its forms—new wine, so to speak, in old flagons" (Cassuto, *Biblical and Oriental Studies*, 2:18). For the second millennium treaty form in the Pentateuch, see Kitchen, *Ancient Orient and Old Testament*; and idem, *The Bible in Its World*. For the covenant lawsuit form in the ancient Near East and the Prophets, cf. Niehaus, "Amos," 1:318–22.

52. Unfashionable as it may be among scholars to make the following observation, it appears to be biblical and I must make it: the immediate source of such extrabiblical revelation is most likely demonic. The Bible does not devote much time to the demonic realm, because its chief interest is the kingdom of God. But what it does say touching this issue makes our interpretation likely. A number of biblical passages declare that demons are the source of false religion and religious ideas (Deut. 32:16–18; 1 Kings 22:1–28; 1 Cor. 10:20; 1 Tim. 4:1).

familiar to God's people so that, when he actually broke into the historical plane and acted, his acts would be recognizable against their cultural background. God's self-revelation was so dynamic and (in his holiness) so challenging (cf. Exod. 20:18–19; Deut. 18:16) that a background preparation for at least some aspects of that revelation was necessary for his people.[53]

God's Ways: A Schema Proposed

We propose to explore primarily the third of these categories in this book. We will consider how God allowed concepts that are true of him and his ways to appear in the realms of common grace. But we will not study a mere random selection of parallels, found, say, in Sumer, Egypt, Hatti, Babylon, and Assyria. Rather, we propose that a shared theological structure of ideas existed in the ancient Near East, a structure that finds its most complete and true form in the Old and New Testaments.

The basic structure of ideas is this: A god works through a man (a royal or prophetic figure, often styled a shepherd) to wage war against the god's enemies and thereby advance his kingdom. The royal or prophetic protagonist is in a covenant with the god, as are the god's people. The god establishes a temple among his people, either before or after the warfare, because he wants to dwell among them. This can mean the founding (or choice) of a city, as well as a temple location. The ultimate purpose is to bring into the god's kingdom those who were not part of it. A simple outline illustrates the process.

god
↓
king/prophet
↓
warfare
↓
covenant
↓
city/temple

---

53. For a recent treatment of comparative studies, which, however, adopts a somewhat different approach from that taken here, see Walton, *Ancient Near Eastern Thought*, 15–40. I will have occasion to both affirm and disagree with Walton's work, e.g., on the matter of divine law giving (287–311), and on the fact that, *pace* Walton, there is no such thing as a "Deuteronomistic History" (141).

In its fullest form, this theological structure contains one more idea. The royal kingdom work is understood to be an act of divine creation or re-creation.

The most perfect extrabiblical parallel comes from Egypt. Perhaps its antiquity and long span of cultural continuity allowed it to develop the scheme with greater completeness than we find elsewhere in the ancient Near East. In Egypt, the sun god, Amon-Ra, wages war through his son and prophet, Pharaoh (who bears the shepherd's crook), to extend his kingdom and bring people into vassaldom to the god (through covenant, international treaty), which includes worship and even temple service. Implicit here, as in all ancient Near Eastern warfare, is a major assumption: When the monarch defeats the foe, it is because his gods in heaven defeat the gods of the enemy. Those gods once claimed the foe as vassals. Now the foe is set free from bondage to other gods to become a vassal of Pharaoh and his father, Amon-Ra. Pharaoh is also creator or re-creator. His monarchy and warfare extend the rule of *maʾat* (approximately, "truth," "proper order") on behalf of his father, Amon-Ra. Pharaoh's work is actually a new creation of both Egypt and conquered lands.

The same process appears in the Bible. In the Old Testament, God wages war through the prophet and shepherd Moses against Pharaoh and the gods of Egypt to liberate Israel and establish them as his people by covenant. He then establishes a temple (tabernacle) presence among them. He eventually establishes a city presence, Jerusalem, with its temple. God's theocratic rule is an act of creation/re-creation. Israel in its promised land is an emblem of humanity in the Garden, and Canaan is compared to Eden (Joel 2:3; in restoration prophecy, Isa. 51:3; Ezek. 36:35). So (symbolically) God re-creates Eden by his theocratic rule.

In the New Testament, God wages war through his Son and prophet, the Good Shepherd, Jesus, against the powers of darkness. He liberates people from those powers and establishes them as his people by a new covenant. He establishes a temple presence, not only among them but in them (the church and individually its members). They look forward to a heavenly city (Gal. 4:26; Heb. 11:10; Rev. 21:2). Theologically it is important to remember that these people were God's enemies ("slaves to sin," Rom. 6:15–17) until he waged the warfare, set them free from their vassaldom to sin, and established his covenant with them, making them his own vassals ("slaves to righteousness," Rom 6:18; cf. Rom. 5:6–8). Christ is also Creator or Re-creator. He creates a "new heaven and a new earth," with a temple presence that recalls Eden with its river and tree of life (Rev. 21:1–2; 22:1–2; cf. Gen. 2:9–10; Ezek. 47:1–12).[54]

God is a wise and good suzerain. He always does what is best for his vassals. Ancient Near Eastern monarchs always claimed to be good: obedient to the gods, careful for the nation's welfare, and faithful to covenants. By contrast, vassals could disobey or even rebel. Ancient Near Eastern treaties make provision for such cases. A variety of curses may befall the rebel, but two stand out as consistently parallel concepts in the ancient Near East and the Bible, and I explore them because of their profound theological interest. First, a rebel and his whole household may be punished or even destroyed because of disobedience. Second, the deity may depart from the temple (and city) of the vassal. Divine temple abandonment is the most profound curse and can bring a host of others. Once God/the gods are gone, once his or their protective cover is removed, the former vassals are exposed to any foe the wrathful suzerain may choose to send against them, including beast, famine, and/or the sword.

We will argue that the structure of thought outlined above (including the covenantal punishments) was prevalent in the ancient Near East. Unfortunately, data from the Hittites (Hatti) and Canaanites (Ugarit) are less abundant than those from Egypt and Mesopotamia, which enjoyed a longer span of continuous cultural development than did the nations around them. Accordingly we have more data from those domains.

The structure we propose was not only prevalent in the ancient Near East. It applies in one sense or another to the whole scope of biblical revelation, from the first Adam to the second. It is the theological backbone of the whole Bible. As it appears in the Bible, the structure of thought described above is primary truth. We have only outlined this proposition here but describe it more completely in the final chapter of this book. The same structure naturally was reflected in pagan worldviews in the ancient Near East, although in darkened forms.

As humankind spread across the globe and cultures arose that were more remote in time from the beginning, the theological outline we find in the ancient Near East became somewhat blurred. Modern Western cultures, of

---

54.   For an extensive biblical-theological study of the temple, see Beale, *Temple and the Church's Mission*.

course, have abandoned it altogether in favor of alternate, secular world-views, except that it is kept alive in the church, God's people, who continue to be his temple and to advance his kingdom, until he returns to establish it once and for all, for all time, and for all who believe in him.

2

God and the Royal Shepherd

According to the schema I am proposing, a god works through a monarch or prophet to advance his kingdom. The god is a suzerain over the monarch and is viewed as a shepherd. But the monarch also can be styled a shepherd, and in this he is like his god. The present chapter explores the royal shepherd idea as it appears in various cultures of the ancient Near East.

Egypt

God as King

For Egyptians the sun god was both creator of all and king.[1] One creation account (ca. 2000 B.C.) says that Ra was a king who "began to rule that which he had made."[2] Like God in the Old Testament, Ra is king over all

---

1. Frankfort, *Kingship and the Gods*, 148–61, offers a fine discussion of the sun god as creator. He observes that even the Memphite theology, which proclaimed Ptah, the chthonic god of Memphis, as creator, could only do so by affirming that the sun god was an emanation of Ptah. As he says, "The sun whose daily rising repeated his appearance on the First Day remained for the Egyptians the Creator" (151; cf. 28). The sun god was known variously as Atum, Amon, and Ra (or Re), among other names.

2. Pritchard, "Another Version of the Creation by Atum," in *Ancient Near Eastern Texts* (hereafter *ANET*), 4. Re is another name for Atum; that is, both Atum and Re are "phases of the sun" (3n. 2). Breasted, *Development of Religion*, 14ff., points out that the sun god came to be conceived of as a former king of Egypt and that as a result, "the qualities of earthly kingship were easily transferred to Re." Among his evidence Breasted cites a five-thousand-year-old hymn to Re (16–17).

creation. A later hymn (ca. 1775–1757 B.C.) celebrates Amon-Ra as "King of Upper and Lower Egypt."[3] The solar creator has become suzerain over one nation, a united Egypt. He is like Yahweh, suzerain over all (as Gen 1:1 implies), who became suzerain over Israel (cf. Deut 33:5).[4]

Amon was originally the breath of life, or the wind. Frankfort observes that "Amon, the venerable god who came into being first . . . he is that breath which stays in all things and through which one lives forever."[5] He is like God the Spirit, who was present at Creation (Gen. 1:2), and breathed life into the first man (Gen. 2:7).

Ancient Egypt thought of a god (and predominantly the solar god) as creator of all and king of the world. He was also creator and suzerain over Egypt. These formulations parallel Old Testament declarations that God was creator of the world and king over it, and also maker and monarch of the nation Israel.

God as Shepherd

Egypt's solar god is also a good shepherd. He is "Creator of all . . . Who came into being by himself. . . . Courageous shepherd driving his sheep and goats."[6]

Egyptian gods can be shepherds. But a god as shepherd, as well as monarch, appears in Egypt mostly in the form of Pharaoh as shepherd king. That is because pharaonic ideology declared that Pharaoh, the shepherd, was not only the son of Amon-Ra but also Ra incarnate. As such, Pharaoh also could be called the creator of Egypt and do miracles. He ruled Egypt on Ra's behalf and imparted the breath of life to all his subjects. These are cardinal ideas in Egypt, and they deserve attention (along with their biblical parallels) individually.

Pharaoh as God: Creator and Miracle Worker

Portrayals of Pharaoh as creator (or re-creator) of Egypt date from the Pyramid Age if not before.[7] In one Pyramid Text the monarch affirms, "I

---

3. Pritchard, "A Hymn to Amon-Re," in *ANET*, 365. For more examples, see Breasted, *Development of Religion*, 3–48; and Pritchard, *ANET*, 3–36, 365–82.
4. In the ancient world, the creator god was always suzerain over all that he had made. Hence Genesis 1:1 makes what to the ancients would have been a very explicit claim for God, that he was suzerain over all, since he was the Creator.
5. Frankfort, *Kingship and the Gods*, 161. Amon was combined with the sun god, Ra, in the New Kingdom (Dynasties 17–20, ca. 1650–1085 B.C.), and added a dynamic element to the creator image (160).
6. Ibid., 159.
7. The Pyramid Age is generally dated ca. 2350–2175 B.C.

am . . . the spirit of the Kings of Lower Egypt; I am the creator who created this land. . . . I am the Great Word."[8]

Because all pharaohs are incarnations of the sun god, a departed pharaoh can, like Amon-Ra, be "the spirit of the Kings of Lower Egypt." The same royal attribute, creator of Egypt (or even all lands), continues in Egypt because each pharaoh is a new incarnation of the creator. For example, Ramses III (1195–1164 B.C.) musters the lands, "creating them like Ptah."[9] Ramses IV (1164–1157 B.C.) is called "Creator of the Two Lands (i.e., Upper and Lower Egypt)."[10] Moreover, word and creation are intimately involved in Egyptian theology. In our Pyramid Text, the king also calls himself the "Great Word." The title has biblical overtones, and with good reason. The monarch apparently identifies himself with Ptah, the god who created all things by the word of his mouth.[11]

Pharaoh was also a miracle worker. He accomplished what he wanted by word of command and by the power of Pharaoh's name alone (cf. John 16:24). For example, Hatshepsut (1486–1468 B.C.) said, "I am the god, the beginning of being, nothing fails that goes out of my mouth."[12] Thutmose IV (1406–1398 B.C.) was one "who spoke with his mouth. . . . All that he commanded happened."[13] A command in Pharaoh's name could even make mountains yield their ore. Ramses II (1290–1224 B.C.) claimed, "Gold comes forth from the mountain at his name, like (that of) his father, Horus."[14]

---

8.   Faulkner, *Ancient Egyptian Pyramid Texts*, 181 (Utterance 506, §§ 1095, 1100).

9.   Breasted, *Ancient Records of Egypt*, 4:36 (§ 62).

10. Ibid., 4:224 (§ 463).

11. As one Pyramid Text, cited by Breasted, *Development of Religion*, 44–45, declares, Ptah "fashioned all gods, even Atum [the sun god]. . . . Every divine word came into existence by the thought of [his] heart and the commandment of [his] tongue. It was he who made the kas (i.e., approximately, 'souls') and created the qualities; who made all food, all offerings, by this word; who made that which is loved and that which is hated. It was he who gave life to the peaceful and death to the guilty. It was he who made every work, every handicraft, which the hands make, the going of the feet, the movement of every limb, according to his command, through the thought of the heart that came forth from the tongue (i.e., of Ptah)."

12. Breasted, *Ancient Records of Egypt*, 2:121 (§ 293).

13. Ibid., 2:331–32 (§ 837). Cf. the clarification of this concept in a stela inscription of Intef, the herald of Thutmose III, "who says, 'Let it be done,' and it is done on [the instant], like that which comes out of the mouth of a god" (298, § 767).

14. Ibid., 3:119 (§ 285). So Ramose, vizier of Amen-hotep IV (Akh-en-Aton, 1369–1353 B.C.), says of his pharaoh, "Thou hast led the mountains; their secret chambers, the terror of thee is in the midst of them, as the terror of thee is in the hearts of the people; they hearken to thee as the people hearken."

Ptah told Ramses, "As for the mountains, the waters, and the buildings upon the land, they remove at thy good name."[15] And Ramses' courtiers flatter him as follows:

> If thou desirest a matter in the night, in the morning it quickly comes to pass. We have been beholding a multitude of thy marvels, since thy appearance as king of the Two Lands; we have not heard, neither have our eyes seen, (yet) do they come to pass. . . . What is that which thou knowest not? . . . If thou sayest to the water: "Come upon the mountain," the flood comes forth quickly after thy word, for thou art Re in limbs, and Khepri with his true form. Thou art the living image on earth of thy father, Atum of Heliopolis.[16]

Pharaoh's oneness with Ra his father explains how he can do miracles ("thou art Re in [his] limbs"). Jesus similarly says, "Believe me when I say that I am in the Father and the Father is in me; or at least believe on the evidence of the miracles themselves" (John 14:11).

Long after Egypt's glory had passed, her monarchs claimed to create by thought or word. The foes of Piankhi (Twenty-third Dynasty, 720 B.C.) must confess, "Lo, the shadow of the god is over thee; the son of Nut, he gives to thee his two arms; the thought of thy heart comes to pass immediately, like that which comes forth from the mouth of a god."[17] As creator, Pharaoh was omniscient and could make things happen by fiat.

Pharaoh as Son of Ra

Egyptians thought Ra had once ruled on earth as first king of Egypt. So from the Fourth Dynasty (2650–2500 B.C.), any Egyptian monarch could be called "Son of Ra."[18] Breasted notes that lineal descent from Ra "was claimed by all Pharaohs from this time on, and was sufficient to justify the assumption of the title."[19]

Now a son has the form of his father. Adam had sons in his "likeness [and] image" (Gen. 5:3). So Pharaoh, as son of Ra, was made in Ra's image.

---

15. Ibid., 3:180 (§ 409).
16. Ibid., 3:120–21 (§ 288).
17. Ibid., 3:431 (§ 854). Nut was the sky goddess, and the son of Nut was Amon-Re.
18. Ibid., 2:75 (§ 187).
19. Ibid., 2:76 (§ 187). See footnote 2 in this chapter.

One Pyramid Text declares: "The King is a sacred image/The most sacred of the sacred images of the Great One. . . ./For the King is a god."[20] A traditional epithet of Pharaoh was "living image" of Amon.[21] Because he was Amon's image, Pharaoh was also the "bright form" or "emanation" of the sun god.[22]

There are biblical parallels: Christ is "the image of God" (2 Cor. 4:4), and "The Son is the radiance of God's glory and the exact representation of his being" (Heb. 1:3). The fact that Pharaoh's body can be "the form of the majesty of Re"[23] recalls Ezekiel's portrayal of God on a chariot throne ("a figure like that of a man," Ezek. 1:26) as "the likeness of the glory of [Yahweh]" (Ezek. 1:28). For Egypt and Israel, the human shape is a formal expression of the glory-spirit of a god.

As son of Ra, Pharaoh has been "given life," often "like Ra" and "forever."[24] So Jesus says, "As the Father has life in himself, so he has granted the Son to have life in himself" (John 5:26). Pharaoh was also the firstborn of the sun god. A Pyramid Text tells the monarch, "You are the eldest son

---

20. Faulkner, *Ancient Egyptian Pyramid Texts*, 82 (Utterances 273–74, §§ 407–8).

21. Breasted, *Ancient Records of Egypt*, 2:322 (§ 812, Thutmose IV); 3:121 (§ 288, Ramses II); 3:26 (§ 47, Ramses III), 419 (§ 817, "of Aton," Piankhi).

22. Ibid., 2:30 (§ 71, Thutmose I), 128 (§ 308, Hatshepsut), 317 (§ 804, Amen-hotep II), 366 (§ 900, Amen-hotep III), 409 (§ 991, of Aton, Akh-en-Aton); 4:140 (§ 246, Ramses III), 419 (§ 817, of Aton, Piankhi).

23. Ibid., 2:366 (§ 900, Amen-hotep III).

24. Ibid., 1:75 (§ 169; Snefru, 2650 B.C.), 83 (§ 176; Khufu, 2600 B.C.), 108 (§ 236; Sahure, 2487–2475 B.C.), 114 (§ 250; Nusure, 2453–2422 B.C.), 119 (§ 263; Menkhure, 2525 B.C.), 132 (§ 285; Teti I, 2345–2313 B.C.), 140 (§ 305; Pepi, 2325 B.C.), 156 (§ 340; Pepi II, 2275–2185 B.C.), 200 (§ 423; Intef I, 2133–2123 B.C.), 201 (§ 423–B; Intef II, 2123–2074 B.C.), 213 (§ 441; Menuhotep IV, 2060–2010 B.C.), 225 (§ 465; Amen-em-het I, 1991–1961 B.C.), 242 (§ 501; Sesostris = Sen-Usert I, 1971–1926 B.C.), 272 (§ 595; Amen-em-het II, 1929–1894 B.C.), 292 (§ 647; Sesostris = Sen-Usert III, 1897–1878 B.C.), 328 (§ 749–50; Amen-em-het IV, 1796–1790 B.C.), 331 (§ 752; Sekhemre-Khutowe, ca. 1745 B.C.), 333 (§ 755; Neferhotep I, 1723–1713 B.C.), 344 (§ 786; Khenzer, ca. 1747 B.C.); 2:12 (§ 27; Ahmose I, 1570–1545 B.C.), 19 (§ 44; Amenhotep I, 1545–1525 B.C.), 31 (§ 73; Thutmose I, 1525–1495 B.C.), 48 (§120; Thutmose II, 1495–1490 B.C.), 303 (§ 779; Thutmose III, 1490–1436 B.C.), 306 (§ 782; Amenhotep II, 1439–1406 B.C.), 322 (§ 812; Thutmose IV, 1406–1398 B.C.), 384 (§ 934; Amenhotep IV = Akh-en-aton, 1369–1353 B.C.); 3:75 (§ 154; Seti I, 1302–1290 B.C.), 105 (§ 259; Ramses II, 1290–1224 B.C.), 241 (§ 575; Mer-ne-Ptah, 1224–1214 B.C.); 4:223 (§ 460; Ramses IV, 1164–1157 B.C.), 270 (§ 473; Ramses V, 1157–1153 B.C.), 253 (§ 510; Ramses IX, 1138–1119 B.C.), 418 (§ 816; Pi-ankhi, 720 B.C.), 498 (§ 976; Necho, 600 B.C.).

of Atum, his first-born."[25] Amenhotep III (1398–1361 B.C.) boasts regarding Amon-Ra, "I am his first born son."[26] Ramses III (1197–1195 B.C.) is likewise "the son of Re—who came forth from his limbs—firstborn of the gods."[27]

Pharaoh as Shepherd

Not only was Pharaoh a ruler, but he also was deemed a shepherd. Sen-Usert I (1991–1961 B.C.) says that Amon "appointed me shepherd of this land."[28] Amen-hotep III (1398–1361 B.C.) is "the good shepherd, vigilant for all people, whom the maker thereof has placed under his authority."[29] Seti I (1302–1290) is "Son of Re, Seti Merneptah, the good shepherd . . . the father and mother of all."[30] Pharaonic iconography portrayed the same theme by placing a shepherd's crook in Pharaoh's hand.

The royal attribute of shepherd continues after death. According to one Pyramid Text, the departed monarch joins Ra in heaven and says, "I have come to you, my father. . . . Place the crook in my hand, that the head of Lower and Upper Egypt may be bowed."[31]

Biblical parallels abound. In the Old Testament, God is a shepherd to his people (Ps. 80:1; Isa. 40:11). In the New Testament, God's Son (like Ra's son) is a good shepherd (John 10:11, 14). Pharaoh ascends to heaven and is shepherd from above. So Jesus ascends to his Father and becomes Shepherd of his kingdom, the church (Heb. 13:20; 1 Peter 2:25; 5:4). In both cultures the shepherd god has other important attributes. Pharaoh claims that the creator of all people has placed them under his authority; so the Son of God declares that "all authority in heaven and on earth has been given to me" (Matt. 28:18). Pharaoh is "the father and mother of all," just as God is the parent of all (Acts 17:28–29; cf. Ps. 27:10, "Though my father and mother forsake me, the LORD will receive me"). Pharaoh is also like a father who

---

25. Faulkner, *Ancient Egyptian Pyramid Texts*, 271 (Utterance 660, § 1871).
26. Breasted, *Ancient Records of Egypt*, 2:366 (§ 900).
27. Ibid., 4:37 (§ 62).
28. Ibid., 1:243 (§ 502).
29. Ibid., 2:365–66 (§ 900).
30. Ibid., 3:86 (§ 195). And Merneptah (1224–1214 B.C.) says of himself, "I am the ruler who shepherds you . . . as a father, who preserves alive his children" (3:243 [§ 580]).
31. Faulkner, *Ancient Egyptian Pyramid Texts*, 49–50 (Utterance 222, §§ 200, 202). Another text celebrates the monarch's rebirth into eternal life: "This King is hale, the Herdsman stands up" (295 [Utterance 685, §2069]; cf. 253 [Utterance 610, § 1711]).

preserves his children alive, just as the Lord compares himself to a father who takes care of his children ("As a father has compassion on his children," Ps. 103:13; "The Lord disciplines those he loves, as a father the son he delights in," Prov. 3:12; cf. Heb. 12:6).

Pharaoh as the Source of Life

Pharaoh, like his father the Sun, radiantly gives life. Such is Pharaoh's glory that to look upon his face can mean life. But Amon is also the breath of life, and Pharaoh, like his father, also gives the breath of life to those under his rule. Pharaonic theophany and vivification go together. Queen Hatshepsut (1486–1468 B.C.) "illuminates like the sun, vivifying the hearts of the people."[32] Chiefs of Lebanon say to Seti I (1302–1290 B.C.), "Thou seemest like thy father, Re; there is life in seeing thee."[33] Vassals of Ramses III (1195–1164 B.C.) declare, "When he appears, he seems like Atum, when he opens his mouth, with breath for the people."[34]

Pharaoh imparts breath to those under his rule, both Egyptians and acquired vassals. Amenhotep II (1439–1406 B.C.) is "King of kings," whose conquered foes "live by his breath."[35] Tributaries of Thutmose IV (1406–1398 B.C.) beg, "Grant us breath, which thou givest, O mighty king."[36] Seti I sustains vassal peoples by "furnishing their nostrils with his breath."[37] Merneptah (1224–1214 B.C.) says, "The people love me, as I love them, and give to them breath for their cities."[38] As late as the Twenty-fifth Dynasty (eighth/seventh century B.C.), those subject to Tanutamon plead, "Give to us breath, O Lord of life, without whom there is no life."[39]

Pharaoh as the giver of breath is also the creator. Sesostris (Sen-Usert) III (1878–1840 B.C.) is "life, cooling the nostrils" (i.e., giving them breath), and "He is the one creating that which is."[40] The court of Ramses II (1290–

32. Breasted, *Ancient Records of Egypt*, 2:137 (§ 325).
33. Ibid., 3:49 (§ 94); cf. 57 (§ 117; Seti I).
34. Ibid., 4:21 (§ 38). His vassals plead, "Give to us breath, that we may breathe it, the life that is in thy grasp, forever" (4:47 [§ 79]).
35. Ibid., 2:311 (§ 792); cf. 2:361 (§ 891; Amenhotep III).
36. Ibid., 2:325 (§ 819); cf. 2:424 (§ 1032; Tutenkhamon).
37. Ibid., 3:73 (§ 147).
38. Ibid., 3:252 (§ 591). Also said of Merneptah, "Lo, when one dwells in the time of this hero, the breath of life comes immediately" (3:262 [§ 614]).
39. Ibid., 4:473 (§ 932).
40. Ibid., 1:327 (§ 747).

1224 B.C.) eulogizes him as follows: "We come to thee, lord of heaven, lord of earth, Re, life of the whole earth . . . who fashioned the people, giver of breath into the nostrils of all, making all the gods live . . . maker of the great, fashioner of the lowly, whose word produces food . . . beloved of truth, in which he lives by his laws."[41] Later, Mer-ne-Ptah (1224–1214 B.C.) is extolled as giver of breath and as the sun who brings healing and deliverance: "King Merneptah, the Bull, lord of strength . . . the Sun, driving away the storm which was over Egypt, allowing Egypt to see the rays of the sun, removing the mountain of copper from the neck of the people so that he might give breath to the people who were smothered."[42] The phrasing and ideology may well bring to mind the "Sun of righteousness [who] will rise with healing in [his] wings" (Mal. 4:2).

The association of Amon, as god of breath, and Ra, as creator, also recalls the "Spirit/breath of God" who hovered over the waters at the Creation (Gen. 1:2).[43] Divine breath into mortals to make them alive recalls the creation of Adam, as God breathed into him the breath of life (Gen. 2:7). Such theological insights in Egypt are far from being innovations; rather, they echo primordial truth.

Sumeria

God as Monarch and Shepherd

The ideal of a shepherd monarch may have its roots in the idea of a god who is both royal and pastoral. Both are very ancient in Mesopotamia. One fourth millennium B.C. poem tells how Dumuzi becomes supreme shepherd.[44]

> Grant him a royal throne, firm in its foundations;
> grant him a sceptre righting (wrongs in) the land . . .
> From sunrise to sunset

---

41. Ibid., 3:108 (§ 265). Ramses III (1195–1164 B.C.) both creates the lands, like Ptah, and gives the breath of life (4:36 [§ 62]).
42. Ibid., 2:259–60 (§ 608).
43. The Egyptian parallel to the biblical account should do something to dispel the erroneous translation of "Spirit of God" as "mighty wind" (NRSV fn.).
44. Jacobsen, *Treasures of Darkness*, 40. Jacobsen has called the poem "The Blessing of the Bridegroom."

from south to north
from the Upper Sea to the Lower Sea . . .
grant him all shepherds' crooks,
and may he perform the shepherdship
over their darkheaded people.[45]

The gods make Dumuzi, also a god, shepherd over all earthly kings, who
are also styled shepherds. Like Pharaoh they have crooks that symbolize
their authority and charge as rulers to keep the "sheep" (that is, "the darkheaded people") in order.[46] A later work, called "The Sumerian King List"
(third millennium B.C.), declares: "(In) Bad-tibira . . . the god Dumu-zi, a
shepherd, ruled (as king) 36,000 years."[47] Dumuzi rules from one city on
our planet as god and royal shepherd. He resembles the Lord, who as God
and royal shepherd will one day rule from Jerusalem.

Monarch as Son of God

Sumerians thought a ruler could be the son of a god. Eanatum of Lagash
(ca. 2400 B.C.) records how a god, Ningirsu, "implanted the semen for
Eanatum in the womb."[48] Lugalzaggisi (ca. twenty-fifth/twenty-fourth centuries B.C.) is "son born by [the goddess] Nisaba."[49] Gudea says to the god
Gatumdug, "I have no mother, thou art my mother, I have no father, thou
art my father."[50]

---

45. Ibid., 42.
46. The phrase translated "darkheaded" simply means those who have (dark) hair on
   the tops of their heads. The word for "dark" is cognate with the Hebrew word traditionally (and mistakenly) translated "shadow of death" in Psalm 23:4.
47. Pritchard, ANET, 265. Cf. "Dumuzi and Enkimdu: the Dispute between the
   Shepherd-God and the Farmer-God" (41–42).
48. J. S. Cooper, Sumerian and Akkadian Royal Inscriptions, 34 (La 3.1.iv–v).
49. Engnell, Studies in Divine Kingship, 16n. 5. Engnell, however, understands such divine sonship chiefly in a figurative way: "That the king is god implies, in my opinion,
   above all two things: the king is the human maintainer of the divine ideology—the
   king as 'law-king-sky-god'. . .—and the king has—as 'executive king'—to represent, especially in the cult, one of several divine characters" (31). This interpretation is too limited. Even Engnell must admit that when all is said and done, the king
   is in no way "just another feeble creature" (31). For us, the very ascription of divine
   sonship is the point. It has biblical resonances and a biblical background, as I shall
   argue below.
50. Ibid., 16n. 7.

Sumerians also thought a king could incarnate a god and be that god's living image. According to Jacobsen, three documents illustrate incarnational divine kingship among the Sumerians. In one account, King Iddin-Dagan undergoes a ritual marriage. He becomes Dumuzi, shepherd god and god of fertility. His wife, or a high priestess, plays the role of Inanna, goddess of the storehouse. But "the king, being a god," is in fact an embodiment of Dumuzi, and his bride an embodiment of Inanna.[51]

Another Sumerian text identifies the god Damu (equated with Dumuzi) and the kings of Ur. Damu has died. Damu's mother and sister lament his death and recount "the graves in which Damu and his various manifestations rest." As Jacobsen notes, "all the dead kings of the Third Dynasty of Ur and of later dynasties" are among those manifestations of Damu.[52]

Jacobsen's final text is a hymn sung by worshippers who accompany the dead god Damu to his father above. Damu and the mortal king Ur-Nammu (2112–2095 B.C.) are paralleled and so equated.

> my Damu, whom I accompany to the father,
>   in whom I rejoice . . .
> shepherd Ur-Nammu, whom I accompany to the father,
>   in whom I rejoice . . .[53]

Jacobsen notes that "with Ur-Nammu, the first king of the Third Dynasty of Ur [ca. 2112–2004 B.C.], the song takes up the series of rulers who during their lifetimes were the god's ritual avatars and who *continued to be his incarnations after their death*" (emphasis added).[54] Sumerian theology parallels Egyptian thought at this point: a monarch was an embodiment of a god. Both also share a royal metaphor: shepherd for monarch ("shepherd Ur-Nammu"; Dumuzi, god and monarch, also a shepherd).

---

51. Called the "Iddin-Dagan Text." See further Jacobsen, *Treasures of Darkness*, 37–40.
52. Ibid., 66. Frankfort, *Kingship and the Gods*, 224, argues from the use of the divine determinative that few kings after Third Dynasty of Ur (and not the first king of that dynasty) claimed divinity for themselves: "After the fall of that dynasty, the kings of Isin, and occasionally a ruler of one of the other city-states . . . assumed the sign of divinity in their inscriptions." But the use of the divine determinative is not the only manner in which a king could claim divinity, as the text just cited shows. See below.
53. Jacobsen, *Treasures of Darkness*, 71.
54. Ibid., 71.

Monarch as Shepherd

The Sumerian King List says kingship was lowered "from heaven." So human kings receive royal authority from the gods. A third millennium text shows how the king, Lipit-Eshtar, had royal authority (and vitality) from the god An, head of the Sumerian pantheon.

> (From) afar he [i.e., An] looked firmly toward him,
> looked firmly toward Prince Lipit-Eshtar,
> granted long life to him,
> granted long life to Prince Lipit-Eshtar,
> An's decree, a decree (as good as) carried out,
> no god will oppose . . .
> from among the exalted offices,
> from among the offices of the foremost row,
> the kingship, being all things precious,
> to Lipit-Eshtar, son of Enlil,
> great An granted as a gift.[55]

An looks upon Lipit Eshtar and grants him life. An's act may illustrate a common ancient Near Eastern idea: that a god's radiant face imparted life to any mortal upon whom the god looked. But An also grants authority. Jacobsen remarks, "As the ultimate source of all authority An was closely associated with the highest authority on earth, that of kingship. It was he who proclaimed the king chosen by the assembly of the gods and he who was, par excellence, the god that conferred kingship."[56] An was the "numinous power in the sky," the father of all the gods and of "innumerable demons and evil spirits." In fact, he was the creator.[57] An parallels God, who is creator of all things, including angels, who are called "sons of God" (Job 1:6 NKJV), and so also (through their fall) of demons and evil spirits. There is also a parallel to God as the one who alone raises up kings and grants authority (Dan. 2:21; 4:35; Rom. 13:1).

Such monarchs were also styled shepherds. One example will suffice. A Sumerian king, Gudea of Girsu, says he is "the shepherd called by Ningirsu," a god who will "place in (Gudea's) hand a long-term sceptre," in order "to

---

55. Ibid., 98.
56. Ibid., 97.
57. Ibid., 95.

guide aright the hand of the righteous man, but to put the evildoer in the neck-stock . . . to issue ordinances for his city."[58]

Sumeria's royal shepherd was a god's offspring, a god incarnate, or at least one chosen and appointed by a god. His task was to keep the human flock in order. It should come as no surprise that we find the same ideas appear later in Mesopotamia.

Babylon

God as King and Shepherd

As in Sumeria, gods later in Babylon were called shepherds. So Iaḫdun-Līm, king of Mari (1825–1810 B.C.), exalts "the god Šamaš, king of heaven and earth, judge of gods and mankind, whose concern is justice, to whom truth has been given as a gift, shepherd of the black-headed (people) . . . who is lord of Mari."[59] In a tradition spanning two millennia, Mesopotamian gods such as Shamash, Enlil, and Marduk were called both king and shepherd.[60]

Monarch as Son

Semitic Mesopotamian kings did not often claim divinity, at least according to the extant evidence. As Frankfort notes, "Hammurabi of Babylon never used [the divine determinative]. Samsu-iluna, and after him a few Kassite rulers, were the last to style themselves gods. Neither the Assyrians nor the neo-Babylonians renew the custom."[61] Hammurapi of Babylon (1792–1750 B.C.) did at least once style himself a god. He said he was the "god of his nation," although whether this means actual or relative deity is unclear: "Hammu-rapi, god of [his] nation, the one whom the god An [has covered] with the aura of kingship."[62] Samsu-iluna on the other hand definitely claimed to be divine offspring. He speaks of "the goddess Ninmaḫ, the mother who created me," and of "the god Sîn, the god who created me."[63] Moreover, Assyrian evidence has appeared of a royal claim to

---

58.   Ibid., 81–82.
59.   Frayne, *Old Babylonian Period*, 605 (E4.6.8.2, lines 1–16).
60.   Tallqvist, *Akkadische Götterepitheta*, 164–65 (*reʾu*), 232–37 (*šarru*).
61.   Frankfort, *Kingship and the Gods*, 224. The divine determinative was a cuneiform star, rather like an asterisk (*) in appearance, prefixed to a name to show that the owner of the name was divine.
62.   Frayne, *Old Babylonian Period*, 344 (E4.3.6.10, lines 1–2).
63.   Ibid., 381 (E4.3.7.5, lines 34–35, 39). Cf. Frankfort, *Kingship and the Gods*, 224.

divinity. But in the main, Frankfort's observation stands. Apparently there was a major difference between Egyptian and Mesopotamian theology at this point. Mesopotamian rulers did not have a steady tradition of claiming to be a god or a god's incarnation.

Monarch as Shepherd

Babylonian monarchs also adopted the pastoral metaphor. As a royal attribute, it was part of Babylon's Sumerian heritage, as well as a figure for monarchs throughout the ancient Near East.

Hammurapi's Law Code tells how Anu and Enlil gave the rule of all humanity to the god Marduk. Hammurapi adds, "Anum and Illil for the prosperity of the people called me by name Hammu-rabi, the reverent, god-fearing prince, to make justice to appear in the land, to destroy the evil and the wicked that the strong might not oppress the weak, to rise indeed like Shamash over the dark-haired folk to give light to the land."[64]

Hammurapi is not only a shepherd, but he also compares himself to Shamash, the solar god, who was both overseer and great judge of covenants for Mesopotamians. As monarch, shepherd, and god, he is like Sumerian Dumu-zi.

Hammurapi's son Samsu-iluna (1749–1712 B.C.) also claimed pastoral monarchy: "The great gods looked at me with their shining faces (and) granted to me as a gift: a life that, like the god Sîn, is renewed monthly; to exercise the shepherdship of the four quarters in well-being forever; to attain the desire of my heart like a god."[65]

He is a royal pastor of almost biblical proportions: "Marduk . . . gave to me, Samsu-iluna, king of his pleasure, the totality of the lands to shepherd (and) laid a great commission on me to make his nation lie down in pastures and to lead his extensive people in well-being, forever."[66]

Ammī-dītāna of Babylon (1683–1647 B.C.) adapts and enhances Samsu-iluna's phraseology. He says he built a fort "by the wisdom that the god Ea gave to me, in order to superbly shepherd the widespread people of my land by means of fine pastures and watering places and to make them lie down in (safe) pastures."[67]

---

64. G. R. Driver and John C. Miles, *The Babylonian Laws*, 2:6–7 (Col. ia.27–44).
65. Frayne, *Old Babylonian Period*, 382 (E4.3.7.5.67–77).
66. Ibid., 381 (E4.3.7.5.13–24).
67. Ibid., 413 (E4.3.9.2.19'–25').

Babylonia was heir to a Sumerian ideology that understood monarchs to be gods and shepherds. According to that ideology, a monarch had divinely given authority over people and nations to lead them, as it were, to good pasture, and even to fine watering places.

Assyria

Against the Mesopotamian background we have observed, we can now turn to the Assyrian evidence. In Assyria, as in Babylon, a god or a monarch could be a shepherd. But Assyrian monarchs claimed another attribute separable from but important to a good shepherd: an ability to triumph over predatory beasts. Assyrian rulers displayed such ability according to annalistic hunting accounts. Such royal triumph over animals—and especially lions—combines with the pastoral ideal to form a biblical model of monarchy.

God, Monarch, and Shepherd

Assyria, like Babylon, was heir to Sumerian traditions adopted in Mesopotamia generally. According to them, a god could be both a king and a shepherd. His elect monarch on earth also could be a shepherd. And a monarch's pastoral role paralleled the pastoral role of his god.

Monarch as Son of God

Like Babylon, Assyria did not claim divine kingship as often as Egypt or even Sumer. Assyrian rulers normally called themselves "governor" and "appointee of Enlil" and considered themselves beloved and chosen by the gods, but not typically divine progeny.[68] Tiglath-pileser I (ca. 1115–1077 B.C.) was a "beloved prince, your [i.e., the gods'] select one, attentive shepherd, whom in the steadfastness of your hearts you chose." Assyrian kings from Shamshi-Adad I (1814–1782 B.C.) to Ashurbanipal (668–627 B.C.) made similar claims.[69]

But some Assyrian monarchs did claim to be sons of heaven. Compare the following from the *Tukulti-Ninurta Epic*:

> By the fate assigned by Nudimmud
> his form is reckoned as divine nature,

---

68. Frankfort, *Kingship and the Gods*, 228–30.
69. Niehaus, *God at Sinai*, 97.

By the decree of the Lord of the Lands
   his forming proceeded smoothly *inside* the divine womb.
He is the eternal image of Enlil,
   who hears what the people say, the *counsel* of the land.
Likewise in utterance he praised the Lord of the Lands
   who designated him to direct the van.
Enlil, like a physical father,
   exalted him second to his firstborn son.[70]

Tukulti-Ninurta (1244–1208 B.C.) asserts divine parentage as graphically as Ur III monarchs or Egyptian pharaohs. Two Assyrian monarchs at least claim that gods created them or altered their progress in the womb. Adad-narari II (911–891 B.C.) says, "Great gods . . . who decree destinies; they properly created me . . . they altered my stature to lordly stature, they rightly made perfect my features and filled my lordly body with wisdom."[71]

Tukulti-Ninurta II (890–884 B.C.) says, "Great gods . . . who decree destinies . . . (the gods) who faithfully [noticed me] in my mother's womb (and) altered my birth to lordly birth . . . [they] rightly [made perfect] my features."[72] Later in Assyria, Ashurbanipal says to the goddess Ninlil, "I am thy servant, Assurbanipal whom thy hands formed without father and mother, whom thou, Queen, caused to reach maturity."[73] He is like Melchizedek, a type of Christ: "Without father or mother . . . without beginning of days or end of life, like the Son of God he remains a priest forever" (Heb. 7:3). Time and archaeology may tell how unusual such claims were in Assyria.

Monarch as Shepherd and Hunter

An Assyrian ruler normally called himself a shepherd.[74] Tiglath-pileser I (1115–1077 B.C.) was a "faithful shepherd."[75] As such he had been appointed

---

70. Lambert, "Three Unpublished Fragments," 50–51 (ital. in original).
71. Grayson, *Assyrian Rulers of the Early First Millennium B.C. I*, 147 (A.0.99.2, 5–7).
72. Ibid., 165 (A.0.100.1, 14–20).
73. Engnell, *Studies in Divine Kingship*, 16n. 7. See also Grayson, *Assyrian Rulers of the Third and Second Millennia B.C.*, 182 (A.0.77.1, i 7–8; Shalmaneser I, 1274–1245 B.C.); and idem, *Assyrian Rulers of the Early First Millennium B.C. I*, 147 (A.0.99.2, Adad-narari II, 911–891 B.C.), 165 (A.0.100.1, 13; Tukulti-Ninurta II, 890–884 B.C.), 199 (A.0.101.1, i 13; Ashurnasirpal II, 883–859 B.C.).
74. Cf. Seux, *Èpithètes Royales Akkadiennes et Sumériennes*, 244–50 (sub *re'u*).
75. Grayson, *Assyrian Rulers of the Early First Millennium B.C. I*, 13 (A.0.87.1, i 34).

"for sovereignty over the land of the god Enlil."[76] He was like Hammurapi of Babylon, "the shepherd, called of Enlil," some 750 years before. Assyria's gods gave Tukulti-Ninurta II complete authority over the "subjects of the god, Enlil, faithful shepherd."[77] Assyria's last emperor, Ashurbanipal (668–627 B.C.), also boasted, "I shepherded the domains of Enlil."[78] Assyria had a long tradition of pastoral monarchy, and the gods who had chosen them to rule had given them that pastoral role.

Assyrian monarchs were not only shepherds, they were also (by their own account) formidable hunters. For some 150 years, from Tiglath-pileser I (1115–1077 B.C.) to Shalmaneser III (858–824 B.C.), Assyrian royal annals vaunted the royal prowess against wild beasts. Standard phraseology, from Tiglath-pileser I onward, portrayed royal valor in the hunt. Tiglath-pileser's boast becomes typical: "I killed on foot 120 lions with my wildly vigorous assault."[79] His grandson, Ashur-bel-kala (1074–1057 B.C.), also claims to have killed many lions on foot.[80] Ashurnasirpal II (883–859 B.C.) colorfully declares, "By my stretched out arm, and through my furious courage, fifteen mighty lions from the mountains and the woods in my hand I captured."[81]

Assyrian royal tradition calls the monarch both a shepherd (divinely appointed) and a hunter (divinely endowed), able to combat lions on foot and even bare-handed.

The Old Testament presents an important parallel. David affirms before Saul, "Your servant has been keeping his father's sheep. When a lion . . . came and carried off a sheep from the flock, I went after it, struck it and rescued the sheep from its mouth. When it turned on me, I seized it by its hair, struck it and killed it" (1 Sam. 17:34–35).

David's account is not merely high drama from the pastures. David builds a case for a chance to fight Goliath, but he also evokes an ancient Near Eastern royal typology. As he does so, David shows (inadvertently?) that he is royal material. He can combat lions on foot as well as any anointed monarch. That is consonant with his prior anointing by Samuel as king (1 Sam.

---

76. Ibid., (A.0.87.1, i 21–22).
77. Ibid., 165 (A.0.100.1, 22–23).
78. Piepkorn, *Historical Prism Inscriptions of Ashurbanipal I*, 30–31 (Col. i. 40).
79. Grayson, *Assyrian Rulers of the Early First Millennium B.C. I*, 16 (Col. vi.77–79).
80. Ibid., 54 (Col. iv.9–11).
81. Budge and King, *Annals of the Kings of Assyria*, 201–2 (Col. iv.22–27); cf. Grayson, *Assyrian Rulers of the Early First Millennium B.C. I*, 236–37 (42), 291 (92–93).

16:13). David's use of ancient Near Eastern typology resonates beyond his own situation, however, for the Bible employs the same ideas in ways that are Christological.

Biblical Parallels

God as Monarch

God is a king in both Old and New Testaments. More, he is a "Great King," an ancient Near Eastern technical term for suzerain, or emperor. The psalmist says, "How awesome is the LORD Most High, the great King over all the earth," who "reigns over the nations" (Ps. 47:2, 8; cf. Ps. 99:1). Jesus warns people not to swear by Jerusalem, for it is "the city of the Great King," whose throne is heaven, and whose footstool earth (Matt. 5:34–35).

As Great King over all the earth, God makes monarchs of men. Daniel says God "changes times and seasons; he sets up kings and deposes them" (Dan. 2:21), and Paul declares, "There is no authority except that which God has established. The authorities that exist have been established by God" (Rom. 13:1; cf. John 3:27; 19:11). So one should "fear God, honor the king" (1 Peter 2:17). But God, who is the Great King over all kings, is also the Good Shepherd.

God as Shepherd

According to Psalm 23, God was David's shepherd. He was also Israel's shepherd: "Give ear, O Shepherd of Israel, You who lead Joseph like a flock" (Ps. 80:1 NKJV). And he will shepherd his folk in a glorious future: "He tends his flock like a shepherd: he gathers the lambs in his arms and carries them close to his heart; he gently leads those that have young" (Isa. 40:11). A similar future appears in a later prophet: "As a shepherd looks after his scattered flock when he is with them, so will I look after my sheep. I will rescue them from all the places where they were scattered" (Ezek. 34:12).

The Lord is a God who is both Monarch and Shepherd, after the pattern of ancient Near Eastern theology. Like the gods of Egypt and Mesopotamia, he also appoints human kings to shepherd various peoples, including his own.

God's Shepherd Kings

God appoints over his people rulers, such as judges or monarchs, and they are called shepherds. The first of them is the great covenant mediator, Moses.

Not long before Moses encounters the Lord on Horeb, we read that "Moses was keeping the flock of his father-in-law Jethro" (Exod. 3:1 NRSV). Moses, the future ruler, was actually a shepherd of sheep. But God made Moses shepherd of his people: "Then his people recalled the days of old, the days of Moses and his people—where is he who brought them through the sea, with the shepherd of his flock?" (Isa. 63:11). Moses, who was a shepherd of sheep, became, like an ancient Near Eastern king, a divinely appointed shepherd over God's kingdom. He was not an ancient Near Eastern monarch, but in many ways he functioned as one (e.g., he judged cases; he served God in his temple/tabernacle). Subsequently, during the monarchy, God's appointed kings and leaders are also called shepherds, in typical ancient Near Eastern fashion (Isa. 56:11; Jer. 10:21; 23:2; Ezek. 34; Zech. 10:3).[82]

Since all authority comes from God, he also appoints pagan monarchs, who also are termed shepherds. God may summon those same shepherds and their armies ("flocks") in judgment against his people (Jer. 6:2–3). Or he may call upon a royal shepherd, Cyrus, to restore his people: "'He is my shepherd, and he shall fulfill all my purpose'; saying of Jerusalem, 'She shall be built,' and of the temple, 'Your foundation shall be laid'" (Isa. 44:28 RSV).

Cyrus is a royal shepherd under common grace. God calls him by name and even anoints him (he is God's "Messiah," i.e., "Anointed") to redeem Israel from captivity (Isa. 45:1–4). Cyrus may have a unique calling and empowering for the sake of God's elect, but he is still only one example of a more general truth: "The Most High rules the kingdom of men and gives it to whom he will" (Dan. 4:32 RSV). Cyrus demonstrates that "kingship was lowered from heaven," as the Sumerian King List long ago taught.[83]

Another royal typology from the ancient Near East that applies to the Bible is a monarch's mastery of ferocious beasts, most typically lions. I have shown how this topic blends with that of royal shepherd in the Old Testament in the case of David. Another important (although less obvious) example is Samson, who was also competent against a lion.

---

82. God can even raise up a bad shepherd as a judgment (Zech. 11:15–16).
83. Pritchard, *ANET*, 265.

Samson went down to Timnah together with his father and mother. As they approached the vineyards of Timnah, suddenly a young lion came roaring toward him. The Spirit of the LORD came upon him in power so that he tore the lion apart with his bare hands as he might have torn a young goat. (Judg. 14:5–6)

Samson's bare-handed combat with a young lion in the late second millennium parallels contemporary Assyrian royal claims to have fought lions on the ground, hand to hand, and slaughtered them. Significant also, perhaps, is the mention of a young goat. Samson was not actually a shepherd, but the young goat simile may allude to an ancient Near Eastern typology of royal shepherd. As God's anointed judge, Samson was a shepherd of Israel, as Moses had been a judge and shepherd before him.

We have seen how two themes, lion-mastering monarch and faithful shepherd, come together in the case of David (1 Sam. 17:34–37). But David is only a type of his greater son, Jesus, who is altogether God, king, shepherd, and lion-master.

Monarch as Son

A pagan monarch in the ancient Near East could be a son of a god, or even a god incarnate. Such attributes (monarch, son, incarnate god) are Christological. The New Testament portrays Jesus Christ as royalty. Jesus approaches Jerusalem consonant with Zechariah 9:9: "See, your king comes to you, gentle and riding on a donkey, on a colt, the foal of a donkey" (Matt. 21:5).

Jesus is both Son of God (Luke 1:35) and God incarnate (John 1:1, 14, 18).[84] His suzerain ("Great King") status appears eschatologically, upon his return as "King of kings and Lord of lords" (Rev. 19:16; cf. 17:14), enthroned as Judge of all nations (Matt. 25:31ff.; cf. Gen. 18:25).

King as Source of Life

Like Pharaoh, the Son of God is also the source of life. Peter rebukes the crowd at Solomon's Colonnade, saying, "You killed the author of life, but God raised him from the dead" (Acts 3:15). Parallels include the Lord

---

84.   The first "son of God" was Adam (Luke 3:37). The first Adam was a king, like the second Adam (1 Cor. 15:45). For Adam as God's vassal king in the suzerain-vassal Creation covenant, see Niehaus, *God at Sinai*, 143–50.

as theophanic life source and as bestower of life's breath. As the face of Pharaoh brought life to his vassals, so we enjoy the glory of eternal life in Christ's presence (2 Cor. 3:7–18). Just as Pharaoh gave the breath of life, the Lord God breathed the breath of life into Adam (Gen. 2:7), and the Son breathes his Spirit upon his followers (John 20:22) and gives them life (John 5:40; 6:33). Jesus does so as the Good Shepherd: "My sheep listen to my voice . . . I give them eternal life" (10:27–28).

Son as Shepherd

Jesus declares, "I am the good shepherd" (John 10:11, 14). Moreover, the day will come when there will be but "one flock and one shepherd" (John 10:16), in fulfillment of the promise, "My servant David will be king over them, and they will all have one shepherd" (Ezek. 37:24).

Among many human monarchs, the royal shepherd par excellence is "David," that more perfect David—Jesus—who comes to rule over a restored nation. God says that "David my servant will be their prince forever" (Ezek. 37:25) in an eschatological kingdom: "I will make a covenant of peace with them; it will be an everlasting covenant. I will establish them and increase their numbers, and I will put my sanctuary among them forever. My dwelling place will be with them; I will be their God, and they will be my people" (Ezek. 37:26–27).

This promise is fulfilled in the Son's eschatological kingdom: "Now the dwelling of God is with men, and he will live with them. They will be his people, and God himself will be with them and be their God" (Rev. 21:3).

The Son on earth was a good shepherd. But his servant leaders also must be such. So Christ instructed Peter, "Tend my sheep" (John 21:16 NRSV; cf. vv. 15–18). Peter, as a fellow elder, exhorts elders, "Tend the flock of God that is your charge" (1 Peter 5:2 NRSV).

According to Assyrian royal typology, their monarchs fought and overcame lions on foot, and even by hand. Christ, the Good Shepherd, also has a lion for a foe. Peter warns both shepherds and flock, "Be self-controlled and alert. Your enemy the devil prowls around like a roaring lion looking for someone to devour" (1 Peter 5:8).[85] As Jesus was a good shepherd on earth,

---

85. Compare God's characterization of sin to Cain: "Sin is crouching at your door; it desires to have you, but you must master it" (Gen. 4:7). The Hebrew verb translated "crouching" is used of a lion (Gen. 49:9; Ezek. 19:2) and of Egypt as a serpent (a sea dragon, Ezek. 29:3; cf. Rev. 12:9).

so from on high he is "that great Shepherd of the sheep" (Heb. 13:20). On earth, as David rescued his sheep from the lion's mouth, Paul can write that "the Lord stood by me and gave me strength to proclaim the message fully, that all the Gentiles might hear it. So I was rescued from the lion's mouth" (2 Tim. 4:17 RSV; cf. Dan. 6).

Son as Creator and Miracle Worker

Just as Pharaoh claimed to be creator and, sometimes, to work miracles (especially in the reign of Ramses II), so the Son of God is Creator and performer of signs and wonders. John's Christology makes the former very clear (John 1:1, 14, 18), and Jesus' ministry is replete with the latter, so that John summarizes: "Jesus did many other miraculous signs . . . which are not recorded in this book. But these are written that you may believe that Jesus is the Christ, the Son of God, and that by believing you may have life in his name" (John 20:30–31).

Conclusion

We have seen a number of parallels between the ancient Near East and the Bible in this chapter. Some of them, such as the notion of king as shepherd, may seem to have arisen naturally as people compared the human situation to a pastoral situation commonly seen: that of a shepherd managing his flock.

We maintain, however, that all of these concepts are true of God and his Son. God always has been supreme ruler over what he made and always has taken perfect care of his creatures. When he made humans to rule the earth, he gave them the capacity and authority to do so. As they were made in his image, they should care for the world as he would. Human terms such as *monarch* and *shepherd* appropriately characterized these attributes and behaviors and were applied to deity in a pagan context and to God as he spoke to humanity in terms they could understand. Some ideas, such as a son of God who is monarch, find their origin in Adam, who was the first son of God and the first (vassal) monarch. Others, such as the son of God who is monarch and also creator and miracle worker, are true of the Messiah and also appear in pagan antiquity, but in polytheistic terms. Most likely, such false theological concepts appeared through the agency of demons, who, we are told, are the source of false religion (1 Cor. 10:20), and of false doctrines (1 Tim. 4:1).

The Christology apparent in pagan literature may be one of the more fascinating aspects of this study. I close this chapter with a strikingly Christological quote from Hammurapi.

> These are the just laws which Hammurabi the able king has stablished and (thereby) has enabled the land to enjoy stable governance and good rule. I, Hammu-rabi, the gracious king, have not been careless nor been slack on behalf of the dark-haired folk whom Illil has granted to me (and) whose shepherding Marduk has given to me.[86]

It is ironic that such a boast comes from the (shepherd) king of Babylon. Its true antitype is found in Jesus' words to his Father: "While I was with them, I protected them and kept them safe by that name you gave me. None has been lost except the one doomed to destruction so that Scripture would be fulfilled" (John 17:12; cf. vv. 6–11). That is the word of the King, the Good Shepherd, whose word is truth.

---

86. Driver and Miles, *Babylonian Laws*, 94–95 (Col. xxivb, r. 1–17).

3

Covenant and Conquest

The Bible and the ancient Near East attest a structure of thought in which a god makes a covenant with a monarch and for a people. The monarch is the god's son, or at least chosen one, and the people are the god's people. The covenant includes two major features: the god commands or imparts laws that the monarch must implement for his people, and the god commands wars of conquest that will bring foreign peoples under the god's dominion.

Covenant

All covenants involve law, that is, stipulations that must be obeyed by one or both parties. In the ancient Near East a god imparts law to his people through a mediator, either a monarch or ruler.[1] So, for example, the Lord

---

1. The following discussion parts ways to some extent with Walton, *Ancient Near Eastern Thought*, 287–97. Walton follows some current scholarship in seeing the ancient law codes as legal treatises (i.e., containing hypothetical examples meant to serve as guidelines) rather than codes, and as humanly produced (albeit with divine help) rather than divinely revealed. While we cannot indulge in a lengthy treatment here, the treatise hypothesis seems to fall short in light of the highly detailed nature of most of the laws contained in the ancient codes. A familiar example is the Codex Hammurapi [hereafter *CH*]. Hammurapi's laws address many different cases with a high degree of specificity and are laws in their own right, not just paradigms in a treatise (although, of course, they often provide models of judgment, just as the Mosaic laws or, for that matter, any secular laws can do, since we understand that no law code can anticipate all the details of every case that will arise). Furthermore, Hammurapi refers to himself as "the king of righteousness, to whom

establishes a covenant of law through the mediator judge, Moses. Much of the evidence for this process from the ancient Near East is indirect. It takes the form of divine commands to the king rather than extant covenant documents between a god and a people. But the evidence, such as it is, supports the idea of divine-royal covenants in the ancient Near East.

Egypt

In Egypt a covenantal kinship relation appears to have been assumed between Pharaoh and the gods, and in particular between Pharaoh and the sun god. Breasted comments on the "nature of the compact between Pharaoh and his god: on the one hand, the god grants the Pharaoh the might which prevails over all the nations; on the other, the Pharaoh offers to the god the captives and the plunder thus gained."[2]

Pharaohs claimed that the sun god Ra, their father, commanded them to promulgate laws the god had in mind and in general to do what Ra was doing. This meant the rule of *ma'at* (the just order the gods desire and make possible in the world) over Egypt and ultimately over all lands. Sen-Usert

---

Shamash has given law/justice/truth (Akkadian *kīnātum*)" (*CH* xxvb.95–98)—a claim that hardly seems refuted by the casuistic and list forms of the codex's contents (cf. Walton, *Ancient Near Eastern Thought*, 288–91). Even if we understand *kīnātum* as "justice/truth," rather than "law," its historical usage indicates a state of being in alignment with divinely given standards of what is right (cf. *The Assyrian Dictionary of the Oriental Institute of the University of Chicago*, 8:383–84; hereafter *CAD*), and, again, it is *given* to the king by Shamash, the Mesopotamian god of laws and covenants. Moreover, this statement and statements by the king that he has given the land its law/judgments (*CH* xxvb.60–74; cf. *CH* xxvb.80–84, "The procedure, the administration, and the law of the land, which I have given") stand in direct contradiction to Walton's statement, "In the ancient Near East we found that neither Shamash (the deity) nor Hammurabi (the king) could be considered a lawgiver" (297). Moreover, the one who reads and benefits from Hammurapi's Codex will declare, "Hammurabi is a ruler, who is as a father to his subjects, who holds the words of Marduk in reverence, who has achieved conquest for Marduk over the north and south, who rejoices the heart of Marduk, his lord, who has bestowed benefits for ever and ever on his subjects, and has established order in the land" (*CH* xxvb.20–39). That is, Hammurapi has received "words" from Marduk, the chief god of Babylon, and those words are noted in the context of the order provided by law, and also of divinely mandated conquest—the very two categories of divine covenantal command that form the subjects of this chapter. Elsewhere, in Sumer, more than one king claimed to have received divine revelation (a "word" from the god of laws and covenants) regarding alterations of common law ("customs"); cf. below.

2.   Breasted, *Ancient Records of Egypt*, 3:37 (§ 80).

(Sesostris) I (1971–1926 B.C.) says, "[Ra] begat me to do that which he did, To execute that which he commanded me to do. He appointed me shepherd of this land. . . . He appointed me lord of mankind."[3] Hatshepsut (1486–1468 B.C.) declares, "I have no enemy in any land, all countries are my subjects, he has made my boundary to the extremities of heaven."[4] Thutmose III (1490–1436 B.C.) says, "Every law, every regulation which I made, for my father, Amon-Re. . . . I knew . . . that which he commanded to do . . . he desired . . . that I do them for him, according as he commanded."[5] Ptah says to Ramses II (1290–1224 B.C.), "I make thy heart divine like me. . . . I prepare thee, that thy heart may discern, that thy utterance may be profitable. There is nothing whatever which thou dost not know, (for) I have completed thee . . . that thou mayst make all men live by thy instruction."[6] So the Lord says through Moses, "Keep my decrees and laws (instructions), for the man who obeys them will live by them" (Lev. 18:5). Like Ramses II, Moses was to "make men live" by imparting to them his God's instruction. Christological implications (to be discussed later) also abound in the pharaonic claims, not least of which is the association of the pharaoh's word with life (cf. Phil. 2:16).

Sumer

Uruʾinimgina of Lagash (twenty-fifth/twenty-fourth century B.C.) was the lawgiver par excellence who made a covenant with the god Ningirsu that emphasized the human observance of laws. He declares, "When Ningirsu, warrior of Enlil, granted the kingship of Lagash to Uruʾinimgina, selecting him from among the myriad people, he replaced the customs of former times, carrying out the command that Ningirsu, his master, had given him."[7]

Uruʾinimgina's words could well characterize Moses, who appeared some thousand years later. Moses' God also "selected him from among the myriad people." Like the Sumerian king, Moses also "replaced the customs of former times, carrying out the command" of his God. For Moses, God's

---

3.   Ibid., 1:243 (§ 502).

4.   Ibid., 2:134 (§ 319).

5.   Ibid., 2:225 (§ 568). The same pharaoh even claims to have been taken to heaven, where he "was sated with the counsels of the gods," 2:61 (§ 142).

6.   Ibid., 3:177 (§ 402).

7.   Cooper, *Sumerian and Akkadian Royal Inscriptions*, 71 (La 9.1.viiff). Cf. earlier, Thureau-Dangin, *Die Sumerischen und Akkadischen Königsinschriften*, 52ff.

commands and laws came in a covenantal context. The same appears to have been the case for ancient Near Eastern rulers.

The sun god often played a major role in such arrangements, because in Mesopotamia that god oversaw laws and covenants. So, somewhat later in Mesopotamia, Ur-Nammu (2112–2095 B.C.), son of the goddess Ninsun, gave laws to his people "in accordance with the true word of Utu [i.e., the sun god]."[8] Ur-Nammu claims that the god of laws and covenants gave him a revelatory "word." That word told him what laws Ur-nammu must give to his people. In Sumer, as in Egypt, law, like kingship, came from heaven, given through a chosen monarch in an apparently covenantal relationship.

Babylon

A parallel situation appears in Babylon. The most famous law code from the ancient Near East is that of the Babylonian king Hammurapi (1792–1750 B.C.). The sun god Shamash gives Hammurapi the law so that he may "make justice to appear in the land, to destroy the evil and wicked that the strong might not oppress the weak, to rise indeed like Shamash over the dark-haired folk to give light to the land . . . (and) so to give justice to the orphan and widow."[9]

From Babylon also comes the "Prophetic Speech of Marduk," probably from the reign of Nebuchadnezzar I (1127–1105 B.C.). The god Marduk foretells that he will make a covenant with a man whom he will raise up: "That prince will rule all lands. And/But I, O gods all, have a covenant with him. He will destroy Elam. Its cities he will cast down."[10] The god raises up a king and makes a covenant with him, which involves the conquest of other lands and (after the standard ancient Near Eastern pattern) the rule of those lands in the name of the god.

If the pagan gods gave laws for their people through intermediaries, where did they deposit those laws? The answer to that question seems clear enough. The divinely revealed and imparted law was placed in the

---

8. Pritchard, *ANET*, 523.
9. Driver and Miles, *Babylonian Laws*, 6–7 (Col. 1a.33–49), 96–97 (Col. xxivb.60–61).
10. Block, *Gods of the Nations*, 175. Cf. the discussion by Longman, *Fictional Akkadian Biography*, 132–42. The term that Longman translates "friendship" is a metonymy for "covenant"; cf. Moran, "Note on the Treaty Terminology of the Sefire Stelas," 174.

temple, just as was the case in Israel. The outstanding case is the law code of Hammurapi. The Codex Hammurapi reads as follows:

> I, Hammurabi, am the king of justice,
>   to whom Shamash committed law.
>   (Rs.xxv.98–99)

> In Esagila, the temple whose foundations stand firm
>   like heaven and earth,
> I wrote my precious words on my stela,
> and in the presence of the statue of me, the king of justice,
> I set (it) up in order to administer the law of the land,
> to prescribe the ordinances of the land,
> to give justice to the oppressed.
>   (Rs.xxiv.64–72)[11]

The law, revealed and imparted to Hammurapi by the sun god Shamash (also the god of justice and overseer of covenants) was deposited in the Esagila temple in Babylon. Significantly, the same was done with copies of covenants made between two earthly rulers and overseen by Shamash. In the ancient Near East, each ruler would deposit his copy of the treaty in the temple of his gods. Although we lack covenant documents themselves, the royal phraseology and the practice of deposition in the temple suggest that the pagan gods gave such laws in a context of covenant with their elect monarch for the people. The deposition of the "Book of the Covenant" with its laws in Israel's temple (tabernacle) is another example of this practice.

Hatti

There is evidence that the Hittites shared the same theology of divine covenant giving and oversight that appears to have been common to the ancient Near East. Our evidence is scanty, but what we have is significant, and comes in the form of a hymn and a private covenant.

One great Hittite hymn celebrates the sun god Shamash as the "just lord of judgement," who rules all lands and "establishes custom and contract

---

11. Pritchard, *ANET*, 178; cf. Driver and Miles, *Babylonian Laws*, 96–97 (Col. xxivb.57–78).

of the land."[12] From Hatti also comes a covenant between a private individual and the god Sanda (a pestilential god written with the logogram MARDUK). In the covenant ritual a goat is slaughtered and its blood smeared on a drinking vessel. An animal is sacrificed to the gods and consumed at a communion meal. O. R. Gurney has rightly paralleled the ritual to "the covenant of Moses (Exod. 24:5-8)."[13]

We await more evidence from the Hittite realm, but what we have shows clearly enough that they thought that gods entered into covenants, even covenants solemnized by the shedding of blood, and that Shamash, god of covenant, was the one who established the laws of the land.

Assyria

As one might expect, Assyria shows great affinity to Babylon in these matters, perhaps because the ideas under discussion are ancient in Mesopotamia, dating back to Sumer. Assyrian kings regularly make claims reminiscent of their Sumerian and Babylonian forerunners.

Like Hammurapi, Tukulti-Ninurta I (1244–1208 B.C.) claims specific divine instruction for legal and administrative purposes: "(Aššur) taught me righteous judgment."[14] The Assyrian king Ashurnasirpal II (883–859 B.C.) relates, "I founded the temples of the great gods within the city, and established the covenant of the great gods, my lords, within them."[15] Esarhaddon says that Sin and Shamash, the moon and sun deities, appointed him "to give just and righteous judgment to the land and the people."[16] The sun god is involved as god of laws and covenants. The moon god is involved as god of wisdom and change. The god who governed change also had (and could give) the wisdom to manage well amid change. So Esarhaddon claims that Sin, as well as Shamash, was involved in his legal appointment. Gods revealed divine law, or

---

12. H. G. Gütterbock, "The Vocative in Hittite," *Journal of the American Oriental Society* 65 (1945): 251.

13. O. R. Gurney, *Some Aspects of Hittite Religion* (Oxford: Oxford University Press, 1997), 29–30.

14. Weidner, "Das Alter der mittelassyrischen Gesetzestexte," 1.I.32–33.

15. Wiseman, "A New Stela of Assur-nasir-pal II," 34 (Col. ii, left Rev., 59–60). We translate *mamītu* "covenant," i.e., "sworn agreement." Wiseman, with some doubt, translates, "the spell (?) of the great gods." But *mamītu + kinnu* is used of covenant establishment; cf. The Tukulti-Ninurta Epic, "v." 16, *u-kin-nu ma-mi-ta*, where the covenant oath is in view; cf. "iv." 9, "I will read aloud the tablet of the covenant/sworn agreement (*mamītu*) between us to the Lord of heaven" (cf. *CAD* 10.1.190).

16. Borger, *Die Inschriften Asarhaddons Königs von Assyrien*, § 2.I.31–34, 2.

instruction, to those priest kings, just as Yahweh did to Moses. Moreover, the gods could impart covenant or "sworn agreement," just as Yahweh did with Moses. Such covenants and laws were deposited in the god's temple.

Because Assyrian kings believed they had received divine instruction for rule of their own lands and people, they could expect that Israel's God would likewise give instruction (*torah*) for his territories. A passage from the history of Israel supports this view. Second Kings 17:24–25 reports that alien elements that had been imported into the northern kingdom after the Assyrian conquest "feared not Yahweh." So Yahweh sent lions among them, which killed some of them.

> And it was reported to the king of Assyria, "The people whom you have transported and settled in the cities of Samaria do not know the law [*mišpaṭ*] of the god of the land, and he has sent lions among them which are even now killing them off because they do not know the law of the god of the land." And the king of Assyria commanded, "Send there one of the priests whom you deported from there, that he may go and live there and teach them the law of the god of the land." And one of the priests whom they had deported from Samaria went and settled in Beth-El, teaching them how to reverence Yahweh. (2 Kings 17:26–28, author's translation)

The remarkable thing about this passage may be that nothing appears remarkable in it. There is no indication that the concept of a "law of the god of the land" was a novel or alien idea to the Assyrian king. This is consistent with what we have seen in the Assyrian and older Mesopotamian sources.

It seems clear enough that gods in the ancient Near East, in effect, could give *torah*, divine instruction, for the people and that they gave this divine law or instruction to their intermediaries, the kings, for the proper rule of the people. Indications are that such *torah* was given as part of a covenantal understanding.

Conquest

Ancient Near Eastern gods chose monarchs to shepherd their land in a covenant relationship. Royal appointment included a divine gift of law, instruction, and wisdom for good rule. But the alliance had another equally important purpose. The supreme god of the pantheon regularly commanded the conquest of other lands so that people who had not known him would come under his dominion.

Egypt

Pharaohs from Sesostris (Sen-Usert) I (1971–1926 B.C.)[17] to Tanutamon (Twenty-fifth Dynasty, ca. 600 B.C.)[18] claimed divine appointment for conquest. Amen-hotep II (1439–1406 B.C.) says that Ra "appointed him to be king of the living . . . king of kings, ruler of rulers . . . victorious lord, who takes every land. . . . It is my father Re who commands that I do it. . . . He assigned me to that which is with him . . . all lands, all countries . . . they come to me in submission like every subject of my majesty."[19]

All lands belong to Ra, as he makes his great circuit over them daily. But this is like saying that all the world belongs to God. That may be so, but it does not mean that all people worship God or consider themselves his people (cf. Heb. 2:8). Pharaoh's task is to bring nations effectively under the rule of Ra, as vassal to his son, Pharaoh. Accordingly the same pharaoh says that he is Amon's "real son, who came forth from his limbs, one with him, in order to rule that which the sun encircles, all the lands, and countries . . . that he might seize them immediately with victory and power."[20] Likewise the Son of God says, "I and the Father are one" (John 10:30), and "All authority in heaven and on earth has been given to me. Therefore go and make disciples of all nations" (Matt. 28:18–19).

The gods not only command conquest, but they even wage war for Pharaoh. Thutmose II (1495–1490 B.C.) says he achieves universal rule because the gods "smite for him his enemies."[21] So Joshua 10:42 says, "All these kings

---

17. Breasted, *Ancient Records of Egypt*, 2:243 (§ 502). The claim of earlier pharaohs that they were "smiter[s] of all countries" probably means much the same. See ibid., 1:108 (§ 236) for Sahure (Fifth Dynasty, early twenty-fifth century B.C.), 114 (§ 250) for Nusurre (Fifth Dynasty), 121 (§ 267) for Dedkere-Isesi (Fifth Dynasty).

18. Ibid., 4:472 (§§ 931–32).

19. Ibid., 2:317 (§ 804). So later Ptah says to Ramses II (1290–1224 B.C.), "I have set for thee the might, victory, and strength of thy sword in every land, I have bound for thee the hearts of all lands, I have set them beneath thy feet" (3:179 [§ 408]).

20. Ibid., 2:311 (§ 792).

21. Ibid., 2:49 (§ 120). See also 2:97 (§ 237; Hatshepsut, 1486–1468 B.C.), 263 (§ 656; Thutmose III, 1490–1436 B.C.), 310 (§ 792; Amen-hotep II, 1439–1406 B.C.), 329 (§ 829; Thutmose IV, 1406–1398 B.C.), 341 (§ 853; Amen-hotep III, 1398–1361 B.C.); 3:179 (§ 408; Ramses II, 1290–1224 B.C.), 262 (§ 615; Mer-ne-Ptah, 1224–1214 B.C.); 4:56 (§ 92; Ramses III, 1195–1164 B.C.).

and their lands Joshua conquered in one campaign, because the LORD, the God of Israel, fought for Israel."[22]

The gods also put the fear of Pharaoh in the heart of his enemies, so that his victory is assured. Amon-Ra declares, in the great victory hymn of Thutmose III (1490–1436 B.C.), "I have given thee might and victory against all countries, I have set thy fame (even) the fear of thee in all lands. The terror of thee as far as the four pillars of heaven."[23] God promises to do the same for Israel when they invade Canaan: "I will send my terror ahead of you and throw into confusion every nation you encounter. I will make all your enemies turn their backs and run" (Exod. 23:27). As a result, Rahab can tell the spies at Jericho,

> I know that the LORD has given this land to you and that a great fear of you has fallen on us, so that all who live in this country are melting in fear because of you. We have heard how the LORD dried up the water of the Red Sea for you when you came out of Egypt, and what you did to Sihon and Og, the two kings of the Amorites east of the Jordan, whom you completely destroyed. When we heard of it, our hearts melted and everyone's courage failed because of you, for the LORD your God is God in heaven above and on earth below. (Josh. 2:9–11)

Rahab articulates the same principles found in pharaonic claims. The god has worked great things through his servant. As a result, the fame and the fear of the servant are now in the land(s) of the foe. Their courage melts, and the servant's victory is assured.

The gods also endow Pharaoh with a theophanic radiance that cows his foes. This can take the form of a flame in battle. Hatshepsut comes into battle "flaming against my enemies."[24] Or Pharaoh can shine like the sun. Amen-hotep III (1398–1361 B.C.) wages war "shining in the chariot, like

---

22. The phrase "in one campaign" is better translated "once," with implications for supposed inconsistencies between the conquest accounts of Joshua 10ff. and Judges 1. Cf. Niehaus, "*Pa'am 'Eḥat* and the Israelite Conquest," 236–39.

23. Breasted, *Ancient Records of Egypt*, 2:263 (§ 656). See also 2:329 (§ 829; Thutmose IV, 1406–1398 B.C.); 3:56–57 (§ 116; Seti I, 1302–1290 B.C.), 179 (§ 408; Ramses II, 1290–1224 B.C.); 4:48 (§ 81; Ramses III, 1195–1164 B.C.).

24. Ibid., 2:126 (§ 303). See also 2:178 (§ 413; Thutmose III, 1490–1436 B.C.), 311 (§ 792; Amen-hotep II, 1439–1406 B.C.); 3:58 (§ 117; Seti I, 1302–1290 B.C.), 137 (§307; Ramses II, 1290–1224 B.C.); 4:27 (§ 49; Ramses III, 1195–1164 B.C.), 357 (§ 721; Sheshonk I, 945 B.C.), 441 (§ 880; Pi-ankhi, 720 B.C.).

the rising of the sun."[25] The monarch's glory is actually an aspect of divine presence in or upon him, a topic to be discussed later. For now it is enough to recognize its role in battle. That role does not appear in the Old Testament, but it has an important parallel in the New Testament. There, at Pentecost, God's people receive a theophanic fire that empowers them to go forth and advance God's dominion (like that of Amon-Ra, "to the ends of the earth," Acts 1:8) in spiritual warfare (Eph. 6:12).

Amon has assigned Pharaoh lands to conquer and suzerainty over them. That is part of the covenantal arrangement between Pharaoh and his god. It is also part of the covenantal arrangement between Yahweh and Abram in Genesis 15.[26] In that covenant, Yahweh assigns Abram land to conquer (Gen. 15:18–21), much as Amon does to Pharaoh (and as, in Assyria, the gods do to Tukulti-Ninurta I, see below). God does the same in the New Testament ("the ends of the earth"), although there the conquest is spiritual, and the form of the kingdom is the church.

Pharaohs claimed that their acts of conquest (in fact all of their acts) were the same as the acts of Amon-Ra. In effect they said that they were doing what their father did. Sesostris (Sen-usert) I (1971–1926 B.C.) said, "[Ra] begat me to do that which he did, To execute that which he commanded to do."[27] Osiris supposedly had fathered Thutmose I (1525–1495 B.C.) "in the uprightness of his heart, to do that which he did in the earth."[28] Amon leads Thutmose IV (1406–1398 B.C.) "upon a goodly road, to do that which his *ka* desired, as a father speaks to his son."[29] Amen-hotep III (1398–1361 B.C.) claimed that Amon "gave to him the thought of every day."[30] Subsequent pharaohs made similar claims.[31] Later, Jesus could say the same of his own kingdom work, and of his whole life: "I tell you the truth, the Son can do nothing by himself; he can do only what he sees his Father doing, because whatever the Father does the Son also does. For the Father loves the Son and shows him all he does" (John 5:19–20; cf. v. 30; 8:28–29).

---

25. Ibid., 2:342–43 (§ 858). See also 3:57 (§ 117; Seti I, 1302–1290 B.C.).
26. Cf. Niehaus, *God at Sinai*, 172–75.
27. Breasted, *Ancient Records of Egypt*, 1:243 (§ 502); cf. 2:317 (§ 304; Amen-hotep II, 1439–1406 B.C.).
28. Ibid., 2:38 (§ 91).
29. Ibid., 2:328 (§ 827).
30. Ibid., 2:366 (§ 900).
31. Ibid., 2:413 (§ 1002; Akh-en-Aton, 1369–1353 B.C.); 3:218 (§ 511; Ramses II, 1290–1224 B.C.); 4:47 (§ 78; Ramses III, 1195–1164 B.C.).

Amon and the gods command Pharaoh to conquer other lands in order to make effective their rule over those lands. But that means the subject lands will be in covenant with Pharaoh, and hence vassals of Amon-Ra. An important aspect of vassaldom is tribute for and service in the temple(s) of Egypt's god(s). So Sesostris I (1971–1926 B.C.) declares, "I will make a work, namely, a great house, for my father Atum. He will make it broad, according as he has caused me to conquer."[32] That is, the magnitude of the temple will reflect Pharaoh's broad conquest, both because much booty will furnish the temple, and because many vassals will serve in it. So Thutmose III (1490–1436 B.C.) says of Amon, "My father caused that I should be divine, that I might extend the throne of him who made me; that I might supply with food his altars upon earth . . . with great slaughters in his temple, consisting of oxen and calves without limit. . . . I filled for him his granaries of barley and spelt without limit. I increased for him the divine offerings."[33] Seti I (1302–1290 B.C.) presents "tribute to his father, Amon, from the rebellious chiefs of the countries that knew not Egypt. Their tribute is upon their backs, in order to fill thy [i.e., Amon's temple] storehouses with slaves, male and female; from the victories which thou givest me in every country."[34] Ramses II (1290–1224 B.C.) boasts that "his might is in all lands; bringing for him the multitudes of workmen from the captivity of his sword in every country. He has filled the houses of the gods with the children of Retenu."[35] Vassals of Ramses III (1195–1164 B.C.) confess, "Utterance of the vanquished of every country who are before his majesty: 'Breath from thee! O lord of Egypt . . . Thy father, Amon, hath put us beneath thy feet forever, that we may see and breathe the breath of life; that we may hail his temple. Thou art our lord forever, like thy father, Amon. Every land is beneath thy feet.'"[36] The same pharaoh says to Amon, "I came at thy command. . . . I carried off their people, all their possessions . . . they are placed before thee, O lord of gods . . . the males thereof to fill thy storehouse; their women to be subjects of thy temple."[37]

Amon has put Pharaoh's enemies beneath his feet so they might serve in

---

32. Ibid., 1:244 (§ 503).
33. Ibid., 2:63 (§ 149).
34. Ibid., 3:70 (§ 138).
35. Ibid., 3:213 (§ 498).
36. Ibid., 4:71 (§ 122).
37. Ibid., 4:75 (§ 128); cf. 251 (§ 591; Mer-ne-Ptah, 1224–1214 B.C.).

his temple. To place an enemy "beneath one's feet" has an obvious symbolism, and it is complemented in the Egyptian records by another figure of speech (metonymy of the adjunct). Sometimes Pharaoh's enemies are put beneath his "sandals." Both images are symbolic of rule, and that symbolism can appear alongside the vassals' fear of Pharaoh (a response that has to do with his divine status). So Thutmose III (1490–1436 B.C.) says, "My terror was in [their] hearts . . . all lands were under my sandals."[38] Hatshepsut (1486–1468 B.C.) declares that vanquished foes "come to her with fearful heart . . . they present to her their children that there may be given to them the breath of life, because of the greatness of the fame of her father, Amon, who hath set all lands beneath her sandals."[39] Amon says to Seti I (1302–1290 B.C.), "I put fear of thee in their hearts. . . . I give to thee all lands, every country is beneath thy sandals."[40] Because of their fear of Ramses II (1290–1224 B.C.), he can rule, "all countries being prostrate beneath his sandals forever."[41] Those subject to Ramses III (1195–1164 B.C.) are told, "Be ye attached to his sandals."[42]

There are important biblical parallels. For example, against this background we read the Lord's claim, "Moab is my washbasin, upon Edom I toss my sandal; over Philistia I shout in triumph" (Pss. 60:8; 108:9). God's promise to Abraham is part of the same symbolic system: "Go, walk through the length and breadth of the land, for I am giving it to you" (Gen. 13:17). Moses restates that promise: "Every place where you set your foot will be yours: Your territory will extend from the desert to Lebanon, and from the Euphrates River to the western sea. No man will be able to stand against you. The LORD your God, as he promised you, will put the terror and fear of you on the whole land, wherever you go" (Deut. 11:24–25). We note the combination of divinely imparted fear and rule symbolized by walking/treading. And the Lord repeats the Mosaic promise to Joshua, saying, "I will give you every place where you set your foot" (Josh. 1:3), and Joshua also conquers with the help of divinely produced fear (Josh. 2:9–11).

The wilderness wandering and conquest narratives may contain related

38. Ibid., 2:62 (§ 148); cf. 193 (§ 451).
39. Ibid., 2:116 (§ 285); cf. 2:126 (§ 303), 263 (§ 656). So earlier Thutmose I, 2:101 (§ 245).
40. Ibid., 3:76 (§§ 155–56); cf. 3:43 (§ 84).
41. Ibid., 3:165 (§ 371); cf. 3:160 (§ 359), 200 (§ 465), 202 (§ 471).
42. Ibid., 4:206 (§ 412).

concepts. Because of God's favor, Moses can tell Israel, "During the forty years that I led you . . . your clothes did not wear out, nor did the sandals on your feet" (Deut. 29:5). By contrast the Gibeonites say, "Our clothes and sandals are worn out by the very long journey" (Josh. 9:13). Although the Gibeonite statement is a lie, it may contain a significant symbolism when contrasted with the true experience of the Israelites. Israel's sandals did not wear out and so were fit to tread upon the land that Israel was to conquer; by contrast, the Gibeonites' sandals were not fit to tread upon anything, and they would conquer no land but become vassals of Israel.

Excursus: Sandals and Ruth

The symbolism of treading or sandal(s) for dominion or ownership also explains, I believe, the practice mentioned in Ruth: "Now in earlier times in Israel, for the redemption and transfer of property to become final, one party took off his sandal and gave it to the other. This was the method of legalizing transactions in Israel" (Ruth 4:7).

The sandal stood for the owner's right to tread upon his land. The transfer of the sandal from owner to purchaser symbolized the transfer of that right. In the case of Boaz and Ruth, the man who had first option to buy the land from Naomi and Ruth gave up that right in favor of Boaz. He symbolized his decision by giving Boaz his sandal, which would have trodden on the land had he acquired it. The use of a sandal to symbolize dominion or ownership of land, as Egyptian records show, helps to clarify this long obscure Old Testament passage.

We have much to say about kingdom theology and note for now that a kingdom theology drove the pharaonic conquests: the conquered became part of the kingdom of Amon, Pharaoh's father. One way the pharaohs characterized this process was to say that they rendered to Amon the lands he had enabled them to conquer. This is implicit in the claim by Thutmose III (1490–1436 B.C.) that Amon-Ra "gave victory by my arms, in order to widen the boundaries of Egypt."[43] Amen-hotep II (1439–1406 B.C.) says more explicitly of himself, "Every land comes to him bowing down. . . .

---

43.   Ibid., 2:62 (§ 148).

It is my father Re who commands that I do it.... He appointed me to be protector of this land, (for) he knew that I would offer it to him."[44] Amenhotep III (1398–1361 B.C.) says that "His two hands hold might, his word bears victory, in order to present to him (Amon) the whole earth, with the impost thereof."[45] Akh-en-Aton (1369–1353 B.C.) "came forth from Aton, and offers the earth to him who placed him on his throne."[46] Later, Amon says to Seti I (1302–1290 B.C.), "I put the fear of thee in their hearts so that thou cuttest down the Curly-Haired . . . in order to make me lord of their heads."[47] The Bible has a Christological parallel. Just as the "son of Amon" offers his newly won kingdom to his "father," so Jesus offers his kingdom to his Father: "Then the end will come, when he hands over the kingdom to God the Father after he has destroyed all dominion, authority and power. For he must reign until he has put all his enemies under his feet" (1 Cor. 15:24–25).

Sumer

The Sumerians also claimed that their gods commanded elect monarchs to do battle to extend the gods' effective dominion, and here, too, enhancement of temple worship was part of the picture. The Sumerian data are fewer and more scattered than those of Egypt, but they document the concepts sufficiently to show that they were a part of a standard Sumerian royal ideology. Inscriptions from monarchs of the twenty-fourth century B.C. are especially germane.

Eanatum of Lagash records how the god Ningirsu approached him while he slept and encouraged him to move against a rebellious vassal.

> He followed after him. Him who lies sleeping, him who lies sleeping—he approaches his head. Eanatum who lies sleeping—[his] be[loved] master [Ningirsu approaches his head . . .] . . . "The sun-(god) will shine at your right . . . O Eanatum . . . you will slay there. Their myriad corpses will reach the base of heaven. [In] Um[ma . . . the people of his own city]

44. Ibid., 2:317 (§ 804).
45. Ibid., 2:365 (§ 900).
46. Ibid., 2:412 (§ 1000).
47. Ibid., 3:76 (§ 155). Cf. the statement of Ramses IV (1164–1157 B.C.) to Osiris: "And thou shalt give to me every land and every country . . . that I may present their tribute to thy ka and to thy name" (4:229 [§ 471]).

will rise up against him [i.e., the rebel ruler] and he will be killed within Umma itself."[48]

Thus encouraged, the king can report, "Eanatum . . . destroyed the foreign lands; Eanatum restored to Ningirsu's control [his] belov[ed fi]eld," and concludes that he is "Eanatum, who subjugates foreign lands for Ningirsu."[49] A subsequent king, Enmetana, is the one "who carries out the commands of the gods," including warfare, temple building, and domestic improvements.[50] Enshakushana, king of Uruk, reports how, as "lord of Sumer . . . when the gods commanded him, he sacked (the cities of) Kish . . . [and Akshak]."[51] As in Egypt, the monarch conquers by divine command. Also as in Egypt, a divine fear is associated with the king and consolidates his victory. So Eanatum can declare, "All the foreign lands trembled before Eanatum, nominated by Ningirsu."[52] Enmetana says he "built the Eshdugru for Ningirsu, built him the Ahush, the temple he looks upon approvingly, and furnished it. He made him 'Ningirsu's chariot that heaps up (defeated) foreign lands . . .' the fear of which is (felt) within the foreign lands."[53]

As we have seen, conquest can be and often is followed by temple building. Eanatum describes several victories he accomplished for Ningirsu and then declares, "Eanatum, who is commissioned by Ningirsu . . . built the 'palace' [i.e., temple] of Tirash for him."[54] As in Egypt, the conquests mean increased supplies for the god's temple. Eanatum boasts, "Eanatum, who subjugates foreign lands for Ningirsu . . . He built the storehouse of the E[za] for him and amassed piles of grain for him (there)."[55] Likewise, his successor, Enanatum I, declares, "[When Lu]galurub granted the kingship of Lagash to Enanatum, put all foreign lands in his control, and [set] the rebellious lands at his feet, then Enanatum [bui]lt the I[bgal] for Inana. . . . For his master who loves him, Lugalurub, he built the 'palace'

---

48.   Cooper, *Sumerian and Akkadian Royal Inscriptions*, 34 (La 3.1, vi–viii).
49.   Ibid., 35 (xiii), 37 (r.xi).
50.   Ibid., 56 (La 5.1, v).
51.   Ibid., 105 (Uk 4.1, i).
52.   Ibid., 44 (La 3.8, vi).
53.   Ibid., 58 (La 5.4, ii).
54.   Ibid., 42 (La 3.5, vii).
55.   Ibid., 44 (La 3.10, ii).

[i.e., temple] of Urub, decorated it for him with gold and silver, and furnished it."[56]

This pattern of conquest followed by temple building and furnishing is apparent not only in Egypt and Sumer but also throughout the ancient Near East. It has a major biblical-theological parallel, as we have suggested. It also helps to clarify one particular Old Testament account, that of David's statement to Nathan in 2 Samuel 7, and Nathan's response: "After the king was settled in his palace and the LORD had given him rest from all his enemies around him, he said to Nathan the prophet, 'Here I am, living in a palace of cedar, while the ark of God remains in a tent.' Nathan replied to the king, 'Whatever you have in mind, go ahead and do it, for the LORD is with you'" (2 Sam. 7:1–3).

What David "has in mind," of course, is to build a temple for the God who has subdued all his enemies for him, just as any other ancient Near Eastern monarch would do. Nathan understands this perfectly well and encourages David accordingly.

Sumerian monarchs claimed a divine call to conquer foreign lands and bring them under the dominion of their god(s). Or they claimed that the gods sent them to reconquer and restore rebellious vassals to the god's domain. As in Egypt, the conquests meant that other lands and peoples were brought under the effective rule of the god by becoming vassals of his chosen monarch. The monarch carried out these commissions and then built and furnished a temple for his god. This structure of thought was common to the ancient Near East and finds its place in biblical theology as well.

Babylon (Old Babylonian)

Sumer's great successor, Babylon, was heir to the same ideas, as a few illustrations will show. Here, too, gods command conquest and even endow a monarch with theophanic glory to help him win the battle.

---

56. Ibid., 51 (La 4.9, iii–iv); cf. 48 (La 4.2, xi). Cf. later Lugalzagesi: "When Enlil, king of all lands, gave to Lugalzagesi the kingship of the nation, directed all the eyes of the land (obediently) toward him, put all the lands at his feet, and from east to west made them subject to him. . . . [Then] Lugalzagesi, king of Uruk and king of the Land, solicitously provided plentiful food offerings and libated sweet water for his master Enlil in Nippur" (ibid., 94 [Um 7.1, i–ii, iii]). Enshakushana, after the gods command him to sack Kish and Akshak, "dedicated their statues [i.e., idols, gods] their precious metals and lapis lazuli, their timber and treasure, to Enlil at [N]ippur" (ibid., 105 [Uk 4.1, 1']).

Samsu-iluna (1749–1712 B.C.), king of Babylon, tells how Enlil sent the god Zababa and the goddess Eshtar to commission the monarch.

> O Samsu-iluna, eternal seed of the gods, one befitting kingship—Enlil has made your destiny very great. He has laid a commission on us to act as your guardians for (your) well-being. We will go at your right side, kill your enemies, and deliver your foes into your hands. (As for) Kiš, our fear-inspiring cult city, build its wall, make it greater than it was previously.[57]

Many of the concepts we have seen in Egypt and Sumeria occur here. The monarch is divine offspring. The king of the gods commands and empowers him to embark upon a career of conquest. The gods will fight for him, even at his side. He has a divinely imparted glory and can boast, "The fearsome splendour and aura of my kingship covered the borders of heaven and earth."[58] And once his victories are won, he raises, if not a temple, at least temple-related architecture (the wall of the god's cult city, making it greater than before). So the Son of God, after his eschatological victory, will appear with the heavenly Jerusalem, the "cult city" par excellence, where his presence and worship can be fully experienced.

Kudur-mabuk, father of Warad Sîn (1834–1823 B.C.), conquers his foe "by the supreme decree of the gods Enlil, Ninurta, Nanna, and Utu, having conquered (Ṣillī-Eštar) (and) having set (his) f[oot . . .] . . . striding with (his) foot placed on (Ṣillī-Eštar's) head."[59] Likewise, Rīm-Sîn (1822–1763 B.C.) of Larsa says, "When the goddess Ninsianna delivered all my enemies into my hands, on account of this, for the goddess Ninsianna . . . I built in a pure place, the Eešbarzida . . . suitable for her divinity, her residence which pleases her."[60] Iaḫdun-Līm (1825–1810 B.C.) of Mari boasts that the god Shamash, "king of heaven and earth" and Mesopotamian god of law and covenant, "quickly came and went at the side of Iaḫdun-Līm." He marched to the sea and "made that land on the shore of the Sea submit, made it subject to his decree, and made it follow him. Having imposed a permanent tribute on them, they now bring their tribute to him." After the campaign, the king

---

57. Frayne, Old Babylonian Period, 4:386 (E4.3.7.7, 63–79).
58. Ibid., 4:382 (E4.3.7.5, 59–66).
59. Ibid., 4:267 (E4.2.13a.1, 10–20).
60. Ibid., 4:298 (E4.2.14.18, 27–40).

"built the temple of the god Šamaš, his lord."[61] The account anticipates Old Testament terminology. Shamash is the "king of heaven and earth." Rahab tells the spies at Jericho that "the LORD your God is God in heaven above and on the earth below" (Josh. 2:11). The Old Babylonian phrase for "follow him" literally means "walk after him." It is covenantal terminology that is also found in the Bible. Moses tells Israel, "Do not follow (Heb., 'walk after') other gods" (Deut. 6:14), because "It is the LORD your God you must follow (Heb., 'walk after')" (Deut. 13:4). Iaḫdun-Līm imposed a suzerain-vassal (covenantal) relationship on the conquered foe, just as the Lord made such an arrangement with Israel. The biblical irony is profound, for in the deepest sense Israel was God's enemy before he brought them into covenant with himself. So Paul can say that "Christ died for us . . . when we were God's enemies" (Rom. 5:8, 10). Indeed, the full truth comes out in the New Testament: God conquered us not by putting us to death but by dying for us. So we can enter into a covenant with him that brings us life.

Assyria

From the beginning, Assyrian monarchs made claims similar to the ones we have seen. Here, too, the gods command the monarch to conquer, and they help him to do so. As in Egypt, he has a theophanic radiance that inspires fear in his enemies. In Egypt Pharaoh did what his father, Ra, was doing, and in Assyria the application of parallel phrasing to the king and the god implies that the king acts in parallel with his god.[62] As Pharaoh does for Ra, the monarch takes tribute for Ashur, who has put all lands beneath his feet, making them vassals of the god Ashur.

The gods command the monarch to conquer. Shamshi-Adad I (1814–1782 B.C.) declares himself, "Šamši-Adad, king of the universe, builder of the temple of the god Aššur, *pacifier* of the land between the Tigris and the Euphrates, by the command of the god Aššur who loves him."[63] Adad-Nārārī I (1307–1275 B.C.) conquers the foe "by command of the god Aššur, my lord and ally."[64] Shalmaneser I (1274–1245 B.C.) marches against the foe

61. Ibid., 4:605–7 (E4.6.8.2, 1–2, 31–33, 60–66, 99–102).
62. Cf. Niehaus, "Joshua and Ancient Near Eastern Warfare," 37–50.
63. Grayson, *Assyrian Rulers of the Third and Second Millennia B.C.*, 48 (A.O.39.1, 1–11).
64. Ibid., 136 (A.O.76.3, 7–8).

"by the command of the great gods."[65] Ashur-resha-ishi I (1133–1116 B.C.) defeats the foe "by the command of the god Ninurta."[66] A claim of divine command, standard among second millennium kings, continues as a standard in the first millennium as well.[67]

The gods also helped their chosen king to carry out the conquest mandate. Among second millennium kings, Shamshi-Adad I claims that the goddess Ishtar-sharratum "goes at his right hand" and so dedicates a bronze kettledrum to her, "befitting his being a warrior."[68] Adad-narari I combats his foes "with the strong weapons of the god Aššur, my lord; with the support of the gods Anu, Enlil, and Ea," and a host of other deities.[69] In the first millennium, Tiglath-pileser I carries out military operations "with the support of the god Aššur, my lord."[70] Ashur-bel-kala sets out to conquer "with the exalted strength [of the god Aššur, my lord, who goes before me]."[71] Ashurnasirpal II even characterizes himself as the "destructive weapon of the great gods, avenger, the king who has always acted justly with the support of Aššur and the god Šamaš, the gods who helped him and cut down like marsh reeds fortified mountains and princes hostile to him."[72] Sennacherib says, "The god Aššur . . . has made powerful my weapons."[73] Ashurbanipal says the gods gave him "Strength, virility, enormous power," and "brought all my heart's desire . . . to perfect fulfillment," because "I walked in their ways."[74] So King David says, "It is God who arms me with strength and makes my way perfect" (Ps. 18:32). A prayer for the king says, "May he (God) give you the desire of your heart" (Ps. 20:4). Not only the

---

65. Ibid., 183 (A.O.77.1, 56–58).

66. Ibid., 310 (A.O.86.1, 6).

67. Grayson, *Assyrian Rulers of the Early First Millennium B.C. I*, 89 (A.O. 89.1, 15'; Aššur-bēl-kala, 1074–1057 B.C.), 133 (A.O.98.1, 19; Aššur-dān II, 934–912 B.C.), 143 (A.O.99.1, 10; Adad-nārārī II, 911–891 B.C.), 165 (A.O.100.1, 22–23; Tukulti-Ninurta II, 890–884 B.C.). Aššur-naṣirpal II (883–859 B.C.) declares, "Aššur, my great lord . . . sternly commanded me to rule, subdue, and direct the lands" (ibid., 196 [A.0.101.1, i 40–42]). See also Luckenbill, *Annals of Sennacherib*, 26 (Col. I, 65); Piepkorn, *Historical Prism Inscriptions of Ashurbanipal I*, 30–31 (Col. i, 46–47).

68. Grayson, *Assyrian Rulers of the Third and Second Millennia B.C.*, 58 (A.O.39.7, 1–15).

69. Ibid., 136 (A.O. 76.3, 21–26).

70. Grayson, *Assyrian Rulers of the Early First Millennium B.C. I*, 14 (A.O.87.1, i 70).

71. Ibid., 91 (A.O.89.2, i 9').

72. Ibid., 195 (A.O.101.1, i 21–22).

73. Luckenbill, *Annals of Sennacherib*, 23 (Col. I, 10–12).

74. Piepkorn, *Historical Prism Inscriptions of Ashurbanipal I*, 28–29 (Col. i, 11–13, 26).

king but also all God's royal priesthood must "observe the commands of the LORD your God, walking in his ways" (Deut. 8:6). Only then will their warfare be successful, their conquest complete.

A divinely imparted fear helps the Assyrian monarch conquer his foes, and that fear often is associated with a theophanic radiance, also endowed by the gods. In the second millennium, Shalmaneser I is the one "whose aggressive battle flashes like a flame."[75] In the first millennium, Tiglath-pileser is a "radiant day, whose brilliance overwhelms the regions, splendid flame which covers the hostile land like a rain storm and, by the command of the god Enlil, having no rival defeats the enemy of the god Aššur."[76] Adad-narari II says, "I am enormously radiant."[77] Moreover, he scorches the foe "like the god Girru (fire god)."[78] Esarhaddon (680–669 B.C.) advances theophanically in battle.

> The king whose march is like a flood-storm,
> whose acts are like a raging lion;
> before him is a storm-demon,
> behind him is a cloud-burst;
> the onset of his battle is mighty;
> a consuming flame,
> an unquenchable fire.[79]

His theophanic battle advent recalls that of Yahweh in Psalm 97:2–3.

> Clouds and thick darkness surround him;
>   righteousness and justice are the foundation of his throne.
> Fire goes before him
>   and consumes his foes on every side.

---

75. Grayson, *Assyrian Rulers of the Third and Second Millennia B.C.*, 182–83 (A.O. 77.1, 12–13).

76. Grayson, *Assyrian Rulers of the Early First Millennium B.C. I*, 13 (A.O.87.1, i 40–45). The word translated "day" in this context (*umu*) is probably better rendered "storm," i.e., a radiant, flashing storm. That would be consistent with Assyrian tradition in which the king compares himself with theophanic Adad, and also with the secondary meaning of *umu*, "wind, storm."

77. Ibid., 147 (A.O.99.2, 15).

78. Ibid., 157 (A.O.99.4, 5').

79. Borger, *Die Inschriften Asarhaddons Königs von Assyrien*, 97 (§ 65, Rs. 12–14).

The essential factor in the monarch's theophanic triumph over his foes was a divinely imparted radiance, the *melammu*. As Oppenheim has observed,

> The sanctity of the royal person is often, especially in Assyrian texts, said to be revealed by a supernatural and awe-inspiring radiance or aura which, according to the religious literature, is characteristic of deities and of all things divine. A number of terms refer to this phenomenon; among them the probably pre-Sumerian term *melammu*, something like "awe-inspiring luminosity," is most frequent.[80]

Marduk conquered Tiamat and her demons by virtue of this radiance: "The awesome radiance [*melammu*] overwhelming, [was] upon his head."[81] Similarly, Assyrian monarchs overcome the evil foes by a divine *melammu*. Tiglath-pileser I says that his "brilliance [*melammu*] overwhelms the regions."[82] Ashurnasirpal II boasts of the divinely imparted "radiance [*melammu*] of his dominion."[83] He declares of his foes, "I razed, destroyed (and) burnt their cities. I unleashed against them my lordly radiance [*melammu*]."[84] Sennacherib (704–681 B.C.) says of the king of Sidon, "The terrifying splendor [*melammu*] of my sovereignty overcame him and far off into the midst of the sea he fled. (There) he died."[85] The last great Assyrian emperor, Ashurbanipal (668–627 B.C.), declares of Taharka of Egypt, "(My) royal majesty [*melammu*], with which the gods of heaven and earth have adorned me, overpowered him."[86]

Not only is the monarch theophanic, as noted above, but parallel phrasing applied to the monarch and the god also implies that the king acts in parallel with the god. Like Pharaoh, he does what the god is doing. Tiglath-pileser says of his foes, "The terror, fear, (and) splendour [*melammu*] of the god Aššur, my lord, overwhelmed them."[87] But he also says that "the splen-

80. Oppenheim, *Ancient Mesopotamia, Portrait of a Dead Civilization*, 98.

81. *Enuma Elish*, IV.5–8.

82. Grayson, *Assyrian Rulers of the Early First Millennium B.C. I*, 13 (A.O. 87.1, i 41).

83. Ibid., 195 (A.O.101.1, i 26).

84. Ibid., 210 (A.O.101.1, ii 111–12a).

85. Luckenbill, *Annals of Sennacherib*, 29 (Col. II, 38–40).

86. Piepkorn, *Historical Prism Inscriptions of Ashurbanipal I*, 32–35 (Col. i, 82–83).

87. Grayson, *Assyrian Rulers of the Early First Millennium B.C. I*, 15 (A.O.87.1, ii 38–39).

dour [*melammu*] of my valour overwhelmed them."[88] Ashurbanipal says, "(My) royal majesty [*melammu*] . . . overpowered" the foe.[89] But also, "The splendor [*melammu*] of Ashur and Ishtar overcame them."[90] For Tiglath-pileser I, the enemies are those "who had fled from my weapons."[91] But they also are those "who fled from the weapons of the god Aššur, my lord."[92] Shalmaneser I says he is "the lord at whose feet Aššur and the great gods have subdued all rulers and princes."[93] But he also "subdued all of the land Uruatri in three days at the feet of Aššur, my lord."[94] Such claims are made by subsequent Assyrian monarchs as late as Ashurbanipal.

The gods choose a monarch in order to extend their kingdom. One way for the king to assert his rule is to say that the gods put lands under his feet. Among second millennium kings, Tukulti-Ninurta I (1244–1208 B.C.) says,

> When Aššur, my lord, faithfully chose me to worship him, gave me the sceptre for my office of shepherd, (presented) me in addition the staff for my office of herdsman, granted me excellence so that I might slay my enemies (and) subdue those who do not fear me, (and) placed upon me the lordly crown; (at that time) I set my foot upon the neck of the lands (and) shepherded the extensive black-headed people like animals. He (Aššur) teaches me just decisions.[95]

Such claims anticipate biblical doctrine. Ashur chose the Assyrian monarch as his worshipper, a standard claim in Assyrian imperial tradition. So, in a context of encouragement and instructions for the advance of God's kingdom (John 14–17), Jesus says to his disciples, "You did not choose me, but I chose you and appointed you to go and bear fruit—fruit that will

---

88. Ibid., 17 (A.0.87.1, iii 2).
89. Piepkorn, *Historical Prism Inscriptions of Ashurbanipal I*, 32–35 (Col. i, 82–83).
90. Ibid., 71 (Col. vi, 4–5).
91. Grayson, *Assyrian Rulers of the Early First Millennium B.C. I*, 14 (A.0.87.1, ii 2–3).
92. Ibid., 23 (A.0.87.1, v 55–56). So Ashurbanipal says the enemy "fled before my weapons," but also "fled before the weapons of Ashur, my lord" (Piepkorn, *Historical Prism Inscriptions of Ashurbanipal I*, 82–84 [Col. viii, 23–24]).
93. Grayson, *Assyrian Rulers of the Third and Second Millennia B.C.*, 183 (A.0.77.1, 20–21).
94. Ibid., 183 (A.0.77.1, 40–41).
95. Ibid., 234 (A.0.78.1, i 26–33).

last" (John 15:16). By the help of his gods, Tukulti-Ninurta "set [his] foot upon the neck of the lands." Assyrian kings before and after made a similar claim.[96] So, after defeating five Amorite kings, Joshua tells his army commanders, "Come here and put your feet on the necks of these kings. . . . This is what the LORD will do to all the enemies you are going to fight" (Josh. 10:24–25). In the New Testament, Jesus "must reign until he has put all his enemies under his feet" (1 Cor. 15:25).

As part of the kingdom agenda, Tukulti-Ninurta declares that the gods have given him lands to conquer as a gift.

> At that time, from Tulsina the . . . mountain, (the region) between the cities Sasila (and) Mashat-sarri on the opposite bank of the lower Zab, from Mount Zuqusku (and) Mount Lallar—the district of the extensive Qutu—the entire land of the Lullumu, the land of the Paphu to the land Katmuhu (and) all the land of the Subaru, the entirety of Mount Kasiliari to the border of Nairi [and] the border of the land M[akan], to the Euphrates—those regions the great gods allotted to me.[97]

So God says to Abram, "To your descendants I give this land, from the river of Egypt to the great river, the Euphrates—the land of the Kenites, Kenizzites, Kadmonites, Hittites, Perizzites, Rephaites, Amorites, Canaanites, Girgashites and Jebusites" (Gen. 15:18–21). In addition to the remarkable parallel between this and the Assyrian passage, God's gift to Abram is prefaced by the characterization, "On that day the LORD made a covenant with Abram" (Gen. 15:18). This strongly implies that the gods also gave Tukulti-Ninurta I lands to conquer as part of a covenant relationship.

Subsequently, Tiglath-Pileser I (1115–1077 B.C.) made similar claims. He says,

---

96. Ibid., 131 (A.O.76.1, 15–17; Adad-narari I), 183 (A.O.77.1, 20–22; Shalmaneser I), 310–11 (A.O.86.1, 7; Assur-resa-isi); and idem, *Assyrian Rulers of the Early First Millennium B.C. I*, 194 (A.O.101.1, i 14–15; Ashurnasirpal II). Sennacherib says, "all humankind . . . he (Aššur) has brought in submission at my feet" (Luckenbill, *Annals of Sennacherib*, 23 [Col. I, 15]). Ashurbanipal declares, "At the command of Ashur and Ishtar the kings who inhabit palaces kissed my feet" (Piepkorn, *Historical Prism Inscriptions of Ashurbanipal I*, 30–31 [Col. i, 46–47]).

97. Grayson, *Assyrian Rulers of the Third and Second Millennia B.C.*, 236–37 (A.O.78.1, iv 24–35). The last great Assyrian emperor, Ashurbanipal, says, "The lands of my enemies they (the gods) counted into my hands" (Piepkorn, *Historical Prism Inscriptions of Ashurbanipal I*, 28–29 [Col. i, 12–13]).

The god Aššur (and) the great gods who magnify my sovereignty . . . commanded me to extend the border of their land. They placed into my hands their mighty weapons. . . . I gained control over lands, mountains, towns, and princes who were hostile to Aššur. . . . I added territory to Assyria and people to its population. I extended the border of my land and ruled over their lands.[98]

The monarch brings under his rule peoples who were "hostile to Aššur."[99] Sometimes Assyrian kings expressed this act in terms of imposing the heavy yoke of the monarch's sovereignty upon them. Tukulti-Ninurta I declares, "I made them swear by the great gods of heaven (and) underworld, I imposed upon them the [exacting] yoke of my lordship."[100] The yoke clearly stands for vassal status in a suzerain-vassal covenant relationship (indicated by the oath sworn "by the great gods"). Tiglath-pileser I says of a newly conquered vassal, "I imposed upon him forever the heavy yoke of my dominion."[101] Sennacherib says the Medes, "To the yoke of my rule I made them submit."[102] Ashurbanipal boasts, "The kings of the East and the West brought their heavy tribute. People living in the sea and those inhabiting high mountains I subjected to my yoke."[103] The Assyrian word for yoke (*niru*) is cognate with a Hebrew noun (*nir*). This fact clears up a long-standing mistranslation of this Hebrew word, which resembles the Hebrew word normally used for "lamp" (*ner*). There are four passages (1 Kings 11:36; 15:4; 2 Kings 8:19; 2 Chron. 21:7) in which we are told that the Lord gave David a "lamp" in Jerusalem. We can now understand that he gave David, not a "lamp," but a "yoke," symbolic of royal rule. Even as late as the Roman Empire, the same figure of speech was used, the word "yoke" (Latin *jugum*) being symbolic of Roman suzerainty: "the yoke, under which the Romans compelled their vanquished enemies to pass in token

---

98. Grayson, *Assyrian Rulers of the Early First Millennium B.C. I*, 12 (A.O.87.1, i 46–61).

99. See also Grayson, *Assyrian Rulers of the Third and Second Millennia B.C.*, 310 (A.O.86.1, 5; Assur-resa-isi); and idem, *Assyrian Rulers of the Early First Millennium B.C. I*, 239–40 (A.O.101.17, i 25–27; Ashurnasirpal II).

100. Grayson, *Assyrian Rulers of the Third and Second Millennia B.C.*, 235 (A.O.78.1, iii 4–5).

101. Grayson, *Assyrian Rulers of the Early First Millennium B.C. I*, 15–16 (A.O.87.1, ii 54–55).

102. Luckenbill, *Annals of Sennacherib*, 29 (Col. II, 36).

103. Piepkorn, *Historical Prism Inscriptions of Ashurbanipal I*, 30–31 (Col. i, 42–45).

of submission" (and compare the Latin phrase for the same, *mittere sub jugum*, "to put/send under the yoke").[104] The Assyrians arrogantly boasted of the heavy yoke (and the harsh burden of tribute) they imposed on their vassals. By contrast, Jesus calls people into his covenant (to be his vassals), with the words, "Take my yoke upon you and learn from me, for I am gentle and humble in heart, and you will find rest for your souls. For my yoke is easy and my burden is light" (Matt. 11:29–30).

Tiglath-pileser expresses well the theological content of Assyrian rule when he says of captured foes, "I imposed upon them tribute and impost (and) regarded them as vassals of the god Aššur, my lord,"[105] and again, "I released them from their bonds and fetters in the presence of the god Šamaš, my lord, and made them swear by my great gods an oath of eternal vassaldom."[106]

Not only are people brought into vassaldom, but foreign gods are as well. For instance, Tiglath-pileser captures foreign gods and makes them subject to his gods: "At that time I donated the 25 gods of those lands, my own booty which I had taken, to be door-keepers of the temple of the goddess Ninlil, beloved chief spouse of the god Aššur, my lord, (the temple) of the gods Anu (and) Adad, (the temple of) the Assyrian Ištar, the temples of my city, Aššur, and the goddesses of my land."[107] (We may recall David, who, as the Lord's vassal, says, "I would rather be a doorkeeper in the house of my God than dwell in the tents of the wicked," Ps. 84:10). Adad-narari II also "gave their [i.e., enemies'] gods as gifts to Aššur, my lord."[108] The gift of captured gods meant that the foes' gods had now become vassals of Ashur. Subdued by Ashur, they had no power to control their former people and make them resist Ashur and his chosen monarch any longer. So Jesus, "having disarmed the powers and authorities . . . made a public spectacle of them, triumphing over them by the cross" (Col. 2:15).

Indeed, the Assyrian monarch can sound almost evangelistic in his sub-jugation of foreigners: "I brought Sēni, king of the land Daienu, who had

---

104.   Simpson, *Cassell's New Latin Dictionary*, 330.
105.   Grayson, *Assyrian Rulers of the Early First Millennium B.C. I*, 20 (A.O.87.1, iv 29–31).
106.   Ibid., 22 (A.O.87.1, v 12–16). See Piepkorn, *Historical Prism Inscriptions of Ashurbanipal I*, 12–13 (Col. ii, 30–31).
107.   Grayson, *Assyrian Rulers of the Early First Millennium B.C. I*, 2:20 (A.O.87.1, iv 32–39).
108.   Ibid., 144 (A.O.99.1, Obverse, 16–17).

not been submissive to the god Aššur, my Lord, in bonds and fetters to my city Aššur. I had mercy on him and let him leave my city Aššur alive in order to proclaim the glory of the great gods. (Thus) I became lord of the vast lands of Nairi in their entirety."[109]

After his conquests, an Assyrian monarch would build or rebuild a temple for the god(s) who helped him conquer. Tukulti-Ninurta I builds a palace with rooms for the gods, a "sanctuary . . . (as a place for the exercise) of my rule . . . [a palace], my royal residence [and rooms] for all the [great] gods."[110] A dynamic affinity between the emperor and his gods was a standard part of Assyrian tradition. It did not always, or even often, mean that the king was divine. But in addition to his own palace, he always built a temple for the god(s) who had commanded his conquests and made them possible. If no new temple were needed, he might restore a dilapidated temple, as did Tiglath-pileser I: "After I had gained complete dominion over the enemies of the god Aššur, I rebuilt (and) completed the dilapidated (portions of) . . . the temples of the gods of my city Aššur."[111] Later, Ashurbanipal, the last great Assyrian emperor, says that after the work of conquest, "The sanctuaries of the great gods, my lords, I restored."[112] If no temple repair were needed, the victorious king would at least offer booty from his conquests to the god(s). By Assyrian reckoning, their enemies were really Ashur's enemies and were counted among those who "*had withheld* tribute *from* Aššur, my lord."[113] On the other hand, good vassals were "bearers of tribute and tithe to the god Aššur, my lord."[114] When the king conquered an enemy, he made them vassals to Ashur, and, as such, they owed tribute. So Tiglath-pileser I says, "I donated to the god Aššur one bronze vat (and) one bronze bath-tub from the booty and tribute of the land Katmuhu."[115] Such claims are standard in Assyrian tradition.

---

109. Ibid., 22 (A.O.87.1, v 22–32; Tiglath-pileser I).
110. Grayson, *Assyrian Rulers of the Third and Second Millennia B.C.*, 242 (A.O.78.3, 26–34).
111. Ibid., 26 (A.O.87.1, vi 85–89).
112. Piepkorn, *Historical Prism Inscriptions of Ashurbanipal I*, 28–29 (Col. i, 16).
113. Grayson, *Assyrian Rulers of the Early First Millennium B.C. I*, 134 (A.O.98.1, 47–48; Assur-dan II). At the latter end of Assyrian tradition, the goddess Ishtar tells Ashurbanipal that his foe "against Ashur, king of the gods, the father who begat thee, has sinned, withheld tribute" (Piepkorn, *Historical Prism Inscriptions of Ashurbanipal I*, 64–65 [Col. v, 41–42]).
114. Grayson, *Assyrian Rulers of the Early First Millennium B.C. I*, 14 (A.O.87.1, i 65–66).
115. Ibid., 16 (A.O.87.1, ii 58–60).

Conclusion

We have seen strong indications that a common theological structure existed throughout the ancient Near East. According to that structure, rulers claimed to be chosen by their gods and in covenant relationship with them. As part of that arrangement, they gave to their people laws, or *torah*, that their gods had given to them so that the people of the gods (and in particular of the chief god) should live as the gods would have them do.[116] Another part of the arrangement had to do with wars of conquest. The gods sought to extend their dominion over more and more peoples. In theory, the chief god of any pantheon was god over all. But that did not necessarily mean that all people would acknowledge his deity. So, the god set about capturing peoples who had not acknowledged him and making them his vassals. He did this by commanding and empowering his chosen (vassal) emperor to conquer those recalcitrants and bring them into covenant. Vassaldom to the emperor meant, ipso facto, vassaldom to his god. Thus tribute paid to the earthly suzerain was considered tribute rendered to his god. We noted also that victory could entail the building or refurbishing of one or more temples as an appropriate response from the emperor to his god for the victories the god had granted and that vassaldom to the suzerain could entail not only tribute to the suzerain's god but even service in the god's temple.

In the course of our discussion, we have seen various parallels between the biblical and ancient Near Eastern materials. Indeed, it seems obvious that the structure of thought found in the ancient Near East is paralleled by the biblical accounts of God's dealing with his people, especially in the Mosaic covenant, but also in the new. We turn now to data that will further demonstrate the extent of that parallelism.

---

116. It seems clear, *pace* Walton and others, that laws, casuistic examples, and divine inspiration and guidance could all be given, and were all claimed, by ancient Near Eastern kings with respect to governance, and apparently in divine-human covenantal contexts, as the examples cited earlier in this chapter indicate.

4

City, Temple, Image

The ideas that form the title of this chapter were an important triad in the ancient world. The city was important because it imaged forth a heavenly city. The temple was important because it represented a heavenly temple. The image, or idol, was important because it represented the god, and actually (it was thought) embodied the god in the earthly temple and city.[1]

City

Not only could an earthly city presuppose a heavenly archetype, but a god could actually build a city and a temple. A god built a city and temple because he wanted to reside in an urban temple among his people. The concept of a divine or holy city, based on a heavenly archetype, was an important one in the ancient Near East.

Egypt

The Pyramid Texts of Egypt attest the concept of a heavenly city as the abode of the gods, and those heavenly realities are paralleled by an earthly

---

1. Cf. Oppenheim, *Ancient Mesopotamia*, 186: "As for the relationship of the image to the sanctuary in which it resided on its pedestal in the cella, it paralleled in all essential aspects that of the king in relation to his palace and, ultimately, to his city. The god lived in the sanctuary with his family and was served in courtly fashion by his officials. . . . In its cella, the image received the visits of lesser gods and the prayers of supplicants." He adds that "it remains a moot question to what degree and under what circumstances it was accessible, if at all, to the common man."

city and temple. Budge says of the Pyramid Texts: "The Pyramid Texts are versions of ancient religious compositions which the priests of the College or School of Anu succeeded in establishing as the authorized version of the Book of the Dead in the first six dynasties."[2] The first six dynasties spanned the period 3100–2185 B.C. Anu was "the metropolis of the XIIIth Nome of Lower Egypt."[3]

The Pyramid Texts contain the idea of a heavenly Anu that corresponds to the earthly Anu: "The abode of the blessed in heaven was called Anu, and it was asserted that the souls of the just were there united to their spiritual or glorified bodies, and that they lived there face to face with the deity for all eternity."[4]

Those who ascended to heaven required "glorified bodies" appropriate to the heavenly environment. The Pyramid Texts tell us that monarchs were transformed for citizenship in the heavenly Anu. According to one text, "Re speaks, he makes a spirit of this king, who receives his spirit-form in front of the gods."[5] Another text has the monarch say, "I am pure. I am conveyed to the sky thereby. . . . I appear in glory before the gods."[6] Much later, in the New Testament, we learn that those who die in Christ receive glorified bodies (1 Cor. 15:42–44) and see God face-to-face for eternity (1 Cor. 13:12; cf. 2 Cor. 3:18). We will discuss later how such a remarkable parallelism of ideas might have come about.

We see, then, that the Anu above was the city of gods and of the spirits of men made perfect. But the Anu below also was the abode of the gods (idols) and of flesh-and-blood people. In Egyptian theology, both cities were sources of divine instruction, or, to use a Hebrew term, *torah*: "The heavenly Anu was the capital of the mythological world . . . and was, to the spirits of men, what the earthly Anu was to their bodies, i.e., the abode of the gods and the centre and source of all divine instruction."[7]

The earthly Anu was the "abode of the gods" because it contained their idols. It corresponded to the heavenly Anu, which was the abode of the gods in their spirit form. Biblical Jerusalem was a (partial) biblical parallel. The earthly Jerusalem had the temple, God's abode. It also had flesh-and-blood

2. Budge, *Book of the Dead*, 24.
3. Ibid., 24n. 1.
4. Ibid., 25.
5. Faulkner, *Ancient Egyptian Pyramid Texts*, 144 (Utterance 437, § 795).
6. Ibid., 220 (Utterance 565, § 1423).
7. Budge, *Book of the Dead*, 25n. 2.

people. But a heavenly Jerusalem is the true abode of God. And "the heavenly Jerusalem, the city of the living God" contains "the spirits of righteous men made perfect" (Heb. 12:22–23). Moreover, Isaiah can say of that eschatological Jerusalem,

> [God] will teach us his ways,
>   so that we may walk in his paths.
> The *law* [*torah,* i.e., divine *instruction*] will go out from Zion,
>   the word of the LORD from Jerusalem.
>   (Isa. 2:3, emphasis added; cf. Mic. 4:2)

Just as the heavenly Anu is the source of divine instruction (*torah*) for humans, so will the eschatological Jerusalem be; and that Jerusalem will come down from heaven (Rev. 21:2).

Parallelism between the heavenly Anu and the earthly Anu is a major installment in the three-part system of heavenly correspondences. It establishes a context in which a similar parallelism may take form between the heavenly and earthly temples and between a god in heaven and his idol on earth. There is a foundational theological idea here: the earthly is patterned after the heavenly, which is ultimately the more substantial, vital, and enduring.

In accord with such parallelism, Egypt attests divine guidance in both city and temple construction. Seti I (1302–1290 B.C.) records that a god (presumably Amon) commanded him to build a city and a temple as an act of gratitude for enabling Pharaoh to build a well—a water station—in a mountainous passage for the refreshment of weary travelers: "Another good thought has come into my heart, at the command of the god, even the equipment of a town, in whose august midst shall be a resting place, a settlement, with a temple. I will build a resting place in this spot, in the great name of my fathers, the gods."[8] The pharaoh goes on to report that a number of gods—including Amon/Re, Ptah, Osiris, Horus, Isis, and Menmare (Seti I—i.e., Pharaoh himself!)—belong in this temple.[9] The statement that Pharaoh also belongs in the temple means he caused a statue of himself to be installed there among the gods, who were his relations.

The henotheist Pharaoh Amen-hotep IV (Akn-en-Aton, 1369–1353 B.C.)

---

8. Breasted, *Ancient Records of Egypt,* 3:82 (§ 172).
9. Ibid., 3:83 (§ 173).

built a cult city for the sun god Aton, "in order to found it as a monument to Aton, according to the command of his father Aton."[10] Of that city he said, "She is lovely and beautiful; when one sees her, it is like a glimpse at heaven."[11] It is apparent that the idea of an earthly holy city that corresponded to a heavenly one was an ancient and enduring belief in Egypt.

Sumer

It is not certain, but Sumerian mythology also may have assumed a primordial (pre-creation) city. J. van Dijk has proposed a Sumerian creation scenario that includes a preexisting embryonic universe conceived as a "primeval city" inhabited by primordial gods.[12] As Richard J. Clifford notes, "The best evidence for a primeval city of gods prior to the act of creation are the parent gods' names. . . . Enurulla and Ninurulla are 'the lord/lady of the primeval city.'"[13] More work needs to be done in this area, but other parallels between Sumerian and ancient Near Eastern thought suggest that the Sumerians also imagined a heavenly city (see below).

Certainly the Sumerians believed that gods could build a city in heaven. One early text says the gods made the city Uruk and its temple in heaven, before those structures descended to earth.

> (The city) Uruk, handiwork of the gods,
>   and (its temple) Eanna, temple descended from heaven . . .
> It is the great gods (themselves who) made their component parts!
> As the great wall that (the former) is—
>   a stormcloud lying on the horizon—
> and as the august abode that (the latter) is—
>   one founded by An.[14]

The city Uruk has a heavenly origin, and therefore it is actually theophanic, "a stormcloud lying on the horizon." The parallelism of the last four lines ("great wall" // "august abode"; "stormcloud" // "one [temple] founded by An") implies that the city also may have "descended from

---

10. Ibid., 2:396 (§ 960).
11. Ibid., 2:412 (§ 1000).
12. Van Dijk, "Le motif cosmique dans la pensée sumeriénne," 13.
13. Clifford, *Creation Accounts*, 19–20.
14. Jacobsen, *Treasures of Darkness*, 78–79.

heaven," and so it has come to rest on the horizon like a storm cloud. Much later, in what appears to be a remarkable analogy, John sees "the Holy City, Jerusalem, coming down out of heaven from God. It shone with the glory of God, and its brilliance was like that of a very precious jewel, like a jasper, clear as crystal" (Rev. 21:10–11). The city of Uruk is called the "handiwork of the gods" who made its "component parts." It may recall the heavenly Jerusalem, "the city with foundations, whose architect and builder is God" (Heb. 11:10). In another parallel, we read that the Eanna temple is "descended from heaven," a claim that may recall a city clerk's statement during the riot at Ephesus: "Men of Ephesus, doesn't all the world know that the city of Ephesus is the guardian of the temple of the great Artemis and of her image, which fell from heaven?" (Acts 19:35). But, to carry the thought further, it is actually Jesus, who is "the exact representation (Gk., *charaktēr*) of his (i.e., God's) being" (Heb. 1:3), who has "come down from heaven" (John 6:38; cf. v. 42).

Babylon (Old Babylonian)

The Babylonians also believed that the gods built cities. In the Babylonian creation epic we read:

> Marduk . . . (said:) "So shall Babylon be, whose construction ye
> [i.e., the gods] have desired;
> Let its brickwork be fashioned, and call (it) a sanctuary."
> The Anunaki wielded the hoe.
> One year they made bricks for it;
> When the second year arrived,
> They raised the head of Esagila on high.
>
> (Tablet VI, lines 55–62)[15]

The gods desired and therefore built Babylon, which is itself called "a sanctuary." We see from this that a city could be both the locus of a temple and itself a temple (we will have more to say about the significance of this). Be that as it may, the belief that gods would build cities continued in Mesopotamia. So Iaḫdun-Līm of Mari could refer to the "early days, when the god El built Mari."[16]

---

15. Heidel, *Babylonian Genesis*, 48.
16. Frayne, *Old Babylonian Period*, 605 (E.4.6.8.2, 34–35).

Gods not only built primordial sanctuary cities, but they also commanded that cities be built and gave men wisdom for the work. A number
of inscriptions from the Old Babylonian period (written in Sumerian) illustrate this fact. Warad-Sîn (1834–1823 B.C.), king of Larsa, says,

> The god Nanna . . . ordered me . . . to strengthen the base of shrine Ebab-
> bar, to build the cities of the gods of the land . . . about enlarging Ur, and
> reinforcing its enforcing wall, of making its foundation greater . . . I im-
> plored the god (Nanna) humbly. The god Nanna, [my] lord, was favorable
> (to my prayer).[17]

The king asks the god for direction concerning the architectural work
commanded by the god, and he receives it. Warad-Sîn was succeeded by his
brother, Rim-Sîn (1822–1763 B.C.), who declared that "[the gods An, Enlil,
Enk]i (and) Ninmaḫ . . . determined the destiny of Larsa . . . , their beloved
abode, (and) by their [un]alterable [word] decr[eed] its creation."[18] He then
undertakes the construction work the gods have commanded. Samsu-iluna,
son of Hammurapi, tells how Enlil decreed the rebuilding of the wall of his
cult city, Sippar, and the restoration of the Ebabbar temple, and how the
god Shamash, his messenger, "gave to me that . . . commission."[19] Clearly,
monarchs of the Old Babylonian period believed that the gods built both
cities and temples and commanded kings to do likewise. Often the latter
involved reconstruction of cities and temples that had fallen into disrepair.

Assyria

For whatever reason (perhaps the randomness of archeological discovery), the evidence from Assyria is very scant on this particular topic. Yet
what little we have (one claim from the annals of one king) makes it clear
that the Assyrians also were comfortable with the idea that a god might
command the construction of both a city and a temple. The Assyrian king
Tukulti-Ninurta I (1244–1208 B.C.) said that Ashur, chief god of the Assyrian pantheon, commanded him to build a great cult city, Kar-Tukulti-
Ninurta, across the river from his capital city, Ashur: "At that time the God
Aššur-Enlil, my lord, requested of me a cult centre on the bank opposite

---

17.   Ibid., 242 (E4.2.13.21, 49–67).
18.   Ibid., 292 (E4.2.14.15, 1–5).
19.   Ibid., 376 (E4.3.7.3, 1–38).

my city and he commanded me to build his sanctuary."[20] Divine revelation
came to the king in the form of a command to build a city.

Temple

Evidence now also shows that people in the ancient Near East believed
that gods could and would reveal temple patterns to their elect priest kings,
just as Yahweh revealed a tabernacle pattern to Moses.

Egypt

A Pyramid Age inscription describes Ptah as creator of all. He made the
gods. He also made the cities and temples they were to inhabit: "He fashioned the gods, he made the cities, he settled the nomes. He installed the
gods [i.e., idols] in their holy places, he made their offerings to flourish, he
equipped their holy places."[21]

We recall how the gods made Uruk and its temple and Babylon and its
temple. In Egypt, it was Ptah who first made the cities and temples. Later
rulers, to be like Ptah, had to do likewise, either building or restoring cities
or temples. Under Pepi II (2275–2185 B.C.), for example, a city god raised up
a nomarch (provincial governor) to restore his temple, "which Ptah [had]
built with his fingers."[22]

Egypt also believed that the gods revealed patterns for temples and related objects. Indeed, the fact that a god "commands" such construction
implies divine instruction as regards the details, because without such
heavenly instruction, the earthly ruler could not possibly know the plan
according to which he was to proceed.

Although it is important to understand the matter of divine construction
commands and plan giving, it is even more important to understand the
context in which the gods were imagined to give such revelations. Amon or
Ptah could command Pharaoh to build a temple because the gods and Pharaoh had a mutual understanding in the form of a compact, or covenant.
Amon or Ptah revealed temple patterns or commanded temple construction as part of that relationship. The divine kinship and covenantal relation

---

20. Grayson, *Assyrian Rulers of the Third and Second Millennia B.C.*, 270 (A.O.78.22, 39–40).
21. Breasted, *Development of Religion*, 46. "Nomes" were Egyptian administrative dis-
tricts, comparable to counties or states.
22. Breasted, *Ancient Records of Egypt*, 1:186 (§ 403).

to the monarch logically led to a temple because the god wanted to reside among Pharaoh and his covenant people.

Accordingly, the pharaohs often claimed that their gods commanded them to build temples and liturgical equipment. Sen-Usert I (1991–1961 B.C.) said that Ra

> begat me to do that which he did,
> To execute that which he commanded to do . . .
> I will make a work, namely, a great house,
> For my father Atum.
> He will make it broad,
> according as he has caused me to conquer.[23]

Ra commands the monarch to build his "great house" (i.e., temple). Pharaoh does build the god's temple, but Atum also builds it ("he will make it broad"), and its magnitude shows the extent of the kingdom the god has caused Pharaoh to conquer. The latest (and final) form of this theology sees God working through Jesus, and building his temple, the church. God has caused Jesus to conquer broadly by the spread of the gospel so that his kingdom (also the church) is broad—indeed global—in scope.

Egyptian royal ideology remained fundamentally consistent on this and many other points for two thousand years or more. It was normal for Egyptian rulers to claim divine commands and instructions for construction of temples, and indeed of other monumental architecture. So carrying on the tradition of the early second millennium, Thutmose I (1525–1495 B.C.) could claim that Osiris had created him, in part, to restore temples.[24] Thutmose III (1490–1436 B.C.) said he was made divine in order to extend the rule and build the temple of Ra.[25] In the monumental vein, Amon commanded Thutmose's queen, Hatshepsut (1486–1468 B.C.), to form commemorative

---

23. Ibid., 1:243–44 (§§ 502–3).
24. Ibid., 2:38 (§ 91); cf. 2:39 (§ 95), 40 (§ 97).
25. Ibid., 2:63 (§ 149). He also said that Ra commanded him to deposit in the temple a record of the victories the god had granted him: "His majesty commanded to cause to be recorded [his victories which his father, Amon, gave him, upon] a tablet in the temple which his majesty made for [his father, Amon, setting forth each] expedition by its name, together with the plunder which [his majesty] carried away [therein. It was according to] all [the command] which his father, Re, gave to him" (2:175 [§ 407]; cf. 2:195 [§ 455]).

obelisks at Karnak, and she could claim of her relationship with Amon, "I conceived not any works without his doing, it was he who gave the directions."[26] Ramses II (1290–1224 B.C.) said Horus shaped his thoughts so that he should finish the mortuary temple begun by his father.[27] And in another Ramesside inscription, Amon says Ramses II was one "whom I brought up from the womb, to make excellent things for my house."[28]

The fact that a god's temple was his house implies a supernatural correspondence. An inscription from the reign of Sen-Usert III (1878–1840 B.C.) characterizes the temple of Osiris as "his palace," and "his house."[29] These terms reflect the most ancient understanding of a temple, according to which it was a god's house or, since he was royalty, his palace. Accordingly, the temple and its furniture should correspond to their heavenly counterparts, just as the idol of the god corresponds to the god (see below).

Egypt usually indicated such a correspondence by comparing the temple (or some aspect of it) with the "horizon," or with the stars or the sun. Temples were furnished with costly jewels and metals, meant to image forth the heavenly realm by their brilliance and splendor. Thutmose III (1490–1436 B.C.), for example, erected a holy of holies for Amon and named it, "'His-Great-Seat-Is-Like-the-Horizon-of-Heaven.' . . . Its interior was wrought of electrum."[30] As with temple construction, there was divine guidance for fashioning the liturgical equipment.

> . . . a great vase of electrum . . . [. . .] silver, gold, bronze, and copper . . . the Two Lands were flooded with their brightness, like the stars in the body of Nut [i.e., the sky goddess], while my statue followed. Offering tables of electrum . . . I made it for him out of the conceptions of my heart, by the guidance of the god himself.[31]

The Old Testament offers an intriguing parallel. We are told that David gave Solomon "the plans of all that the Spirit had put in his mind for the courts of the temple of the LORD and all the surrounding rooms, for the

---

26. Ibid., 2:131 (§ 316).
27. Ibid., 3:109 (§ 266); cf. 3:112 (§ 271).
28. Ibid., 3:218 (§ 511).
29. Ibid., 1:300 (§ 669); cf. the earlier claim by Sen-Usert I, 1:243 (§ 502).
30. Ibid., 2:64 (§ 153); cf. 2:65 (§ 155).
31. Ibid., 2:68 (§ 164). The same king refurbished an Amon temple and made it "like the heavens" (2:239 [§ 601]; cf. 2:240 [§ 604]).

treasuries of the temple of God and for the treasuries of the dedicated things" (1 Chron. 28:12). The plans included the weight of gold and silver for the lamp stands and their lamps, the tables, and the weight of gold for the forks, sprinkling bowls, pitchers and dishes, as well as for the altar of incense (1 Chron. 28:14–19). "'All this,' David said, 'I have in writing from the hand of the LORD upon me, and he gave me understanding in all the details of the plan'" (1 Chron. 28:19).

We cite the Davidic analogy now because of its remarkable parallelism with the statements of Thutmose III, a parallelism that by itself would suggest that God's temple was meant to reflect a heavenly original, as in Egypt, had the point not been made already in the book of Exodus.

Subsequent Egyptian rulers made analogous claims, and from them we can discern some further theological points. Queen Hatshepsut (1486–1468 B.C.) made a house of Amon with a floor of gold and silver and declared, "Its beauty was like the horizon of heaven."[32] Amen-hotep II (1439–1406 B.C.) said of Amon's temple equipment, "I made for him many vessels; they were more beautiful than the bodies of the stars."[33] Amen-hotep III (1398–1361 B.C.) said of a temple he made for Amon in the Karnak complex that it was "of gold, unlimited in malachite and lazuli; a place of rest for the lord of gods, made like his throne that is in heaven."[34] And of the pylons of the Karnak temple, he declared, "Its pylons reach heaven like the four pillars of heaven."[35] The same pharaoh even made a sacred barge for Amon,

> adorned with silver, wrought with gold throughout, the great shrine is of electrum so that it fills the land with its brightness . . . its bows make Nun [i.e., the water that reflects it] to shine as when the sun rises in heaven, to make his beautiful voyage . . . of a million millions of years.[36]

That sacred barge-shrine was supposedly an ectype of a heavenly archetype, in which Amon-Ra sailed across the heavens each day.

---

32. Ibid., 2:156 (§ 375).
33. Ibid., 2:318 (§ 806).
34. Ibid., 2:355 (§ 881). He says of the Amon temple in Thebes, "It . . . resembles the horizon in heaven when Re rises therein" (2:356 [§ 883]).
35. Ibid., 2:360 (§ 889); cf. the same king's Luxor temple: "Its towers reach heaven, and mingle with the stars" (2:358 [§ 886]; cf. 2:362 [§ 894]).
36. Ibid., 2:359 (§ 888).

For the next six hundred years, pharaohs constructed temples and monuments meant to image forth their counterparts in heaven. These included Ramses I (1303–1302 B.C.),[37] Seti I (1302–1290 B.C.),[38] Ramses II (1290–1224 B.C.),[39] and Ramses III (1195–1164 B.C.),[40] and even Pi-ankhi I (720 B.C.), during his brief and insignificant reign, could boast that he made temple court furnishings "of gold like the horizon of heaven."[41] Clearly, the tradition of earthly constructions mirroring heavenly archetypes and employing precious metals and gemstones to create the heavenly effect was of long standing in Egypt.

Pharaohs often used those same materials to make temple floors, as the Hatshepsut inscription cited above suggests.[42] Predictably, such flooring made a temple more like its numinous archetype in the "horizon." The Bible contains several parallels, both heavenly and earthly. Moses, Aaron, Nadab, Abihu, and the seventy elders on Sinai saw "something like a pavement made

---

37. Ibid., 3:36 (§ 79). He made for Amon "a temple like the horizon of heaven, wherein Re [rises]."

38. Ibid., 3:96–97 (§ 232). He made for Osiris "a temple like heaven; its divine ennead are like the stars in it; its radiance is in the faces (of men) like the horizon of Re, rising therein at early morning" (cf. 3:97 [§ 236]). The same temple was called, "horizon of eternity, place for performing the pleasing ceremonies in the presence," and "a house like the heavens, its beauty illuminating the Two Lands" (3:98 [§ 240.7,12]). Seti I also made a model of a Heliopolis temple, "an august holy of holies in the likeness of the horizon of heaven, a resting-place of the two horizons, in which the lords of Heliopolis rest, like Atum" (3:100 [§ 246]; cf. 3:101 [§ 248]).

39. Ibid., 3:218 (§ 512). He said of the Karnak temple, "Its august columns are of electrum, made like every place that is in heaven. (It is) mistress of silver, queen of gold, it contains every splendid costly stone" (cf. 3:217 [§ 510]). The pharaoh declared on a Heliopolis obelisk that he "made his monuments like the stars of heaven, whose works mingle with the sky, rejoicing over which Re rises in his house of millions of years" (3:230 [§ 548]).

40. Ibid., 4:115 (§ 192). He said of the Medinet Habu solar temple, "I made for thee an august palace . . . like the great house of Atum which is in heaven. The columns, doorposts, and doors were of electrum; the great balcony . . . was of gold." Cf. similarly, "I made for thee an august house in Nubia . . . the likeness of the heavens" (4:123 [§ 218]; cf. 4:143 [§ 251], 165 [§ 314], and especially 180 [§ 357]).

41. Ibid., 4:495 (§ 970); cf. a barque "like Re in his horizon" (4:491 [§ 958K]), and similarly, earlier, Ramses III (4:180 [§ 35–38]).

42. Pavements of silver and/or gold are mentioned in a number of temple descriptions, e.g., Hatshepsut (Breasted, *Ancient Records of Egypt*, 2:156 [§ 375]), Amenhotep II (2:318 [§ 806]), and Amen-hotep III (2:356 [§ 883], 358 [§ 886], 360–61 [§ 889–90]).

of sapphire, clear as the sky itself" under God's feet (Exod. 24:10). John saw "what looked like a sea of glass, clear as crystal" before God's throne (Rev. 4:6). And Solomon actually copied that supernal floor with gold pavement in both inner and outer rooms of his temple (1 Kings 6:30).

We have seen that divine construction of both city and temple was a fundamental part of Egyptian religion: the gods made both at the beginning. Indeed, city and temple construction go together, because the gods wanted to live among their covenant people. We also have seen parallel ideas in Sumer, Babylon, and Assyria. Sumerian gods supposedly constructed Uruk and its temple. Marduk founded Babylon and the *Esagila* temple for his own worship. Ashur commanded Tukulti-Ninurta I to build a cult city. All probably were understood as earthly ectypes of heavenly archetypes, since the gods either did the construction or gave wisdom or instruction to the king who did it for them. All anticipate the New Testament revelation concerning God's city. There we learn that God's people "have come to . . . the heavenly Jerusalem, the city of the living God" (Heb. 12:22), a "city with foundations, whose architect and builder is God" (Heb. 11:10; cf. 11:16; 13:14). That heavenly city also contains a temple—the archetype of God's earthly tabernacle/temple, revealed by God to Moses.

Sumer

Both Egyptian and Sumerian theology declared that gods made cities and temples. In Sumer, as we have seen, a temple could actually "descend from heaven," like the statue of Diana at Ephesus.[43]

The Sumerians, like the Egyptians, also claimed that the gods would give a king instruction on how to build a temple. The greatest Sumerian example was cited at the beginning of this book. It appears in an inscription of Gudea of Lagash (2143–2124 B.C.), who informs us that the great destinies of Enlil's city and its *e-ninnu* temple have been divinely determined. He narrates that he had a dream that he did not understand, so he described it to the goddess Nina.

> In the dream a man, whose stature reached up to heaven [and] reached down to earth, who according to the *tiara* around his head was a god . . . at whose feet was a storm, to whose right and left a lion was at rest, com-

---

43.   Jacobsen, *Treasures of Darkness*, 78–79.

manded me to build his house [i.e., temple] . . . a second [man], like a
warrior . . . held in his hand a tablet of lapus-lazuli, [and] outlined the
pattern of a temple.[44]

The goddess explained the dream to the king: it was a vision of her
brother Ningirsu, who was commanding Gudea to build his temple. The
second god was Nindub, who was showing Gudea the temple pattern.[45]

In this ancient vision, a pagan god prescribes for his worshipper the pattern after which his temple should be built. It shows how ancient was the
concept of a heavenly archetype for an earthly temple. It also shows how
ancient in Mesopotamia was the concept of divine revelation of a temple
pattern. When Yahweh revealed a pattern for a tabernacle to Moses on
Mount Sinai, he was doing something a pagan god (Ningirsu) supposedly
had done for Gudea of Lagash some eight or nine hundred years before. Evidence shows that the concept of such divine revelation persisted in pagan
contexts into the second and first millennia.

Another important idea related to the temple appears in Sumerian theology. Jacobsen has noted that a temple was not only a god's abode, but in
some sense it was also the image of the god.

> The Sumerian and Akkadian words for temple are the usual words for
> house. . . . They imply between the divine owner and his house not only
> all the emotional closeness of a human owner and his home, but beyond
> that a closeness of essence, of being, amounting more nearly to embodi-
> ment than to habitation. In some sense the temple, no less than . . . the
> cult image, was a representation of the form of the power that was meant
> to fill it.[46]

Jacobsen's observation has major implications for biblical theology and
anthropology, not because Sumerian theology is a hermeneutical key for
the Bible, but because the Bible contains parallel ideas. We briefly state

---

44. Thureau-Dangin, *Die Sumerischen und Akkadischen Königsinschriften*, 94–95 (Cyl-
inder A, 4,14–5,4).

45. The dream is also significant because of its storm theophany aspect. A storm was at
Ningirsu's feet as he revealed that temple pattern to Gudea. A combination of storm
theophany and temple revelation recalls the theophany at Sinai and God's revelation of a tabernacle pattern to Moses. Cf. Niehaus, *God at Sinai*, 108–20.

46. Jacobsen, *Treasures of Darkness*, 15–16.

two of those ideas now and will discuss them more fully at the end of this chapter.

First, we understand that human beings are made in God's image and likeness (Gen. 1:26) but are also temples of the Holy Spirit (1 Cor. 6:19). It follows that the human form is the form of the Holy Spirit, "a representation of the form of the power that was meant to fill it," to use Jacobsen's phrasing. But not only the human form. God's form is also the form of the Holy Spirit. Ezekiel saw an exalted human form on God's chariot throne, and that *human* form was "the likeness of the glory of the LORD" (Ezek. 1:28). But, what is the "glory of the LORD"? According to 1 Peter 4:14, the Holy Spirit is "the Spirit of glory and of God." So, for now, we boldly equate the "glory of the LORD" with the "Spirit of the Lord," and will add further evidence below. Therefore, God's form and the human form made in his image and likeness are both the form of the Holy Spirit. That is, the human form that Ezekiel sees is the "likeness" (Ezek. 1:28, Heb. *demuth*) of the Spirit. But the human form, as image and "likeness" (Gen. 1:26, Heb. *demuth*) of God, is therefore also a "likeness" of the Holy Spirit, and this is also one aspect of the *imago dei*. Humans are made in the image and likeness of the Glory Spirit, the power that is meant to fill them. When that power does fill one, the human form becomes a temple of the Holy Spirit.

Second, not only are individual humans temples of the Holy Spirit, but God's church, the corporate faithful, also form a temple of God's Spirit (1 Cor. 3:16; 2 Cor. 6:16; cf. Eph. 2:22, "And in him you too are being built together to become a dwelling in which God lives by his Spirit"). So the church is also made in God's image (a body with a head, Christ), and is "a representation of the form of the power that was meant to fill it."

Babylon (Old Babylonian)

The Babylonians also believed that gods could build, or command the construction of, temples. The Babylonian creation epic portrays the gods as builders, not only of Babylon, but also of the Esagila temple.

> The Anunaki wielded the hoe.
> One year they made bricks for it;
> When the second year arrived,

They raised the head of Esagila on high
(Tablet VI, lines 55–62)[47]

Apparently, according to this poem, the Anunaki gods even got their hands dirty building Babylon and its Esagila temple. Moreover, as noted above, Babylon itself was called a temple ("call it a sanctuary"), because the city, like its temple, was to be the god Marduk's residence.

Divine revelation also was given for the building of other temples or cities. Sīn-iddinam (1849–1843 B.C.) of Larsa says the god Utu (the sun god, also Shamash) commissioned him to enlarge his residence (i.e., temple).[48] Warad-Sīn of Larsa declares, "The god Enki gave to me the broad wisdom to create eternal works," and, on account of this, he enlarges the temple of Inanna.[49] Kudur-Mabuk of Larsa, father of Warad-Sīn, claims that he built a temple for Shamash, "with the wise understanding that the god gave to him."[50] Ammi-ditana (1683–1647 B.C.), king of Babylon, can even declare that he built a fort named after himself "by the wisdom that the god Ea gave to me."[51]

As in Egypt, such construction work apparently was done as part of the covenant relationship between the god and his chosen king. So, for example, Warad-Sīn claims, "At that time, for the god Nergal, his lord, having (established) a colleagueship (with him), he built for him, he built for him Emetegira ('House—suitable for the mighty one') his residence of valour, filled with a radiance and a fearsome splendour."[52]

The king built the temple as part of a covenant relationship ("colleague-ship") with Nergal, and, because it is the god's residence, the temple is also theophanic (it has a "radiance and a fearsome splendour"). When the same king builds another theophanic temple at the command of the god Ašimbabbar, he declares, "O god Nanna, my lord, it is you who has done it; (as for) myself, what am I?"[53] Perhaps, as in Egypt, the closeness of monarch and god also may be accounted for (in part) by sonship. At least, Warad-Sīn

---

47. Heidel, *Babylonian Genesis*, 48.
48. Frayne, *Old Babylonian Period*, 165 (E4.2.9.6, 212–24).
49. Ibid., 253 (E4.2.13.27, 27–41).
50. Ibid., 267 (E4.2.13a.1, 8–20).
51. Ibid., 413 (E4.3.9.2, 19–26).
52. Ibid., 206 (E4.2.13.3, 20–26).
53. Ibid., 234 (E4.2.13.16, 42–44).

claimed an immaculate conception, for he says he was "purely formed in the womb of the mother who bore me, whom (the god Nanna) appointed (for) shepherdship of his nation."[54] His brother, Rīm-Sîn, likewise had a covenant with his god: "When the gods An, Enlil, Enki and the great gods entrusted Uruk, the ancient city, into my hands, on account of this, I established a colleagueship with the god Ninšubur my lord, I built for my own life the Emekilibasagil . . . a residence suitable for his divinity."[55]

Assyria

Like their counterparts in the ancient Near East, Assyrian emperors also claimed divine guidance for temple construction. Since the cult in Assyria was long established in ancient temples, the issue there was often not so much building as renovating a temple. Assyrian tradition describes the procedure with stock phrasing. The kings say that the gods, "who love my priesthood,"[56] "commanded me to rebuild their shrine."[57] Whether the command came by way of oracle or by way of dream vision is not specified. But a command there was, and divine command is divine revelation.

The Middle Assyrian king, Tiglath-pileser I (1115–1077 B.C.), is a typical example. Toward the end of his fifth-year annals, he declares,

> In my accession year the gods Anu and Adad, the great gods, my lords, who love my priesthood, commanded me to rebuild their shrine. . . . Its interior I decorated like the interior of heaven. I decorated its walls as splendidly as the brilliance of rising stars. . . . (Thus) did I please their great divinity.[58]

---

54. Ibid., 242 (E4,2,13,21, 42–45).
55. Ibid., 289 (E4.2.14.13, 23–31).
56. Cf. Grayson, *Assyrian Rulers of the Early First Millennium B.C. I*, 200 (A.0.101.1, i, line 99, Ashurnasirpal II); Luckenbill, *Annals of Sennacherib*, 107 (line 48, Sennacherib); and Borger, *Die Inschriften Asarhaddons Königs von Assyrien* (§ 65.Vs.1–12, 96, Esarhaddon).
57. Cf. Grayson, *Assyrian Rulers of the Third and Second Millennia B.C.*, 273 (A.0.78.23, I, 88–91, "the god Aššur . . . commanded me to build his sanctuary," Tukulti-Ninurta I); Luckenbill, *Annals of Sennacherib*, 137 (30, Sennacherib); and Borger, *Die Inschriften Asarhaddons Königs von Assyrien* (§ 11 Ep. 14.41–45, 18, Esarhaddon).
58. Grayson, *Assyrian Rulers of the Early First Millennium B.C. I*, 28–29 (A.0.87.1, vii, 71–114).

The king renovates the temple, which is the earthly home of Anu and Adad. The use of the word *bītu*, Assyrian equivalent of Hebrew *bayit*, "house," for the temple of the god (regularly in Assyrian tradition) illustrates this point. Moreover, the similarity of the earthly temple to the heavenly is a salient feature in Assyria, as in Egypt. Tiglath-pileser stresses that he made the interior of the temple "like the interior of heaven . . . as splendidly as the brilliance of rising stars," so that the gods would feel at home.

Like the pharaohs, Assyrian monarchs used gold and other precious materials to achieve a likeness of heaven in their temples. Tukulti-Ninurta I (1244–1208 B.C.) said of the Ishtar temple, "I rebuilt Eme . . . her joyful dwelling, the shrine, her voluptuous dais, (and) the awesome sanctuary . . . and made (the temple) as beautiful as a heavenly dwelling" [lit., "like a dwelling of heaven"].[59] Centuries later, Ashurbanipal (668–627 B.C.), the last great Assyrian emperor, could declare, "The sanctuaries of the great gods, my lords, I restored, with gold and silver I decked . . . Ešarra . . . I made shine like the writing of heaven. Every kind of gold and silver adornment of a temple I made, I added to that of my royal ancestors."[60]

As we have seen, Assyrian rulers (like those of Egypt, Sumer, and the Old Babylonian period) built temples at divine behest. The temples were made to be like heaven (or a heavenly archetype) so that the gods would feel at home. In Assyria as elsewhere, just as the temple was patterned after heaven, so the idol was patterned after the god.

Image: Divine Presence in the Temple

We have spoken of divine revelation by way of commands and instructions for the construction of temples and their equipment and other monumental architecture. But the ultimate form of divine revelation is the very presence of a god, accessible to the worshipper. The pagan world desired such presence and achieved it by means of idols. The idol (or "image" or "likeness" in ancient Near Eastern parlance) not only represented the god, but, it was thought, also embodied the god in his earthly temple and city.

59. Grayson, *Assyrian Rulers of the Third and Second Millennia B.C.*, 254–55 (A.0.78.11.38–51).

60. Piepkorn, *Historical Prism Inscriptions of Ashurbanipal I*, 28–29 (i.16–23). See the similar claim by his father, Esarhaddon, in Borger, *Die Inschriften Asarhaddons Königs von Assyrien*, 5 (§ 2.V.37–39).

Egypt

Idol as "Image"

Egyptian theologians of the Fifth Dynasty (2500–2350 B.C.) had a very spiritual concept of idolatry. According to them, the gods were spirit, or spiritual bodies. Yet a god might enter a concrete form that humans had made for him.

> The form in which Ra was worshipped in the large Sun-temples which were built by some of the kings of the Vth dynasty was that of a stone. The stone had the shape of a massive, truncated obelisk, with a pyramid above it, and it stood on a strong masonry base. The spirit of the Sun-god was supposed to enter the stone at certain periods, and on these occasions human sacrifices were offered to it.[61]

One Pyramid Age inscription portrays Ptah as creator, who made not only the gods but also idols ("bodies") for the immaterial gods to enter.

> He fashioned the gods, he made the cities, he settled the nomes. He installed the gods [i.e., idols] in their holy places, he made their offerings to flourish, he equipped their holy places. He made likenesses of their bodies to the satisfaction of their hearts. Then the gods entered into their bodies of every wood and every stone and every metal.[62]

According to Egyptian theology, Ptah created both the gods and their earthly temples and images. The Pyramid Texts also gave a rationale for idolatry that probably any idolater in the ancient world could have affirmed: "He made likenesses of their bodies to the satisfaction of their hearts." That is, the creator god made idols of the gods that resembled the gods in form, visage, and color. Because the images were faithful likenesses, the gods felt that their "souls" (see below) could be at home in them. So they "entered into their bodies of every wood and every stone and every metal." But how did the gods do that?

---

61. Budge, *Book of the Dead*, 165–66. Budge further remarks, "The victims were probably prisoners of war who had been captured alive, and foreigners, and when these failed, the priests must have drawn upon the native population, as priests have done in Africa from time immemorial."

62. Breasted, *Development of Religion*, 46.

Egyptian theology answered that question with a greater sophistication than any other ancient nation. Other nations also believed that a god, an immaterial being, would enter his idol, a shapen image. But only Egypt understood that a god had not only a body and a spirit but also something in between, known as the "Ka," and the Ka possessed the idol. Both gods and humans had Kas. Regarding the human Ka, Budge has observed,

> . . . in addition to the Natural-body and the Spirit-body, man also had an abstract individuality or personality endowed with all his characteristic attributes. This abstract personality had an absolutely independent existence. It could move freely from place to place, separating itself from, or uniting itself to, the body at will, and also enjoying life with the gods in heaven. This was the KA.[63]

Funeral donations of meat, cakes, ale, wine, unguents, and so on were intended for the Ka, which apparently needed them to survive.[64] Because both people and gods were made in Ptah's image, a god also had a Ka. Consequently such gifts must be made continually to both gods and departed humans. Those offerings were made in the temples of gods and in the mortuary temples of humans. They were made to images of the gods and statues of the pharaohs because "the KA dwelt in the man's statue just as the KA of a god inhabited the statue of the god."[65]

Two biblical parallels come to mind, which we will mention briefly now but will discuss in a different context later in this chapter. First, one cannot help but notice the parallel between the Egyptian model (body, Ka, spirit) and the biblical model (body, soul, spirit, 1 Thess. 5:23). Second, just as the Ka of a god can inhabit an idol made in his image, so the Spirit of God can inhabit a human made in God's image.

---

63. Budge, *Book of the Dead*, 73. As Budge notes, translations of the word *Ka* vary and include "genius, double, character, disposition, and mental attributes" (74).

64. Budge remarks that "it seems as if the Egyptians thought that the existence of the KA depended upon a constant supply of sepulchral offerings. When circumstances rendered it impossible to continue the material supply of food, the KA fed upon the offerings painted on the walls of the tomb, which were transformed into suitable nourishment by the prayers of the living" (ibid., 75).

65. Ibid., 74. An idol can be "mysterious" because a god can inhabit it. So Thutmose I (1525–1495 B.C.) commanded idols to be shaped, and said, "Mysterious and splendid were their bodies" (Breasted, *Ancient Records of Egypt*, 2:39 [§ 95]).

We have considered one ancient account that says that Ptah made all things, including the images of the gods "to the satisfaction of their hearts." A later account, however, says it was a divine council that decided what form the images should take.[66] So Pharaoh Neferhotep (1751–1740 B.C.) addresses his counselors:

> My heart hath desired to see the ancient writings of Atum; open ye for me . . . a great investigation; let the god know concerning his creation, and the gods concerning their fashioning . . . (let) me know the god in his form, that I may fashion him as he was formerly, when they made the statues in their council, in order to establish their monuments upon earth.[67]

Breasted explains, "The reference is apparently to a council of the gods in which the form of the god's statue was determined once for all. This the king expects to find in the ancient writings."[68] The "investigation" is successful, and once the numinous pattern is located, the king declares, "I will fashion him, his limbs—his face, his fingers according to that which my majesty has seen in the rolls [—] his form as King of Upper and Lower Egypt, at his coming forth from the body of Nut."[69] He adds, "May I make his monuments according to 'the beginning.'"[70] When Pharaoh says, "the beginning," he means the god's original form at the beginning of the world, which Pharaoh has just learned from the rolls.[71]

We see here another, further parallelism between Pharaoh and his heavenly father. Just as Ptah originally had made the gods' first earthly images, subsequent pharaohs had to create new earthly images according to that primordial divine archetype (which was Ptah, or Amon as Ptah). Pharaohs made those idols in Ptah's image because Ptah had once made the gods in

---

66. The later version posits a council where the earlier one had Ptah alone, but that may or may not be an inconsistency. As Budge remarks on the doctrine of eternal life, there may be "many difficulties . . . in harmonizing the statements made in different works of different periods," but there remains a consistency in the core ideas of the doctrine—and one might add, of Egyptian religion itself (*Book of the Dead*, 66).

67. Breasted, *Ancient Records of Egypt*, 1:333 (§ 755–56).

68. Ibid., 1:333n. e.

69. Ibid., 1:334 (§ 759). "Nut" is the divine sky.

70. Ibid., 1:335 (§ 760).

71. Ibid., 1:335n. b.

his own image. Ramses II (1290–1224 B.C.) told his "father," the god Ptah-Tatenen, "I have wrought the gods' forms from thy limbs, even to their color and to their bodies."[72] That is, he patterned the idols after ("wrought the gods' forms from") Ptah's limbs, and colored them the same as Ptah's body. Later, Ramses III (1195–1164 B.C.) could say to Amon-Ra, "Thou art divine among the gods who are in thy image."[73] The gods are in Amon's image because (as Ptah) he created them so.

It is clear from the foregoing that in Egypt an idol, like a temple, was made to represent a heavenly archetype. So it comes as no surprise that, as in temple construction, gold, silver, and precious stones were used to make the idol shine with a heavenly glory. Ramses III (1195–1164 B.C.) says to Amon-Ra, "I fashioned thy great statue . . . 'Amon-Endowed-with-Eternity' was its august name; it was endowed with real costly stone like the horizon."[74] The same king reports that in Ra's temple, "I fashioned the gods in their mysterious forms of gold, silver, and every costly stone, as everlasting works."[75]

Moreover, the same was true of statues of living monarchs since they were gods on earth, or of departed monarchs since they were gods in heaven. Amen-hotep III (1398–1361 B.C.) could say of the Amon temple at Thebes, "It is numerous in royal statues. . . . Their stature shines more than the heavens, their rays are in the faces (of men) like the sun, when he shines early in the morning."[76] Ramses III (1195–1164 B.C.), who made a statue of himself serving Amon-Ra in the Medinet Habu temple, describes it in the following way: "I bring to thee myrrh for thy temple, a statue kneeling upon the ground, my figure of gold and every costly stone, mounted in Asiatic gold."[77] Later, we read that a statue of Psammetichus I (664–610 B.C.), along with statues of his daughter, Nitocris, was installed in a palace chapel of Osiris: "The portable image of his majesty was fashioned of electrum,

---

72. Ibid., 3:181 (§ 411).
73. Ibid., 4:112 (§187).
74. Ibid., 4:114 (§ 190). Breasted notes that in this case, "the horizon" may mean "the horizon god," 114n. h.
75. Ibid., 4:143 (§ 250).
76. Ibid., 2:356 (§ 883). Statues, obelisks, temple doors, and temples themselves "shine" in the inscriptions because they are made of precious metals.
77. Ibid., 4:15 (§ 26). Breasted observes, "The neighboring reliefs show this statue; on a rectangular base kneels a figure of the king, bearing in his outstretched hands an ointment jar" (4:15n. e).

inlaid with every genuine costly stone, together with statues of her body of electrum."[78]

As we have seen, Egyptians thought that a royal image or a divine image could contain the Ka of the one in whose likeness it had been made. When a god entered his earthly image, he thereby became accessible to the worshipper. In such a state, the god might even make the image nod, as a way of showing what the god wanted.

One such case dates from the reign of Mer-ne-Ptah (1224–1214 B.C.), who reports that "Amon nod[ded] approval" when Pharaoh wanted to campaign against a coalition of northern foes.[79] The idol literally gave Pharaoh the nod, functioning as an oracle.

An idol also could be a judge, who might nod in order to render a judgment, as two cases from the Twenty-first Dynasty (1090–945 B.C.) illustrate. In the first case, Menkheperre, high priest of Amon, asks his god to judge murder cases.

> Then the High Priest of Amon, Menkheperre, triumphant, went to the great god, saying: "As for any person, of whom they shall report before thee, saying, 'A slayer of living people . . . is he;' thou shalt destroy him, thou shalt slay him." Then the great god nodded exceedingly, exceedingly.[80]

Amon's image is a judge who can find murderers guilty and condemn them accordingly. For an Egyptian that made sense according to "the beginning," because, as we learn from the Pyramid Age, Ptah, who originally made the idols, was also a judge who "gave life to the peaceful and death to the guilty."[81] So, now, Amon (another form of Ptah) inhabits an image and, in Menkheperre's day, carries on his perennial function as judge.

In the second case, Menkheperre's son, who like his father was also high priest of Amon, tells how Amon's idol acquitted a person accused of embezzlement. Two tablets were placed before the idol. One tablet declared there were no matters to be investigated in the case of the accused; the second tablet said there were matters to be investigated.

---

78.   Ibid., 4:491 (§ 958K).
79.   Ibid., 3:244 (§ 580).
80.   Ibid., 4:320 (§ 658); cf. 4:318 (§ 655), 319 (§ 656).
81.   Breasted, *Development of Religion*, 45.

This great god appeared upon the pavement of silver in the house of
Amon at the morning hour. The High Priest of Amon-Re . . . came before this great god. This great god saluted violently . . . He placed the two
tablets of writing before the great god. . . . The [High Priest] of Amon-Re,
king of gods . . . repeated before this great god, saying, "O my good lord,
thou shalt judge . . . thou prosperest beyond all wonders." [The] great god
saluted violently.[82]

Amon's salute affirmed that he was present, available to judge. Then
Amon "took [i.e., selected, nodded toward] the writing" that exonerated
the accused. The god is present in the image and ready to help decide knotty
cases. Indeed, this second account draws unusual attention to the image's
vitality, perhaps in order to affirm how truly Amon indwells that image
made in his likeness.

Pharaoh as a Sacred Image

Egyptians taught that their creator god made lesser gods in his image
and likeness. This tenet of Egyptian theology may have a biblical parallel.
In the Old Testament, angels are called "gods" (Gen. 35:7) and "sons of
God" (Job 1:6; 2:1 RSV).[83] It is well understood, in biblical parlance, that
a "son" of someone (or something) reflects or partakes of his father's nature. If angels are "sons of God," then they also may have been created in
God's image, just as Adam was a "son of God" (Luke 3:38) and was created
in God's image (Gen. 1:27). Moreover, the "Son of God" par excellence is
Jesus, who is also the very image and likeness of God (Heb. 1:3). In a way
that remarkably anticipates these truths about the Messiah, every pharaoh
also was considered to be the "Son of God," namely, the son of Amon-Ra,
and as such also was made in that god's image.

Very early, in a Pyramid Text, we read the following:

> For the King is a great Power
> Who has power over the Powers;
> The King is a sacred image,
> The most sacred of the sacred images of the Great One . . .
> For the King is a god,

---

82. Breasted, *Ancient Records of Egypt*, 4:327–28 (§ 672).
83. Cf. Dickason, *Angels Elect and Evil*, 60.

> Older than the oldest.
> Thousands serve him,
> Hundreds offer to him.[84]

However, there appears to be a contradiction here. On the one hand, the king is a sacred image of the Great One (i.e., the creator); on the other hand, he is also older than the oldest god (presumably including his creator)! This conundrum may be resolved by another claim, that "the King was fashioned by his father Atum before the sky existed, before earth existed, before men existed, before the gods were born."[85] In other words, the text is not claiming that the king existed before Amon, but rather Amon made the king before he made any other god. Be that as it may, there are two possible biblical parallels to this material. First, we read that the king is made in the creator's image. We recall that the first king, Adam, also was made in the image of his Creator. Second, the king is portrayed in terms that surely recall the Ancient of Days in Daniel 7, who was also "older than the oldest." As "thousands serve" the king and "hundreds offer to him," so for the Ancient of Days

> Thousands upon thousands
> attended him;
> Ten thousand times ten thousand
> stood before him.
>
> (Dan. 7:10)

The Ancient of Days may have multiple thousands who attend him, but a Pyramid Age monarch would claim the same.

Although we encounter the concept of Pharaoh's creation as a divine image often after the Pyramid Age, I will cite just one example here. Ramses II (1290–1224 B.C.) declares, "I am thy son whom thou hast placed upon thy throne. Thou hast assigned to me thy kingdom, thou hast fashioned me in thy likeness and thy form, which thou hast assigned to me and hast created."[86]

---

84. Faulkner, *Ancient Egyptian Pyramid Texts*, 82 (Utterances 273–74, §§ 407–8); cf. "the King is unique, the eldest of the gods" (ibid., 68 [Utterance 258, § 309]).
85. Ibid., 226 (Utterance 571, § 1466).
86. Breasted, *Ancient Records of Egypt*, 3:181 (§ 411).

Pharaoh's claim that the creator god "fashioned" him in his own "likeness" and "form" recalls word for word the Genesis account, when God says, "Let us fashion man in our image ["form"], according to our likeness" (Gen. 1:26, author's translation). Moreover, some theologians have argued that the plural, "let us," shows that a divine council planned what form the man should take, and they decided he should be in the image of God. If so, that would parallel the Neferhotep account, cited above, that a council of gods decided to make their idols in their own image (which was also the image of the creator god).[87]

Many generations of pharaohs claimed to be the image of (Amon) Ra, or of one of the gods equated with Ra. Consequently, a standard epithet of Pharaoh was "son of Ra."[88] But Pharaoh not only was created or formed in his god's image; he also *contained* Ra (or one of the gods identified with Ra). For example, one Pyramid Text says, "Horus has caused the gods to join you. . . . Horus has acted on behalf of his spirit in you."[89] In another such text, the king declares, "I am the essence of a god, the son of a god, the messenger of a god."[90] In fact, one Pyramid Text avers, "O King, you are the essence of all the gods, and Horus has protected you, you having become the essence of him."[91] We can see, then, that the king is not only a god's son, but he also has a god's spirit within him; that is, the monarch is also a god essentially or the god incarnate. Moreover, he also can be called "the messenger of a god." These ideas are astounding precisely because they are not unique to Egypt. The biblical parallels are striking. Jesus, the King of Kings, is also God's Son. On earth he had God's Spirit within him, without measure (John 3:34). He was essentially God, or God incarnate. In addition, we can recall those cases in the Old Testament when the "angel/messenger of the LORD" apparently is God himself (e.g., Gen. 16:7, 9–11; 18:1ff.; Exod.

---

87. The topic of divine councils, which has come clearly into focus in the last few decades of scholarship, will not form part of this enquiry. For a good, brief introduction to the topic of the biblical divine council and the pagan councils of the gods, see Walton, *Ancient Near Eastern Thought*, 92–97.

88. See chapter 2, "God and the Royal Shepherd."

89. Faulkner, *Ancient Egyptian Pyramid Texts*, 122 Utterance 370, §§ 645, 647).

90. Ibid., 160 (Utterance 471, § 920). Budge, *Book of the Dead*, 87, translates, "an angel of God." The word *angel* originally meant simply "messenger," whether divine or human.

91. Faulkner, *Ancient Egyptian Pyramid Texts*, 242 (Utterance 589, § 1609); cf. the command to the dead king, "Come into being as the essence of every god" (ibid., 307 [Utterance 715, § 2219]).

3:6). Finally, we noted that Pharaoh was "the essence of all the gods"—a concept not far from the idea that "in him [that is, Christ] we live and move and have our being" (Acts 17:28).

Sumer

Like the Egyptians, the Sumerians also believed a god would inhabit the idol made in his image and so become accessible to the worshipper. As Oppenheim notes concerning idols in Sumero-Babylonian culture, "Fundamentally, the deity was considered present in its image if it showed certain specific features and paraphernalia and was cared for in the appropriate manner."[92] He adds that, as in Egypt, "they had to undergo an elaborate and highly secret ritual of consecration to transform the lifeless matter into a receptacle of the divine presence. During these nocturnal ceremonies they were endowed with 'life,' their eyes and mouths were 'opened' so that the images could see and eat."[93]

Babylon (Old Babylonian)

Monarchs of the Old Babylonian period claimed that gods gave them the wisdom or direction needed to make appropriate idols. In light of what we have seen, the meaning of such a claim is clear: divine wisdom was necessary if the idol was to correspond to the deity, so that the deity would be pleased to enter it.

Abī-sarē (1905–1895 B.C.) of Larsa said, "[. . . the god *Enki* . . .] gave to me su[preme intellig]ence, surpassing everything," as a result of which he was able to make "a statue fashioned of silver and *carnelian*, expertly formed as a masterpiece . . . fashioned with jewels . . . an etern[al] thing that [should not be] removed [from] the temple of the god Nann[a]."[94] Sīn-iddinam of Larsa says he was "given broad wisdom and surpassing intelligence by the god Nudimmud," and so fashions a cult statue (idol) and throne on which the statue may rest.[95] Kudur-mabuk, father of Warad-Sīn, says that the gods An, Enlil, Enki, and Ninmaḫ had given him authority to rule. Then, in a sadly broken context, we read, ". . . shining star(s) . . . awe-inspiring radi-

---

92. Oppenheim, *Ancient Mesopotamia*, 184.

93. Ibid., 186.

94. Frayne, *Old Babylonian Period*, 122 (E4.2.6.1, ii 1'–17'). Apparently it was a royal statue placed in the presence of (the idol of) Nanna.

95. Ibid., 178–79 (E4.2.9.15, 41–84).

ance . . . a th[rone] . . . that throne [was inlaid] with red gold . . . statue of
the god Nanna [whose] fo[rm] was fashioned correctly . . . grandly I. . . . A
pair of protective genii . . . [giving] good omens . . . being there daily. . . . I
set up on either side of it."[96] Even from such a damaged text the major ideas
are clear: the monarch has made a throne like the heavenly throne of the
god (made of gold), and "fashioned correctly" the statue of the god, that is,
made it in the god's image so the god would enter it; he then placed these in a
temple decorated as with "shining stars" and having a heavenly/theophanic
"radiance." The temple has a pair of "protective genii," an added touch that
may find a parallel in the cherubim who guarded God's Eden temple (Gen.
3:24) and later his tabernacle/temple (see below).

Assyria

Later in Mesopotamia, Assyrian rulers also claimed heavenly guidance
for the production of divine images (idols). They likewise believed that divine guidance was needed if the earthly idol was to be an accurate image of
the deity. Ashurnasirpal II (883–859 B.C.) says,

> With the wisdom (and) understanding of, (and) according to the desire
> of, the great gods who love me, I created an icon of the goddess Istar, my
> mistress, which had never before existed. (I created it) from the finest
> stones, fine gold, and red gold (thus) making her great divinity resplen-
> dent. I set up in (the temple) her dais (with the icon) for eternity. I made
> this temple suitably resplendent.[97]

As was the case with temple construction, so too with idol manufacture,
gemstones and gold are supposed to make the image heavenly like the goddess herself. Once the temple is complete, the Assyrian king establishes the
deity in the temple by taking the idol into its new home in a grand proces-
sion. And, although we have not here documented instances of such idol
installation, it was standard and was the normal and logical conclusion of
the temple-building process: once the house is complete, the god who owns
it enters it to take possession.

---

96. Ibid., 221 (E4.2.13.13, 48–71).
97. Grayson, *Assyrian Rulers of the Early First Millennium B.C. I*, 296–97 (A.0.101
.32.11–12).

In a somewhat parallel fashion, the Lord comes into his temple once it is completed and dedicated.

> And King Solomon and all the congregation of Israel, who had assembled before him, were with him before the ark, sacrificing so many sheep and oxen that they could not be counted or numbered. Then the priests brought the ark of the covenant of the LORD to its place, in the inner sanctuary of the house, in the most holy place, underneath the wings of the cherubim. . . . There was nothing in the ark except the two tablets of stone which Moses put there at Horeb, where the LORD made a covenant with the people of Israel, when they came out of the land of Egypt. And when the priests came out of the holy place, a cloud filled the house of the LORD, so that the priests could not stand to minister because of the cloud; for the glory of the LORD filled the house of the LORD. (1 Kings 8:5–11 RSV)

Egyptian and Mesopotamian kings caused idols to be installed in their temples. Solomon caused the ark to be installed in the Lord's temple. Pagan rulers thought the gods inhabited their idols. The Lord had no idol, but his temple had the ark (which the Philistines naturally assumed held a divine presence, cf. 1 Sam. 4:5–9; 5:1–11), and Solomon knew the Lord sat enthroned *above* the ark (1 Kings 8:6–11; 9:1–3).[98] The interiors of Egyptian and Mesopotamian temples were made heavenly. The interior of the Lord's temple was made heavenly by the gold pavement and walls and by the presence of cherubim. Mesopotamian kings installed the law/covenant of their gods in their temples. Solomon installed in the Lord's temple the ark that housed the two tablets of the Decalogue (also referred to as "the two tablets of the covenant" in Deut. 9:15; cf. 9:9, 11; Exod. 34:28).

We have observed a number of parallels between the ancient Near East and the Old Testament on the topics of city, temple, and image. Those parallels now provide a foundation for some final reflections.

Conclusion

We have seen how the pagan world (theologically speaking, the realm of "common grace") contained adumbrations of truth revealed in Scripture,

---

98. The Lord was celebrated as the one "enthroned between the cherubim" (1 Sam. 4:4; 2 Sam. 6:2; 2 Kings 19:15; Pss. 80:1; 99:1; Isa. 37:16) that stood guard over the ark (Exod. 25:20–21; 1 Kings 8:7).

regarding heavenly cities or cities made by gods or commanded by the gods
to be made, the revelation of temple patterns, the revelation of the law/
covenant to be deposited in those temples (see chapter 3), and the divine
presence to reside within those temples. I would now like to review and
summarize biblical data evocative of these themes.

One theme alluded to in the concept of heavenly cities or temples is that
of a cosmic temple. Some ancient Near Eastern data imply that the cosmos
is a temple. The same theme appears in the Old and New Testaments. For
example, Psalm 104 says of the Lord,

> He wraps himself in light as with a garment;
> he stretches out the heavens like a tent
> and lays the beams of his upper chambers on their waters. . . .
> He waters the mountains from his upper chambers.
>
> (Ps. 104:2–3, 13)

Here the Lord implicitly lives in a heavenly tent, like the Canaanite
gods; and he has "upper chambers" above the heavenly "waters" (cf. Gen.
1:7). The term "upper chambers" is significant in this discussion, because
it is used elsewhere in the Old Testament for domestic architecture (e.g.,
1 Kings 17:19, Elijah's "upper room" in the widow of Zarephath's house;
2 Kings 1:2, Ahaziah's "upper room" in Samaria).

Amos portrays a similar picture of the Lord, "who builds his lofty palace
in the heavens and sets its foundation on the earth, who calls for the waters
of the sea and pours them out over the face of the land—the LORD is his
name" (Amos 9:6). Isaiah, like the psalmist, speaks of the Lord's heavenly
tent:

> He sits enthroned above the circle of the earth,
> and its people are like grasshoppers.
> He stretches out the heavens like a canopy,
> and spreads them out like a tent to live in.
>
> (Isa. 40:22)

Not only are the heavens likened to a tent, reminiscent perhaps of the heavenly tents of the Canaanite gods, but also the enthronement idea naturally
implies a palace or temple, and recalls the assertion of Psalm 2:4, "The One

enthroned in heaven laughs (at his foes)." We also should note that in Job Elihu refers to the heavens in architectural terms: "Who can understand how he spreads out the clouds, how he thunders from his pavilion?" (Job 36:29). All of these portraits point to a cosmic tent or palace or temple concept, and indeed the three are ultimately the same, since a "temple," be it a tent or a palace, is the god's dwelling.[99] David illustrates this point in Psalm 27:4–5.

> One thing I ask of the LORD,
>   this is what I seek:
> that I may dwell in the *house* of the LORD
>   all the days of my life,
> to gaze upon the beauty of the LORD
>   and to seek him in his *temple*.
> For in the day of trouble
>   he will keep me safe in his *tent*;
> he will hide me in the shelter of his *booth*.
>   (author's translation,
>   emphasis added)

When David wrote this, the ark of the Lord was in the tabernacle. Yet consistent with the ancient Near Eastern concept of "temple," David could refer to it as both a "tent," or even "booth," and a "house" or "temple." Such usage helps us to understand that when the other passages we have cited refer to the Lord's heavenly "tent" or "pavilion," they are really speaking of, or at least implying, his heavenly or cosmic temple.

In the New Testament, Jesus apparently alludes to the cosmic temple idea: "I tell you, do not swear at all: either by heaven, for it is God's throne; or by the earth, for it is his footstool; or by Jerusalem, for it is the city of the Great King" (Matt. 5:34–35). Heaven is God's throne, and earth is his footstool. Figuratively the cosmos is therefore the "big house," or "temple," in which this throne and footstool are located. Moreover, the heavenly city, implied by its earthly counterpart, Jerusalem, also belongs to this mixture of ideas, as we have noted.[100]

---

99. We note that the Hebrew word for both "temple" and "palace" is the same (*heykal*), a loanword from Sumerian E.GAL, which means, literally, "big house."
100. As we have seen, city and temple are different forms of expression for the same ultimate reality, forms, as Jacobsen said, of "the power that was meant to fill" them.

We have seen that there is a correspondence between the heavenly temple and the earthly. The latter was patterned after the former, as in the case of the Mosaic tabernacle. As a type of what was to come, that tabernacle/temple is more fully expounded in the New Testament. As the earthly temple had sacrifices of bulls and goats, the heavenly has Christ, the perfect sacrifice (Heb. 9:11–14). As the earthly temple had the law/covenant, so the heavenly one has Christ, who is the fulfillment of the law (Matt. 5:17) and whose blood is the blood of the new covenant (Matt. 26:28). As the earthly temple had the theophany and the ongoing presence of the Lord (cf. Exod. 40:34–35; 1 Kings 8:10–11; 9:3), so the heavenly (Rev. 11:19) has the ongoing presence of the Lord, who ultimately is the temple (Rev. 21:22).

As Jacobsen insightfully noted, a god's temple is also that god's image. What the Sumerians dimly sensed, the New Testament makes wonderfully clear. Humans who contain God's Spirit are God's temple, yet they are also God's image. Jesus himself was the epitome of this equation. He was himself God's temple (cf. John 1:14; 2:19–22). He was also the Son of God par excellence, made in God's image and likeness. The author of Hebrews tells us that the Son "is the radiance of God's glory and the exact representation of his being" (Heb. 1:3). The term translated "exact representation" is Greek *charaktēr*, used also of an image or likeness on a coin, meant to be a faithful representation of the original—usually an emperor or king.[101] Thus Jesus is an exact image or likeness of the Great King. Moreover, he is the "radiance of God's glory." This comment by the author of Hebrews sheds further light on the relation between the Son and the Spirit. One scholar who understood this relationship wrote, "Since God's glory has impressed itself on Him as the One exalted by God, He is its reflection and image."[102] That is, the Son is the reflection and image of God's glory. But God's glory is nothing other than God's Spirit, as Peter makes clear when he speaks of "the Spirit of glory and of God" (1 Peter 4:14). Moreover, the phrases in Hebrews and 1 Peter may recall Ezekiel's inaugural vision, in which he saw the Lord on his chariot throne. That human figure was "the likeness of the glory of the LORD" (Ezek. 1:28). In other words, if the "glory of the Lord" has any likeness, it is the human form. And, lest there be any doubt, the term for "likeness" is the same used of Adam and Eve, made in the image

101.   See G. Kittle and G. Friedrich, eds., *Theological Dictionary of the New Testament*, trans. G. W. Bromiley (Grand Rapids: Eerdmans, 1974), 9:418–22.
102.   Ibid., 9:421.

and "likeness" of God (Gen. 1:27; cf. 5:1), and also of Adam's offspring, who were in his image and "likeness" (Gen. 5:3).

These data invite the conclusion that humans, like Jesus, are made in the image or likeness of God's glory or Spirit. It follows logically that this human image has been fashioned to contain that glory and so to become a temple of God's Spirit (cf. 1 Cor. 6:19; 2 Cor. 4:16–5:10). Ezekiel's phraseology makes it clear that God's own image or form is the likeness of his glory or Spirit. Consequently, God's own form is a temple of his own Spirit; or, stated otherwise, God is a temple of himself. John confirms the same, stating the "the Lord God Almighty and the Lamb" are together a "temple," in fact, the temple that he sees in the heavenly Jerusalem (Rev. 21:22). The "Lord God Almighty" (the Father) and the "Lamb" (the Son) are the temple and contain the unmentioned third person of the Trinity, the "Spirit of glory and of God" (1 Peter 4:14). So humans made in God's image may contain that same Spirit and become temples of the Spirit.

When one becomes a temple of God's Spirit, another temple truth appears. In that body/temple, God, the Great King, deposits his law/covenant, written on the heart: "But this is the covenant which I will make with the house of Israel after those days, says the LORD: I will put my law within them, and I will write it upon their hearts" (Jer. 31:33 RSV). Far more than the law, God himself now resides in such a temple, in fulfillment of the promise made through Ezekiel, "I will put my Spirit in you and move you to follow my decrees and be careful to keep my laws" (Ezek. 36:27). We have, in fact, "Christ in [us], the hope of glory" (Col. 1:27), who has fulfilled the law.

And these things, true of us individually, also are true of us corporately. We are a temple of "living stones" (1 Peter 2:5). As the apostle Paul writes to the Corinthian church, "Do you not know that you are God's temple and that God's Spirit dwells in you?" (1 Cor. 3:16 NRSV).

Moreover, eschatologically we look forward to the heavenly city. That complex is also resplendent with gold and precious stones.

It shone with the glory of God, and its brilliance was like that of a very precious jewel, like a jasper, clear as crystal. . . . The wall was made of jasper, and the city of pure gold, as pure as glass. . . . The first foundation was jasper, the second sapphire, the third chalcedony, the fourth emerald, the fifth sardonyx, the sixth carnelian, the seventh chrysolite, the eighth beryl, the ninth topaz, the tenth chrysoprase, the eleventh jacinth, and the twelfth amethyst. The twelve gates were twelve pearls, each gate made of a single pearl. The great street of the city was of pure gold, like transparent glass. (Rev. 21:11, 18–21)

The account may recall the gold and bejeweled splendor of Egyptian temples or cult cities. But the temple of the heavenly Jerusalem far surpasses any previous temple, being God himself.

Another logical step is warranted by these data. If both image and temple are in some sense forms of the power that is meant to fill them, and if the cosmos is also a temple, then the cosmos is somehow also a form of the power that fills it. In other words, all of creation is somehow made in God's image. This is not so strange a conclusion as it may seem. It is a way of saying that every created thing has its archetype in God, who has made each type of creature after some aspect of his image. C. S. Lewis appears to have understood this, when he says of Jane's encounter with the divine presence,

She had come into a world, or into a Person, or into the presence of a Person. Something expectant, patient, inexorable, met her with no veil of protection between. . . . There was nothing, and never had been anything, like this. And now there was nothing except this. Yet also, everything had been like this; only by being like this had anything existed.[103]

---

103. C. S. Lewis, *That Hideous Strength* (New York: Macmillan, 1965), 318. Plato also appears to have understood this truth, although in a pagan and darkened form, e.g., in his *Republic*.

5

City and Temple

Abandoned and Restored

The ancient Near Eastern cultures we have surveyed all believed that their gods not only ruled over them but also dwelt among them and sought to extend their rule through their people by wars of conquest. The gods' temples were their earthly bases of operation (or "central command") in cities and kingdoms out of which such imperial expansion was to take place. The ancient inscriptions are full of glamorous propagandistic accounts of the emperor's success in conquering other lands and bringing them under the rule of his gods, and every ancient monarch claimed that he had achieved such success because his gods had fought on his side against the foe.

But what happened when a god's army suffered reversal, when a city and its temples were sacked? The ancients accounted for such an event theologically in several ways. The fundamental explanation was always that the gods had abandoned their temples. But why did they abandon them? Sometimes, and particularly in Sumer, an inscrutable divine decree would cause the gods to abandon their cities and temples. Later, in Assyria, the gods would abandon their cities and temples as a judgment on the sin, or covenant breaking, of their earthly shepherd, the king. Alternately, the gods might have to abandon their homes in the face of the more powerful gods of the enemy. Whichever of these causes (inscrutable decree, divine judgment, or flight in the face of more powerful gods) might lead the gods to abandon their homes, such abandonment left the empire or kingdom, and more particularly the capital city and its temples, open to hostile gods and the armies they empowered.

Sumer

Late in the third millennium B.C., the Sumerians faced a crisis. As Piotr Michalowski notes, "During the twenty-fourth year of the reign of King Ibbi-Sin (2028–2004 B.C.) the city of Ur fell to an army from the east. The extensive empire that had been founded by Ur-Namma approximately one hundred years earlier . . . had already been tottering for over a generation, and this final act was nothing more than a *coup de grace* that affected only the old capital city and its immediate environs."[1] In the ancient Near East, the fall of an empire and its capital required a theological explanation, and the Sumerians provided one for the fall of Ur.[2] According to the poem titled by modern scholars "The Lament over the Destruction of Sumer and Ur," we read that "(the gods) An, Enlil, Enki, and Ninmah decided its fate," which was "to quickly subdue it like a yoked ox, to bow its neck to the ground."[3] The poem says that in order to accomplish this,

> Enlil brought down the Elamites, the enemy, from the highlands . . .
> (Enlil) has handed over (the city to the) storm,
> He has handed (it) over to the storm that destroys cities,
> He has handed (it) over to the storm that destroys temples! . . .
> Daily the evil wind returns to (attack) the city.[4]

Such destruction, however, was possible only because "the god of that city turned away, its shepherd vanished."[5] Moreover, all the other gods agree with him and leave their temples as well. So we read that the god "Ningirsu took an unfamiliar path away from the Eninnu."[6] Likewise, "An evil storm swept over Ninhursag at the Enutura,/Like a dove she flew from the window, she stood away on the plain."[7] We may recall how the Lord departed his temple and stood on the mountain east of Jerusalem (Ezek. 10:18–19;

---

1. Michalowski, *Lamentation over the Destruction of Sumer and Ur*, 1. See also S. N. Kramer, "Lamentation over the Destruction of Sumer and Ur," in *ANET*, 611–19.
2. For other laments in Sumerian, similar in outlook and theology to what we are about to consider, see S. N. Kramer, "Lamentation over the Destruction of Ur," in *ANET*, 455–63; idem, "Lamentation over the Destruction of Nippur," 89–93; Kutscher, *Oh Angry Sea*; Green, "The Eridu Lament," 127–61; and idem, "The Uruk Lament," 253–79.
3. Michalowski, *Lamentation over the Destruction of Sumer and Ur*, 39 (lines 54–55).
4. Ibid., 47, 61 (166, 174–76, 386a).
5. Ibid., 41 (68).
6. Ibid., 47 (160).
7. Ibid., 49 (207–8).

11:22–23).[8] And the advent of the foe is described as a "storm," or "wind," just as in the Old Testament prophets.[9]

Once the gods have abandoned their temples, they also leave the city.

> Nanna, who loves his city, left his city,
> Su'en took an unfamiliar path away from his beloved Ur.
> Ningal . . . in order to go to an alien place,
> Quickly clothed herself (and) left the city.
> (All) the Anunna stepped outside of Ur.[10]

Moreover, a god might not only abandon his temple, city, and people, but he might even go over to the enemy. So we read, "Inanna abandoned Uruk, went off to enemy territory."[11]

As a result of this divine abandonment, the enemy is able to attack and destroy the city and the temple, because both now lack divine protection.

> The enemy seized the Ekišnugal of Nanna . . .
> The statues that were in the treasury were cut down . . .
> The great *door ornament* of the temple was felled,
>   its parapet was destroyed,
> The wild animals that were intertwined on its left and right
> Lay before it like heroes smitten by heroes,
> Its open-mouthed dragons (and) its awe-inspiring lions
> Were pulled down with ropes like captured wild bulls and
>   carried off to enemy territory.
> The fragrant aroma of the sacred seat of Nanna was destroyed
>   like that of a cedar grove,
> Its architrave . . . gold, silver, and lapis.
> The admired temple that used (to receive) first class oil,
>   its admiration was extinguished.[12]

---

8. For other gods departing their temples, see ibid., 49 (211: Ningizzida abandoning the Gisbanda), 49 (219: Lugalbanda forsaking "his beloved dwelling"), 51 (246: Enki forsaking Eridu), 59 (347: Enlil abandoning the Kiur), etc.

9. For "storm," see Isaiah 28:2; Jeremiah 4:13–17; Ezekiel 38:7–9; for "wind," see Hosea 13:15–16; Jeremiah 4:11–13; Habakkuk 1:6–11.

10. Michalowski, *Lamentation over the Destruction of Sumer and Ur*, 58–61 (373–77).

11. Ibid., 45 (150).

12. Ibid., 63 (407b, 408, 420–26).

Once the gods abandon their temples, the protective cover, so to speak, of those temples is removed. That leaves the temples open to invasion, destruction, and pillage by the foe.

One major difference between this example and the Lord's temple abandonment is its motive. The Lord abandons the Jerusalem temple because of sin. But Enlil and the gods abandon Ur simply because they have decreed an end to its imperium. Thus Enlil says to his son, the god Su'en (Nanna, the chief deity of Ur),

> O Nanna, the Noble Son . . . why do you concern yourself
>   with crying?
> The judgment of the assembly cannot be turned back,
> The word of An and Enlil knows no overturning,
> Ur was indeed given kingship (but) it was not given an
>   eternal reign . . .
> Who has ever seen a reign of kingship that would take
>   precedence (forever)?
> The reign of its kingship had been long indeed but had
>   to exhaust itself.[13]

The poem explains Ur's defeat as a result of a divine decree that the gods must leave Ur and take its protection and suzerainty with them. The only reason given is that the gods do not give endless preference to any empire: every empire must pass away when its predestined term has expired. Still, the ultimate reason for such a decree remains a mystery. As Su'en says in despair, "O father Enlil, the fate that you have decreed cannot be explained!"[14]

The gods may relent, however, once they consider their decree fulfilled. In this case Enlil's son, the god Su'en, intercedes for Ur; as a result, the father promises to restore what has been destroyed.

> Enlil then provides a favorable response to his son:
> "My son, the city that was built for you in joy and prosperity,
>   it was given to you as your reign . . .

---

13. Ibid., 59 (363–66, 368).
14. Ibid., 65 (457).

> Ur shall be rebuilt in splendor, may the people bow down
> (to you)."[15]

As a result, the gods and goddesses come back to their restored city and temples.

> Father Nanna stood in his city of Ur with head raised high
> (once again),
> The hero Su'en entered into the Ekišnugal.
> Ningal refreshed herself in her sacred living quarters,
> In Ur she entered into her Ekišnugal.[16]

After Enlil's decree, the poet also addresses Nanna and invites him back.

> O Nanna, your kingship is sweet, return to your place!
> May a good abundant reign be long lasting in Ur!
> Let its people lie down in safe pastures . . .
> O Nanna—oh, your city! Oh, your temple! Oh, your people![17]

The gods have built and destroyed, but now they restore the city and temples and can dwell among their people again. In a parallel fashion in the Old Testament, the Lord judges and destroys Jerusalem and its temple and afflicts his people; but once the judgment is past, he restores them all. One important difference in this case is that Enlil's destruction of city and temple is arbitrary, whereas the Lord's judgment on Jerusalem and its temple comes because of sin.

Assyria

The most famous example of temple abandonment in Assyria appears in a thirteenth-century B.C. poem, the "Tukulti-Ninurta Epic." Here, as in the Old Testament, divine temple abandonment occurs because of human sin. The poem celebrates the victory of the Assyrian king Tukulti-Ninurta I

---

15. Ibid., 64–67 (460–61, 465).
16. Ibid., 67 (475–77a).
17. Ibid., 69 (514–16, 518). Like the complex of city, temple, and image, the triad of city, temple, and people was normal in the ancient Near East.

(1244–1208 B.C.) over his adversary Kashtiliash IV, the vassal king of Cassite Babylon. It portrays the vassal as a covenant breaker from a long line of covenant breakers. His fathers broke their covenants with former kings of Assyria, and he has followed in their footsteps. By doing so he has outraged the current Assyrian emperor, who appeals to Shamash, the sun god and overseer of covenants in Mesopotamia. He calls upon Shamash to judge between himself and his Babylonian vassal and grant victory to the one who has been a faithful keeper of the covenant. The god's judgment, of course, goes against Kashtiliash, and the poem has the Babylonian vassal condemn himself out of his own mouth.

> The (covenant) oath of Shamash oppresses me . . .
> I have delivered my people into a ruthless hand, a bondage
>   [unyielding],
> Into an inextricable impasse without escape I have [led them].
> Punished are my sins before Shamash, the wrongdoing . . .
> Who is the god who will rescue my people . . . ?[18]

The Assyrian king wins the victory, but it is the gods who make his triumph possible. Angry at the sin of Kashtiliash IV, they abandon their temples in his cities, and thus leave him open to defeat.

> . . . impious Cassite king . . .
> Against the covenant-breaker Kashtiliash the gods of heaven
>   [and earth]
> They showed [. . .] against the king of the land and the peop[le . . .
> They were angry with the overseer, their shepherd, and [. . .
> The Enlilship of the Lord of the Lands was distressed and [. . .]
>   Nippur,
> So that he did not approach the dwelling of Dur-Kurigalzu [. . .
> Marduk abandoned his lofty shrine, the city of [. . .
> He [cu]rsed his beloved city Kar [. . .
> Sin left Ur, [his] cult center [. . .
> With Sippar and Larsa Sha[mash . . .
> Ea [. . .] Eridu, the House of Wisdom [. . .

---

18.   Thompson and Mallowen, "British Museum Excavations at Nineveh," 20:120–21 ([Akkadian], 125 [English]).

> Ishtaran was angry [. . .
> Anunitu does not approach Akkad [. . .
> The mistress of Uruk forsook [. . .
> The gods were wrath [. . .[19]

Despite the lacunae, it is clear that the gods are angry with the Babylonian king and abandon their temples and holy cities as an indication of their displeasure. The sinful king is, indeed, called the gods' "shepherd," in accordance with the royal shepherd typology of the ancient Near East. But the gods abandon him because he has been a bad shepherd, who has broken covenant and thus exposed himself and his people to judgment.

Later in Assyria, Sennacherib (704–681 B.C.) tells how the gods abandoned seven rebellious cities on the border of Qutmuhu.

> who from days of old, in (the time of) the kings, my fathers,
> were strong and proud, not knowing
> the fear of (Assyrian) rule,—in the time of my rule,
> their gods deserted
> them and left them
> empty.[20]

The king then states: "I pursued and [defeated them]. A memorial stela I caused to be made, and I had them inscribe (thereon) the might and power of Ashur, my lord."[21] Sennacherib's record makes theological statements that imply more than they say. The Assyrian is able to defeat his enemies because "their gods deserted them." However, the reason for the divine abandonment is not stated. From what we know of ancient Near Eastern thinking on the topic, there seem to be two possible answers. Either the gods abandoned the cities as a judgment on them, or the gods fled in retreat from the onslaught of Assyria's gods (or, to borrow a phrase from the inscription, in the face of "the might and power of Ashur").

We have seen that the Assyrians believed gods could abandon temples and cities because of sin, and an inscription of Esarhaddon (680–669 B.C.) portrays the Babylonian gods doing just that, forsaking their temples for a

---

19. Lambert, *Three Unpublished Fragments of the Tukulti-Ninurta Epic*, 42–45.
20. Luckenbill, *Annals of Sennacherib*, 64 (19–24).
21. Ibid., 66 (48–49).

period of seventy years because of heavenly wrath at the sinfulness of the people.

> The Lord of the gods, Marduk, was angry. He planned evil;
>> to wipe out the land, to destroy its inhabitants . . . an evil curse was on his lips.[22]

> The gods and goddesses who dwelt in it (i.e., the temple Esagila) fled like birds and went up to heaven.
> The protective gods [. . . ran] off and withdrew.[23]

The curse on the land and the people for a seventy-year period recalls Jeremiah's prophecy that the Lord would send his people into Babylonian exile for seventy years (Jer. 25:11–12; 29:10). From this parallel, some scholars draw the conclusion that Jeremiah (or a hand involved in his book) borrowed the idea from some Babylonian source. However, there is no way to determine this. The concept of divine temple abandonment (like the concept of exile) was long established in the ancient Near East and in that sense required no borrowing from any particular source by anyone who wished to employ it. At the present time, there is not enough information to enable us to account for the presence of the particular number, seventy, in both Jeremiah and the Assyrian inscription.

Spoliation of Images

We have seen some literary accounts of divine temple abandonment, which perhaps give the impression that the invisible gods left their temples and went back to heaven. But their departure from their temples could take a more concrete form. Sometimes the idols, which represented the gods, were physically removed from the temples. Morton Cogan has noticed the significance of this act in the Assyrian realm: "NA spoliation of divine images was meant to portray the abandonment of the enemy by his own gods in submission to the superior might of Assyria's god, Ashur."[24]

---

22. Borger, *Die Inschriften Asarhaddons Königs von Assyrien*, 11, ep. 5, A + B.
23. Ibid., 11, ep. 8, A + B.
24. Cogan, *Imperialism and Religion*, 40. "NA" stands for "Neo-Assyrian" (ca. 1180–609 B.C.). As we have noted, the related theme of divine abandonment occurs in the second millennium "Tukulti-Ninurta Epic." Cogan is mistaken, therefore, when he

Such spoliation certainly occurred in second-millennium Assyria, and the earliest known example comes from the annals of Tiglath-pileser I (1115–1077 B.C.), as Cogan notes.[25] The Assyrian king battles against the Qumanu and overwhelms Hunusu, their fortified city. He then declares, "I conquered that city. I took their gods (and) brought out their booty, possessions (and) property."[26] The same practice is attested later, in the annals of Sennacherib, who states: "But Sidka, the king of Ashkelon, who had not submitted to my yoke,—the gods of his father-house, himself, his wife, his sons, his daughters, his brothers, the seed of his father-house, I tore away and brought to Assyria."[27]

When an Assyrian king captured and removed the idols of his enemies, he was making a theological statement about the superiority of Assyria's gods over the gods of the conquered. As though to emphasize that point, Esarhaddon actually had the name of Ashur inscribed upon the idols of his defeated vassals before he returned their gods to them. The symbolism is clear: just as the conquered people were now the property of Esarhaddon, so the conquered gods were now the property of his god, Ashur.

Abandonment of the Individual

The Assyrians believed that gods could abandon individuals just as they could abandon cities and temples. The concept has intriguing Old Testament and New Testament parallels, to be considered below. The Assyrian emperor Sennacherib comments on one such abandoned individual: "Kirua, prefect of Illubru, a slave, subject to me, whom his gods forsook, caused the men of Hilakku (Cilicia) to revolt, and made ready for battle."[28]

The word translated "slave" (Akkadian *amardu*) by Luckenbill is better translated "vassal" in this context. The vassal has been disloyal and fomented a revolt. The Assyrian monarch reconquers the vassal, flays him, and, as we read subsequently, reestablishes Assyrian suzerainty ("The weapon of Ashur, my lord, I established in its midst").[29] It is not clear whether Kirua's

---

maintains that "Before the NA period, no conqueror has thought to enlist this thesis [i.e., that of divine abandonment] in justifying his conquests" (21).

25. Ibid., 27.
26. Grayson, *Assyrian Rulers of the Early First Millennium B.C. I*, 24 (vi, 9–10); cf. 15 (ii, 30–32), 19 (iii, 81–82).
27. Luckenbill, *Annals of Sennacherib*, 30 (Col. II, 60–64).
28. Ibid., 61 (Col. IV, 62–65).
29. Ibid., 62 (Col. IV, 89).

gods forsook him because he chose to rebel or whether they abandoned him earlier and for some other reason. If the latter was the case, then the withdrawal of their tutelary cover may have produced an unstable mental state, in which he made the disastrous decision to rebel.

Biblical Evidence

Our survey of Near Eastern antiquity shows that a concept of divine temple abandonment was part of Mesopotamia's theological outlook for nearly two millennia. One possible explanation for such divine action was inscrutable fate: the gods might simply decree an end to a city's rule for no apparent reason and so cause its temples to be abandoned, as in Sumer. Or the gods might abandon their temples and cities because of some sin on the part of their chosen ruler or people. Whatever the cause, divine abandonment paved the way for judgment, which took the form of military defeat with its disastrous consequences for the human inhabitants of the cities. For once the heavenly presence and protection were withdrawn, the people on the ground were exposed to any foreign army who still had their gods present and waging war on their behalf. We saw that divine abandonment sometimes took concrete form in the removal of the gods' idols from their temples. Gods also could abandon individuals as a judgment upon them, as in the case of Kashtiliash IV of Babylon and Kirua, prefect of Illubru. The Old Testament and the New Testament have their counterparts to these ideas.

Jeremiah implies divine abandonment when he warns Jerusalem not to place false confidence in the temple that stands in their midst: "This is what the LORD Almighty, the God of Israel, says: Reform your ways and your actions, and I will let you live in this place.[30] Do not trust in deceptive words and say, 'This is the temple of the LORD, the temple of the LORD, the temple of the LORD!'" (Jer. 7:3–4). On the strong basis of the Davidic covenant (2 Sam. 7:1–17), a popular but false theology had arisen, which maintained that the Lord would never abandon his temple; the corollary in the popular mind was that Jerusalem could never be defeated. But Jeremiah makes it clear that God will abandon his temple if his people continue to sin:

---

30. Or, "I will live with you in this place" (also in v. 7), depending on which vowels ought to be understood in the verb forms (the Hebrew consonants are the same for either reading). In fact, both promises are true, and the one (the people's continuance in the place) depends on the other (the Lord's continuance there).

Will you steal and murder, commit adultery and perjury, burn incense to Baal and follow other gods you have not known, and then come and stand before me in this house, which bears my Name, and say, "We are safe"—safe to do all these detestable things? Has this house, which bears my Name, become a den of robbers to you? . . . Therefore, what I did to Shiloh I will now do to the house that bears my Name, the temple you trust in, the place I gave to you and your fathers. I will thrust you from my presence, just as I did all your brothers, the people of Ephraim. (Jer. 7:9–15)

The Lord will abandon his temple. As was the case in Mesopotamia, temple abandonment also would mean abandonment of the holy city (the Lord will do to both his "house" and to "the place I gave to you" as he did to Shiloh, apparently an allusion to the departure of the ark from the tabernacle at Shiloh and its capture by the Philistines when they defeated Israel and killed Eli's sons [1 Sam. 4:1–11]).[31] Such abandonment would mean a removal of divine protection and would result in military defeat, foreign domination, and exile.

God already had warned Solomon of such a possibility, just after David's son had consecrated the newly built temple: "But if you or your sons turn away from me and do not observe the commands and decrees I have given you and go off to serve other gods and worship them, then I will cut off Israel from the land I have given them and will reject this temple I have consecrated for my Name" (1 Kings 9:6–7). Therefore, when Jeremiah warns Judah of a possible temple abandonment, he is not telling them a new thing. The Lord had already given Solomon the same warning years before.

The Lord does at last abandon his temple, and Ezekiel is the one who must see and report that tragic event. The reason, as God explains, is Judah's sin, and in particular idolatry.

They were proud of their beautiful jewelry and used it to make their detestable idols and vile images. Therefore I will turn these into an unclean thing for them. I will hand it all over as plunder to foreigners and as loot to the wicked of the earth, and they will defile it. I will turn my face away from them, and they will desecrate my treasured place; robbers will enter

---

31. Although Keil and Delitzsch, *Jeremiah*, 157, maintain that the event alluded to in this passage remains obscure.

it and desecrate it. Prepare chains, because the land is full of bloodshed and the city is full of violence. (Ezek. 7:20–23)

God's judgment is highly ironic. Jeremiah had rebuked the people because they were making God's temple a den of robbers (Jer. 7:11; cf. Jesus' later accusation, which, as an allusion to Jeremiah's warning, also implies a coming temple abandonment [Matt. 21:13]). But now, as judgment for Judah's sin, the temple will be exposed to other robbers—pagan robbers who will sack and profane the Lord's temple. He will turn his face from them, thus abandoning his temple and his people to judgment.

Now comes a visionary transport, in which Ezekiel sees the abominations committed in the temple. The Lord says, "Son of man, do you see what they are doing—the utterly detestable things the house of Israel is doing here, things that will drive me far from my sanctuary?" (Ezek. 8:6).[32] Of the "utterly detestable things," idolatry is the grossest. It is a renunciation of the first commandment, and because of it the Lord will abandon his sanctuary. But other sins necessarily follow upon idolatry. When a person abandons the Lord to worship other gods, he also abandons the Lord's *Torah*, and begins to live falsely. "Bloodshed and . . . violence" (Ezek. 7:23) are natural consequences of idolatry, in Ezekiel's day as in our own.

Because of idolatry and the spiritually "detestable things" that are its fruit, the Lord abandons his temple.

Then the glory of the LORD departed from over the threshold of the temple and stopped above the cherubim. While I watched, the cherubim spread their wings and rose from the ground, and as they went, the wheels went with them. They stopped at the entrance to the east gate of the LORD's house, and the glory of the God of Israel was above them. (Ezek. 10:18–19)

The Lord has departed the Holy of Holies and has come to the east gate of the temple. From there he departs to a point east of Jerusalem: "Then

---

32. When Ezekiel sees idolaters in the Jerusalem temple, he also hears them declare, "The LORD does not see us; the LORD has forsaken the land" (Ezek. 8:12). Both statements, of course, are false: the Lord does see them, and his ability to see them is not contingent upon his being in the land. Ironically, however, their second statement comes true. Because of their covenant breaking, the Lord will abandon the land. As a result, both temple and city will be destroyed.

the cherubim, with the wheels beside them, spread their wings, and the glory of the God of Israel was above them. The glory of the LORD went up from within the city and stopped above the mountain east of it" (Ezek. 11:22–23).

City abandonment follows temple abandonment in Judah as in the ancient Near East. The glory of the Lord departs Jerusalem and comes to rest on the mountain east of it. God's departure, of course, is a prelude to disaster: the desolation of Jerusalem and its temple by the armies of Babylon. The New Testament offers a parallel. After a strong indictment of Israel's sin, Jesus declares, "Look, your house is left to you desolate" (Matt. 23:38). Then we read:

> Jesus left the temple and was walking away when his disciples came up to him to call his attention to its buildings. "Do you see all these things?" he asked. "I tell you the truth, not one stone here will be left on another; every one will be thrown down." As Jesus was sitting on the Mount of Olives, the disciples came to him privately. "Tell us," they said, "when will this happen, and what will be the sign of your coming and of the end of the age?" (Matt. 24:1–3)

The pattern is the same as in Ezekiel: an indictment for sin followed by temple abandonment. God's abandonment of a temple always leads to its destruction. Thus, Jesus prophesies such destruction after he himself leaves the temple. He then goes to the mountain east of Jerusalem (the Mount of Olives), just as the Glory had done in Ezekiel's day. In effect, the incarnate Lord abandons the second temple just as the preincarnate Lord had abandoned the first.

Theme	Ezekiel	Matthew
indictments and warning of abandonment	8–9	23
temple and city abandonment	10:18–19 (temple)	24:1
	11:22–23 (city)	24:1–2
session east of Jerusalem	11:22–23	24:3

The Lord in his Glory Spirit departs the temple in Ezekiel's day because of idolatry and its fruit. The Lord incarnate also departs the temple in Jesus' day because of spiritual idolatry and its fruit.

But God is gracious. As the Lord abandoned his city and temple, so he will return. Ezekiel prophesies God's return to the temple (Ezek. 43), and Zechariah portrays God's return to the city.

> Then the LORD will go out and fight against those nations, as he fights in the day of battle. On that day his feet will stand on the Mount of Olives, east of Jerusalem, and the Mount of Olives will be split in two from east to west, forming a great valley, with half of the mountain moving north and half moving south. You will flee by my mountain valley, for it will extend to Azel. You will flee as you fled from the earthquake in the days of Uzziah king of Judah. Then the LORD my God will come, and all the holy ones with him. On that day there will be no light, no cold or frost. It will be a unique day, without daytime or nighttime—a day known to the LORD. When evening comes, there will be light. On that day living water will flow out from Jerusalem, half to the eastern sea and half to the western sea, in summer and in winter. The LORD will be king over the whole earth. On that day there will be one LORD, and his name the only name. (Zech. 14:3–9)

The Lord will return on that eschatological day of the Lord. He will return to the Mount of Olives and do combat for his city and people. The "living water" (Zech. 14:8) that flows from Jerusalem actually flows from the Lord's throne/temple presence (Ezek. 47:1–12; Rev. 22:1–5). Zechariah portrays the Lord's eschatological temple presence among his people, with the heavenly Jerusalem (Rev. 21:2), the cult city par excellence, as world capital (cf. Isa. 2:1–5; Mic. 4:1–5), and the Lord as Suzerain, "king over the whole earth" (Zech. 14:9).

Spoliation of Images

In Mesopotamian theology, spoliation of divine images represented the departure of the gods and, therewith, the withdrawal of their protection from their temples and cities. Typically the defeated gods became vassals of the conqueror's god and joined that god's pantheon. The conqueror could, and often did, install those captured images in the temple of his god as a physical representation of their new vassal status. In the Old Testament David captures the gods of his foes, but he does not add them to a pantheon. Rather, he destroys them: "The Philistines abandoned their gods there [at Baal Perazim], and David and his men carried them off" (2 Sam. 5:21); and then we read, "and David gave orders to burn them in the fire" (1 Chron. 14:12).

The closest analogy to spoliation of a divine image in Israel is the removal of the Lord's ark from the tabernacle and its capture by the foe. The ark is lost in a battle against the Philistines, when the army of Israel brings the sacred object onto the field of battle. The Israelites have a pagan mentality. The Lord sits enthroned above the ark, so (they reason) he must go with them into battle if they carry the ark into the fray. The Lord disproves that theology by handing them over to defeat and allowing the Philistines to capture the ark (1 Sam. 4:1–11). To pagan thinking, such an event would mean that the Philistine gods (and perhaps Dagon in particular) were more powerful than the God of Israel, because the Philistines had won the battle and captured Israel's "god." The Lord proves that theology wrong by making Dagon fall, and finally be shattered, at the foot of his ark (1 Sam. 5:1–5), in an apparent analogy to the ancient Near Eastern practice by which conquered vassals bowed down at the feet of their conquerors. Because of his encounter with the Lord, Dagon loses both his hands and his head (1 Sam. 5:4). Those losses are important, because one thinks with the head and one acts with the hands (cf. Rev. 13:16). (In a literal enactment of such symbolism, Assyrian monarchs often boasted that they amassed the severed hands and heads of rebel troops outside their city gates.) Consequently, the god of the Philistines is shown to be one who cannot think or act, as opposed to the God of Israel, who can and does do both (cf. Ps. 115:2–8; Isa. 41:21–24; 44:12–18). Once more, later in Israel's history, God's ark will depart from its house, the temple, but this time at the hands of Babylonian conquerors, and only after the Lord himself has abandoned it.

Abandonment of the Individual

There is an analogy in the Old Testament between an individual and a temple, but it is only an analogy. The similarities become clear as we consider both the temple and the individual in relation to God's Spirit, or Glory Presence. We will see that just as the Lord can abandon his temple, he also can abandon an individual.

God's Spirit descends upon the tabernacle (Exod. 40:34–35) and later upon the temple (1 Kings 8:1–11). Although God resides in the tabernacle (and then in the temple) and not within individuals in the Mosaic covenant, one account of God's descent upon the tabernacle does imply a relationship between the temple (tabernacle) and the individual.

> When Moses entered the tent, the pillar of cloud would descend and stand at the door of the tent, and the LORD would speak with Moses. And when all the people saw the pillar of cloud standing at the door of the tent, all the people would rise up and worship, every man at his tent door. (Exod. 33:9–10 RSV)

There is a clear and important parallel between the Lord at his tent door and the men of Israel at their tent doors. Both the Lord and the men "stand" at the doors of their tents. Moreover, the verb "to stand" is the same root from which the word "pillar," in the phrase "pillar of cloud," derives. The posture of God's Glory-Spirit Presence ("pillar of cloud") and the posture of his people are the same. Both dwell in tents, and both are standing at their tent doors. A similar parallel is evident in Ezekiel, where the foreign robbers who despoil the Lord's "house" (so termed in Ezek. 8:14) also will despoil the "houses" of his people (Ezek. 7:23–24, declared just after Yahweh says that they will "profane my precious place" [v. 22 RSV]). Moreover, as the Lord abandons the land, so his people will be forced to abandon it. That is, as the Lord abandons his "house," his people will be forced to abandon their houses. All of these parallels suggest a correspondence between human households and the Lord's "house" or temple. And if there is such a correspondence, it may be rooted in the *imago Dei*. Humans are made in God's image, and they live in houses, just as the Lord does. The parallel does not exhaust the "house" or "temple" idea, as we know from the New Testament, but it is one part, and a part worth noticing, of a larger system of correspondences between heaven and earth that informs the Bible.

Just as God's Glory Spirit descends upon his tabernacle and temple, so his Spirit comes upon his chosen kings, Saul and David. The prophet Samuel says to Saul, "The Spirit of the LORD will come upon you in power, and you will prophesy with them [the prophets]; and you will be changed into a different person. Once these signs are fulfilled, do whatever your hand finds to do, for God is with you" (1 Sam. 10:6–7). Promptly, the promise is fulfilled: "As Saul turned to leave Samuel, God changed Saul's heart, and all these signs were fulfilled that day" (1 Sam. 10:9). The Lord's Spirit came upon David in a similar way when Samuel anointed him: "So Samuel took the horn of oil and anointed him in the presence of his brothers, and from that day on the Spirit of the LORD came upon David in power" (1 Sam. 16:13).

Although the Holy Spirit came upon Saul at the beginning, the Spirit later abandoned Saul because of his sin. "Now the Spirit of the LORD had departed from Saul, and an evil spirit from the LORD tormented him" (1 Sam. 16:14; cf. 1 Sam. 18:10–12). As God's Spirit abandoned Saul because of his disobedience to his covenant Lord, so God's Glory Spirit later abandoned his temple and holy city because of the disobedience of his covenant people, Israel.

God, then, could take his Holy Spirit from his own disobedient king, as David had seen in the case of Saul. Considering Saul's torment and his end, it comes as no surprise that David, after his own sin with Bathsheba, cried out to the Lord, "Do not cast me from your presence or take your Holy Spirit from me" (Ps. 51:11). Much as the Glory Spirit had come upon the tabernacle (and would come upon the temple), so God's Holy Spirit had come upon his anointed kings, Saul and David. And just as that Glory Spirit would one day abandon God's temple and holy city (Ezek. 8–11), so the Holy Spirit had already abandoned Saul—and, so David feared, might abandon Saul's successor.

In both cases (Saul and the temple), the departure was caused by sin, and the result was oppression by a force hostile to the Lord and his people. For the temple and Jerusalem, the hostile force was Babylonian. For Saul, it was an evil spirit. For both, the result was devastating.[33]

If there was an analogy between temple abandonment and individual abandonment in the Old Testament, there is even more of an analogy in the New Testament. In Jesus' day, God abandoned his temple and city yet again, but he also abandoned a person who really was a temple of the Spirit, namely, his Son.

In the New Testament, as in the Old Testament, the nation (on the whole) rejects its covenant Lord. Jesus therefore pronounces judgment on both temple and city. The temple will be destroyed: "Truly, I say to you,

---

33. The Lord abandoned his rebellious servants. Another way of saying this is that he turned away from them: from Israel ("I will turn my face away from them" [Ezek. 7:22]), and from Saul ("God has turned away from me" [1 Sam. 28:15]). When the Lord turns his face away from someone, it is a curse (Deut. 32:20)—the opposite of the Aaronic blessing (Num. 6:24–26). Since God's face/presence is the source of life (hence the blessing of Aaron), it means death if God turns away, or hides his face. For further discussion, see Niehaus, *God at Sinai*, 313–15.

there will not be left here one stone upon another, that will not be thrown down" (Matt. 24:2 RSV). The same is true of Jerusalem.

> As he approached Jerusalem and saw the city, he wept over it and said, "If you, even you, had only known on this day what would bring you peace—but now it is hidden from your eyes. The days will come upon you when your enemies will build an embankment against you and encircle you and hem you in on every side. They will dash you to the ground, you and the children within your walls. They will not leave one stone on another, because you did not recognize the time of God's coming to you." (Luke 19:41–44)

As in the Old Testament, rejection of the Lord leads to temple and city abandonment.[34] God's people will forfeit the peace that could have been theirs. But the loss of their temple will lead to a better temple, and the loss of their peace to a better peace. Those things happen when a person becomes a temple of the Spirit through faith in Christ and receives the peace that the world cannot know.

But the temple presence of the Spirit in Christians became possible only because the Spirit once abandoned the Messiah-temple. We saw how the theme of abandonment became individualized in the Old Testament. God's Spirit presence came upon a chosen king but also could depart if the king effectively rejected God through disobedience. We also saw that Saul, who had that experience, was not exactly a temple of the Holy Spirit and that likewise David, who feared such abandonment, was not a temple. The Spirit dwells in God's people only after Christ's death and resurrection (John 7:37–39; cf. Ezek. 36:27). But in the New Testament one person, Jesus, actually was a temple of the Spirit. And the Son was abandoned by the Father at the time of his crucifixion (hence his cry, "My God, my God, why have you forsaken me?" [Matt. 27:46]). Jesus referred to this event as a temple abandonment/destruction.

---

34. Some question whether the Lord actually was present in the temple in Jesus' day, and it was a matter of disagreement among the Jews. It is certainly true that no theophanic entry into the Second Temple was reported, as was the case with the Lord's documented entry into the tabernacle (Exod. 40:34ff.) and the Solomonic temple (1 Kings 8:10ff.) But whatever Jesus' contemporaries may have thought, Jesus himself settled the issue when he said that, "he who swears by the temple swears by it and by the one who dwells in it" (Matt. 23:21). For a general overview, see Green, McKnight, and Marshall, *Dictionary of Jesus and the Gospels*, 813–16.

Jesus answered them, "Destroy this temple, and I will raise it again in three days." The Jews replied, "It has taken forty-six years to build this temple, and you are going to raise it in three days?" But the temple he had spoken of was his body. After he was raised from the dead, his disciples recalled what he had said. Then they believed the Scripture and the words that Jesus had spoken. (John 2:19–22)[35]

Jesus implies a parallel between himself and the Solomonic temple, and in order to understand what he implies, it is important to have two facts firmly in mind. First, the Solomonic temple was polluted by the sin of Judah and was itself a good representation of Judah's sin. Second, God abandoned the Solomonic temple as a judgment on his rebellious vassals, but he restored the temple when that judgment was over. Because of the implied parallel between himself and the temple, the same two facts apply to Jesus. Jesus the Messiah-temple was without sin, but he "became sin" for us (2 Cor. 5:21), that is, he was a good representation of the sin of God's people and indeed of humanity. After God abandoned the Jesus-temple he also restored it, and, as in the Old Testament, that restoration meant the end of judgment (cf. Heb. 7:27; 10:10; Rom. 6:10).

The consummate example, then, of temple abandonment is Jesus Christ himself, whose body/temple was forsaken and then destroyed as a divine punishment for sin but restored ultimately to an eternal glory when that punishment had been accomplished. Those who receive him also receive authority to become temples of the Holy Spirit, as we have seen (e.g., 1 Cor. 6:19–20). One who does so experiences that better peace that was mentioned above. The Hebrew word *shalom* is the background concept of peace in the New Testament. It means wholeness, and it comes as the Holy Spirit works in those who have accepted God and his Messiah. The Spirit works to re-create, to rebuild the human temple he has entered. So Paul says that we "are being transformed into his likeness with ever-increasing glory, which comes from the Lord, who is the Spirit" (2 Cor. 3:18), so that "if anyone is in Christ, he is a new creation" (2 Cor. 5:17).

---

35.   The "Scripture" referred to is Hosea 6:1–2, where the resuscitation of Israel on the third day is affirmed. Jesus apparently took this passage and applied it in a *razpesher* and corporate solidarity fashion to himself, just as Matthew did with Hosea 11:1 in Matthew 2:15.

The question that naturally arises is whether such a temple also can be abandoned. The author of Hebrews warns,

> It is impossible for those who have once been enlightened, who have tasted the heavenly gift, who have shared in the Holy Spirit, who have tasted the goodness of the word of God and the powers of the coming age, if they fall away, to be brought back to repentance, because to their loss they are crucifying the Son of God all over again and subjecting him to public disgrace. (Heb. 6:4–6)

How are we to understand this passage? People who receive the Holy Spirit are temples of the Spirit, that is, temples of God, and the people described in the Hebrews passage appear to have been such people. They have "shared in the Holy Spirit," and have "tasted . . . the powers of the coming age."[36] Calvin seems to have been correct in identifying them as apostates, who have committed the one unforgivable sin, the sin against the Holy Spirit (Mark 3:29).[37] On that understanding, the Holy Spirit departs from the apostate, leaving him unable to be renewed (Heb. 6:4, 6). If this understanding is correct, there is a real possibility of divine temple abandonment under the new covenant, even if it happens only rarely.

The Last Days

In the Old Testament, the Lord abandons his city and temple, and both are destroyed by the Babylonians. But he restores the temple and Jerusalem after the time of judgment has passed. In the New Testament, Jesus abandons the temple and city, and both are destroyed by the Romans. But he establishes a new temple, his church, who have no city on earth but are members of a heavenly city. Yet the New Testament anticipates a day when God's temple will be occupied by his foe, the "man of lawlessness," who "will oppose and will exalt himself over everything that is called God or is worshiped, so that he sets himself up in God's temple, proclaiming himself

---

36. The verb "tasted" is the same Greek word used in Hebrews 2:9, which states that "Jesus . . . suffered death, so that by the grace of God he might *taste* death for everyone." The verb, therefore, can imply not a slight tasting but rather a full experience: for Jesus, a full experience of death; for the people of Hebrews 6, a full experience of the Holy Spirit.
37. Calvin, *Epistle of Paul*, 75.

to be God" (2 Thess. 2:3–4). Perhaps the best understanding of this prophecy is the appearance of Antichrist as the head of the church. That event
will be possible because God has withdrawn his Holy Spirit.

> And now you know what is holding him back, so that he may be revealed
> at the proper time. For the secret power of lawlessness is already at work;
> but the one who now holds it back will continue to do so till he is taken
> out of the way. And then the lawless one will be revealed, whom the Lord
> Jesus will overthrow with the breath of his mouth and destroy by the
> splendor of his coming. (2 Thess. 2:6–8)

Like some interpreters, I understand that "the one who holds back" the
power of lawlessness is the Holy Spirit. When God withdraws him, it is another way of saying that God abandons the cosmic temple. Once that happens, lawlessness can hold sway and "the lawless one will be revealed."

Jesus will destroy that foe with "the breath of his mouth" and "the splendor of his coming." He will restore the cosmic temple, for there will be "a
new heaven and a new earth" (Rev. 21:1).[38] And he himself will become the
new temple (Rev. 21:22) for his people in a heavenly Jerusalem.

Conclusion

Divine abandonment of temple and city is a major idea in the ancient
Near East, and in particular in Mesopotamian theology and in the Bible.
In Mesopotamia the gods may simply, and inscrutably, decree the end of a
dynasty or empire. Or disobedience to the gods may provoke their wrath so
that they abandon the temple and holy city. Such abandonment results in
defeat and conquest by the foe and, usually, destruction of the city and temple.
This scenario describes a major aspect of theodicy in Mesopotamia and in
the Old and New Testaments. It also applies in a somewhat analogous way to
individuals. In Mesopotamian theology, a god or gods can abandon a sinful
individual and derange that individual, making him ripe for destruction (so
in Cassite Babylon, Kashtiliash IV, the sinful covenant breaker). The same
can occur in the Old Testament, as demonstrated by Saul. Such cases are
only analogous to temple abandonment, however, because the individuals

---

38. He will be like a Mesopotamian monarch, who overthrows the foe with the "splendor" (*melammu*) of his attack. And, like a Pharaoh, he will restore all things "as at
the beginning" (cf. chap. 7, "The Restoration of All Things").

involved were not temples. The New Testament presents what appears to be a warning of individual temple abandonment in the book of Hebrews, a warning that Calvin took seriously and that, because of its presence in the Bible, deserves to be taken seriously by the church.

6

The Covenantal Household

Destruction and Salvation

The destruction of households is a major biblical theme, and the salvation of households is its counterpart. Household destruction can take one of two forms: a corporate solidarity form, in which the head of the household, and the whole household with him, are subject to slavery or destruction; or an internecine warfare form in which household members wage war against each other. This intrafamilial form has a further refinement: family members may war against other family members because the latter are faithful to God and the former are not. On a larger scale, international conflict is a form of intrafamilial warfare since all humans are part of the fallen, Adamic family. On any scale we will find that household destruction or salvation is a covenantal event according to the Bible. In fact, this concept is common in the ancient Near East. As a point of departure, We note that the New Testament assumes and teaches all of the covenantal judgment forms mentioned above.

Jesus illustrates the first form of judgment—the corporate solidarity form—in a well-known parable.

> Therefore, the kingdom of heaven is like a king who wanted to settle accounts with his servants. As he began the settlement, a man who owed him ten thousand talents was brought to him. Since he was not able to pay, the master ordered that he and his wife and his children and all that he had be sold to repay the debt. (Matt. 18:23–25)

The parable explores forgiveness as a major aspect of the kingdom of heaven. The servant is pardoned a great debt but fails to pardon his fellow servant. When the king hears of it, he sends the servant to jail because he was unwilling to forgive as he had been forgiven. The gospel of forgiveness is of paramount importance. But what concerns us now is the parable's statement of corporate solidarity. Not only the servant, but also his whole family—"his wife and his children and all that he had"—stand to be sold into slavery in order to pay the debt the servant has incurred. The parable is covenantal in its implications because it is told against the background of Israel's covenantal relationship to God, who is the king in the parable.

Jesus also teaches, or rather prophesies, about the second form of household destruction, the internecine warfare form. He portrays future household division over the gospel.

> Do not suppose that I have come to bring peace to the earth. I did not come to bring peace, but a sword. For I have come to turn
> "a man against his father,
> a daughter against her mother,
> a daughter-in-law against her mother-in-law—
> a man's enemies will be the members of his own household."
> (Matt. 10:34–36)

Jesus quotes Micah 7:6 to show how rejection of his gospel covenant will produce intrafamilial warfare—with the nonbelievers in a household warring against the believers.

The internecine form of household destruction appears in a broadened form in Jesus' eschatological prophecy about the nations: "You will hear of wars and rumors of wars, but see to it that you are not alarmed. Such things must happen, but the end is still to come. Nation will rise against nation, and kingdom against kingdom" (Matt. 24:6–7). The prophecy deals with a broad form of family warfare, namely, warfare between large groups of the human or Adamic family (nations and kingdoms), which also must be understood against a background of God's covenantal dealings with humanity.[1]

Household salvation also appears in the Lord's dealing with people, and

---

1. All of humanity are vassals under God according to the legal package formed by the creation (Adamic) and re-creation (Noahic) covenants; cf. Jeffrey J. Niehaus, "An Argument Against Theologically Constructed Covenants," *Vetus Testamentum* 50, no. 2 (June 2007): 259–73.

although we will explore that topic further below, a notable example is the salvation of the Philippian jailer and his household. Paul and Silas assure the jailer, "Believe in the Lord Jesus, and you will be saved—you and your household" (Acts 16:31). It is interesting that the jailer drops down on his knees, trembling before them as he asks for salvation (Acts 16:29–30). His posture is much like that of a rebellious vassal in the ancient Near East, kneeling and trembling before the suzerain against whom he has rebelled and asking for salvation.

We suggest, then, that the forms of household destruction or salvation articulated above occur against a background of covenant. The same is true both in the Bible and in the ancient Near East. As we explore the outworkings of such household punishment, we also will be able to appreciate more fully the converse idea of household salvation, which appears so rarely in the ancient Near East but is a governing idea in the Bible.

The Ancient Near East

The covenantal punishment of households is well attested in the ancient Near East. Egypt, Hatti, Assyria, and Babylon offer good examples. Most of the evidence comes from royal annals, and this is so for obvious reasons. Monarchs were naturally in a position both to encounter covenantal disobedience and to deal with it. Indeed, suzerains often were faced with rebellious vassals who had to be caught and punished.

Egypt

One passage in the Old Testament pronounces upon Egypt a family curse that would not have been strange to Egyptians.

> I will stir up Egyptian against Egyptian—
> brother will fight against brother,
> neighbor against neighbor,
> city against city,
> kingdom against kingdom.
>
> (Isa. 19:2)

We know the concept of household judgment was familiar in Egypt because it appears in the Pyramid Texts, in Egyptian annals, and in a royal mortuary papyrus. It can be a condition of enemies of the dead king, of rebellious vassals in Palestine, and of leaderless Egyptians. Isaiah's curse involves the internecine warfare form of household punishment, and for convenience we consider that form first in Egypt.

Internecine Warfare Form

The internecine warfare form of household punishment appears in Egypt as a result either of rebellion against Pharaoh or of an absence of strong pharaonic rule. An example of the former comes from the reign of Seti I (1302–1290 B.C.), in the context of a set of Karnak temple reliefs that portray the successful campaigns of the pharaoh.[2] During the first year of his reign, he brings a number of Canaanite and Phoenician cities, as well as Bedouin tribes, into vassalage. Pharaoh returns to the Egyptian border with a train of captives. But he can scarcely celebrate his conquests when news comes that his recently acquired vassals have begun to rebel. The rebels' condition is significant.

> One came to say to his majesty: "The vanquished Shasu . . . plan a rebellion. Their tribal chiefs are gathered together, rising against the Asiatics of Kharu. They have taken to cursing, and quarreling, each of them slaying his neighbor, and they disregard the laws of the palace."[3]

The various Bedouin tribes (Shasu) are making common cause against the Palestinians (Kharu). The rebels are in a state of chaos among themselves, cursing, quarreling, and slaying each other. It is no accident that this portrayal is followed by the statement that they "disregard the laws of the palace." Those laws are the institutes of pharaonic rule, which the vassals should obey. The implication is that chaos naturally follows when one abandons the suzerainty of Pharaoh. That should come as no surprise, since Pharaoh is (supposedly) the source of light and life to the foreign lands he has conquered. Rejection of his imperial rule means loss of life and light. The outworking of that loss already appears in the increasingly chaotic state of the rebels.

The same chaotic condition could occur in Egypt itself during a period when no strong pharaoh ruled. So, for example, Ramses III (1195–1164 B.C.) portrays Egypt's sad estate during the Syrian interregnum (1202–1197 B.C.).

---

2. Breasted, *Ancient Records of Egypt*, 3:37–76.
3. Ibid., 3:52 (§ 101).

> Hear ye that I may inform you of my benefactions which I did while I
> was king of the people. The land of Egypt was overthrown from without,
> and every man was thrown out of his right; they had no chief mouth [i.e.,
> ruler] for many years formerly. . . . The land of Egypt was in the hands of
> chiefs and of rulers of towns; one slew his neighbor, great and small.[4]

The state of internecine warfare is a cursed condition. It follows upon
the absence of pharaonic rule. Pharaoh alone can bring life and order to
the land. He does so in his capacity as son of Ra, who gives both light and
life to all. If Ra's son is not upon the throne, the land finds itself in a state of
darkness and lawlessness. Each person does what he or she wants, and the
inevitable result is internal chaos.

Corporate Solidarity Form

The other major form of household punishment is the corporate solidarity form, in which the head of the household, along with his wife, children,
and possessions, are taken into slavery or even killed.

The corporate solidarity form appears as early as the Pyramid Texts in
Egypt. One Pyramid Text inscription portrays the dead king as one who is
able to curse his mortal foes: "I am stronger than they . . . their hearts fall
to my fingers, their entrails are for the denizens of the sky, their blood is for
the denizens of the earth. Their heirs are (doomed) to poverty, their houses
to conflagration, and their courtyards to the high Nile."[5] In another Pyramid Text the king proclaims, "As for anyone who shall lay a finger on this
pyramid and this temple which belong to me . . . his affair will be judged by
the Ennead and he will be nowhere and his house will be nowhere."[6]

The most drastic application of the corporate solidarity form of punishment is the slaughter of all the enemies, and it appears in the accounts of
many pharaohs. Pepi I (ca. 2325 B.C.), the first Egyptian king to be called
"Pharaoh," says of his conquests in southern Palestine, "I came and smote
them all and every revolter among them was slain."[7] Much later Ramses III
(1195–1164 B.C.) declares of the chief of the Meshwesh, "Their chief is fet-

---

4. Ibid., 4:198–99 (§ 398); cf. 4:87–206.
5. Faulkner, *Ancient Egyptian Pyramid Texts*, 64 (Utterance 254, §§ 291–92).
6. Ibid., 202 (Utterance 534, §§ 1278–79).
7. Breasted, *Ancient Records of Egypt*, 1:144 (§ 315). For Pepi I as the first "Pharaoh,"
   see ibid., 1:141 (§ 309).

tered before his (Pharaoh's) horses, his son, his wife, his family are slain."[8] Similar claims appear regarding the slaughter of rebels and their children (or occasionally servants, where the children are unavailable) during the 1100 years between those two pharaohs: e.g., Pepi II (2275–2185 B.C.),[9] Ahmose I (1570–1545 B.C.),[10] Thutmose II (1495–1490 B.C.),[11] and Ramses II (1290–1224 B.C.).[12] Ramses III particularly records how he cut off the *phalli* of his foes, a practice that is obviously symbolic of the household destruction under discussion.[13]

A treaty made by Ramses II with the Hittites articulates the same ethos, clearly in a covenantal context.

> Now, these words, which are upon this silver tablet, are for the land of Kheta (Hatti) and for the land of Egypt. As for him who shall not keep them, the thousand gods of the land of Kheta, and the thousand gods of the land of Egypt shall desolate his house, his land, and his subjects.[14]

By contrast, those who keep the covenant are, along with their households, to be blest by the gods.

> Now as for him who shall keep these words, which are upon this silver tablet, whether they be of Kheta, or whether they be people of Egypt . . . the thousand gods of the land of Kheta, together with the thousand gods of the land of Egypt, shall preserve his health, and his life, together with his issue, with his land, and his subjects.[15]

---

8. Ibid., 4:61 (§ 103). Zedekiah suffers a similar fate at the hands of the Babylonians (2 Kings 25:6–7).
9. Ibid., 1:163 (§ 358); chiefs' children.
10. Ibid., 2:9 (§ 16); rebel leader and his servants.
11. Ibid., 2:49 (§§ 121–22); chief of Cush and his children, and all of their males, except one of the chief's children who was taken prisoner.
12. Ibid., 3:142 (§ 314); family of the prince of Kheta (Hatti).
13. Ibid., 4:29 (§ 52), 31 (§ 54); cf. Ramses III's boast of the foe that his "seed is not," ibid., 4:21 (§ 39), 52 (§ 87); cf. ibid., 4:48 (§ 81).
14. Ibid., 3:172 (§ 387). For the whole treaty, see ibid., 3:163–74. Although this is a parity treaty, the same applies to vassals in a suzerain-vassal arrangement.
15. Ibid., 3:172 (§ 388). Interestingly, the treaty also provides for the extradition of any fugitives from Egypt to Hatti, or vice versa, in household terms: "let not his house be injured, nor his wives, nor his children, let him not be killed, and let no injury be done to his eyes, to his ears, to his mouth, nor to his feet. Let not any crime be set up against him" (173 [§§ 389–90]).

As long as the monarch obeys the covenantal stipulations, the "thousand gods" will bless his household and the nation under him with life and health. This is another way of saying that the salvation of the king, his family, and his nation depends upon his own faithfulness to the parity covenant.

Pharaoh has another covenant, however, a covenant with the gods in which he, as son of Ra, is vassal. In that covenant also, the life, prosperity, and health of the households in his kingdom depend directly on the pharaoh himself. We note this now as a reflex of the household judgment of enemies, to be studied more closely later. Ramses III, for example, says of his reign:

> I planted the whole land with trees and verdure, and I made the people dwell in their shade.... Their bows and their weapons reposed in their magazines, while they were satisfied and drunk with joy. Their wives were with them, their children at their side; they looked not behind them [i.e., in fear], (but) their hearts were confident, (for) I was with them as the defense and protection of their limbs. I sustained alive the whole land, whether foreigners, (common) folk, citizens, or people, male or female.[16]

We have seen that the salvation of the king, his family, and his nation can depend upon his own faithfulness to a covenant and that Pharaoh himself gives life and peace to the households in his kingdom. Both of these ideas have biblical ramifications, which we shall discuss below.

The ancient records may picture covenantal blessings, but they more generally portray the punishment of rebels. This is so because most of the records are annalistic and record the king's punitive expeditions against rebellious vassals.

We have seen how an insubordinate vassal could be killed along with his household for his rebelliousness. The same fate that could befall a rebellious vassal also might befall a citizen of Egypt who had a mind to instigate rebellion. The "Teaching for Merikare" (2100 B.C.)—a piece of wisdom literature imparted by a pharaoh to his son—urges such punishment.[17]

> A talker is a mischief-maker; suppress him, kill [him], erase his name, [destroy] his kinsfolk, suppress the remembrance of him and his par-

---

16. Ibid., 4:204–5 (§ 410).
17. For a discussion of this teaching and its place in the tumultuous First Intermediate period, see Wilson, *Burden of Egypt*, 106–12, 119–20.

tisans who love him . . . accuse him before the entourage and suppress [him], for he is a rebel indeed; a talker is a mischief-maker. Bend the multitude (i.e., to your will) and drive out hot temper from it.[18]

The same household penalty incurred by a rebellious vassal applies, in this passage, to a rebellious member of Pharaoh's kingdom.[19] No one may arise against the suzerain, for the people of Egypt are also Pharaoh's vassals (see discussion below).

A milder application of household judgment involves not the annihilation but the capture of the family, a form of punishment well attested in Egyptian royal annals. Usually it involves the capture of rebellious foes, who then become slaves in the temples of Amon-Ra or other Egyptian gods. It is important to understand that any foe of Egypt was ipso facto a rebel, since Amon-Ra had decreed that his son, the pharaoh, should conquer all lands and bring them into submission to the sun god.

The milder application of the household punishment form currently under discussion is also the more common. Thutmose III (1490–1436 B.C.) boasts of a campaign against Retenu, saying, "Lo, my majesty carried off the wives of that vanquished one, together with his children, and the wives of the chiefs who were [there, together with their] children."[20] Amenhotep II (1439–1406 B.C.) conducted a campaign of conquest beyond the Orontes. He says of the chief of the tribe of Khatithana, "His chiefs, his wives, his children were carried captive, and all his people likewise."[21] Such claims were a standard part of pharaonic tradition: e.g., Pepi II (2275–2185 B.C.),[22] Ahmose I (1570-1545 B.C.),[23] Thutmose I (1525–1495 B.C.),[24] Amenhotep III (1398–1361 B.C.),[25] and Merneptah (1224–1214 B.C.).[26]

---

18. Simpson, *Literature of Ancient Egypt*, 181.
19. Indeed, much later, a similar curse is invoked on anyone who maltreats the statue of Pharaoh Ramses VI (1153–1149 B.C.): "As for anyone who disregards it, Amon, king of gods, shall pursue him, Mut shall pursue his wife, Khonsu shall pursue his children; he shall hunger, he shall thirst, he shall faint and sicken" (Breasted, *Ancient Records of Egypt*, 4:235 [§ 483]).
20. Ibid., 2:236 (§ 596); cf. also 2:67 (§ 162), 198 (§ 467.70), 188 (§ 436), 203 (§ 480), and 205 (§ 490).
21. Ibid., 2:308 (§§ 789–90).
22. Ibid., 1:163 (§ 359).
23. Ibid., 2:8 (§ 15).
24. Ibid., 2:34 (§ 80).
25. Ibid., 2:356 (§ 884).
26. Ibid., 3:246 (§ 584).

The captives normally were taken to serve in the temples of Egypt's gods. So Seti I (1302–1290 B.C.) boasts,

> There is none that thrusts aside his [i.e., Pharaoh's] hand, carrying away their chiefs as living captives, with their tribute upon their backs, presenting them to his august father, Amon, and his associate gods, in order to fill their storehouse with male and female slaves, the captivity of every country.[27]

Similarly Ramses III declares,

> I destroyed the people of Seir, of the tribes of the Shasu, I plundered the tents of their people, their possessions, their cattle likewise, without number. They were pinioned and brought as captive, as tribute to Egypt. I gave them to the gods, as slaves into their house[s].[28]

The pattern is one that we have noted before. Pharaoh, who is the son of the sun god, has been commanded by his heavenly father to conquer other lands and bring them into submission to Amon-Ra. As the son does this, he brings those he has captured to serve in the house (i.e., in the temple) of his father or in the temples of the other Egyptian gods. The biblical parallels in this theological construct are outstanding and will receive further discussion below.

We conclude our survey of the Egyptian data with two examples of special interest. Each is unique because of its irony—an irony, in each case, that has a certain affinity with biblical data.

The first example is the account of the "Capture of Joppa."[29] Pharaoh Menkheperre Thutmose III apparently secures the vassalage of Joppa (modern Jaffa) during his first campaign into Syro-Palestine. Subsequently Joppa rebels against Egyptian domination. Djehuty, a prominent general and garrison commander under Thutmose III, recaptures the city for Pharaoh by a ruse. He offers to deliver himself and his family into the hands of

---

27. Ibid., 3:42 (§ 82).
28. Ibid., 4:201 (§ 404); cf. 4:202 (§ 405). Ramses III also sacrificed captive princes on at least one occasion; cf. 4:38 (§ 80). For other captures by this pharaoh, cf. 4:53 (§ 90), and 66 (§ 111).
29. For translation and comment, see Simpson, *Literature of Ancient Egypt*, 81–84.

the prince of Joppa, along with two hundred baskets of possessions. Each basket actually conceals a soldier.[30] Once the prince of Joppa allows the baskets into his city, the Egyptians break out of concealment and capture the rebels. At the end we read:

> At nightime Djehuty sent to Egypt to King Menkheperre, l.p.h., his lord, saying: "Be of good cheer! Amon, your good father, has delivered to you the Rebel of [Jo]ppa and all his people as well as his town. Send men to take them away captive that you may fill the estate of your father Amon-Re, King of the Gods, with male and female slaves, who have fallen beneath your feet forever and ever."[31]

Djehuty's ruse is twofold. He conceals the soldiers in baskets, and that enables him to take over the city. But he also offers himself and his family as a prize of war, and that makes the basket trick possible. When he offers his own flesh and blood, he lulls any suspicions the prince of Joppa might have about his entry into the city. It is an ironic offer. Djehuty acts as though he were the rebellious vassal, who must be taken captive with his family. But at the end it is the prince of Joppa and his family, as well as his whole city, who are taken captive and become slaves to "fill the estate of your father Amon-Re, King of the Gods." It is interesting to consider a biblical parallel to this event. Jesus also offers his own flesh and blood, and it might be argued that by doing so he lulls any suspicions the prince of darkness might have about his power or plans. It is an ironic offer. Jesus acts as though he were the rebellious vassal, who must be taken captive and executed. But at the end it is the prince of darkness and his household who suffer, because Jesus, "having disarmed the powers and authorities . . . made a public spectacle of them, triumphing over them by the cross" (Col. 2:15). Of course there is not and cannot be any intentional parallel (unless one considers that God in his comprehensive sovereignty over all of human history allowed such an event to antedate the cross). The parallel that exists depends upon the irony by which a faithful vassal takes on the role of a rebel and thereby defeats the true rebel. In either case, a household punishment is on display.

---

30. A ruse that may recall the tale of the Trojan horse.
31. Simpson, *Literature of Ancient Egypt*, 84. The tag "l.p.h." traditionally attached to royal names stands for "may he live, prosper, and be in health," or, more briefly, "life prosperity, health" (cf. ibid., 11).

A similar punishment can befall any servant who deceives his master to the latter's (even potential) hurt. Such is the case in the Egyptian "Tale of the Eloquent Peasant" (action ca. 2100 B.C., possibly set down ca. 1991–1786 B.C.).[32] The main characters are an important court official, the high steward, Rensi, and one of his tenants, named Djehutinakhte. Djehutinakhte tricks an itinerant peasant into trespassing on his barley field. He then seizes the peasant's goods as compensation. The peasant appeals to the high steward, and the hyperbolic eloquence of his ninefold appeal forms part of the humor of the story. But the outcome is not humorous for the villainous tenant. Pharaoh counsels Rensi to pass judgment according to the latter's wisdom. So the high steward

> caused two apparitors to go to [fetch Djehutinakhte], and he was brought in. An inventory was made of [all his goods . . .], his [servants], six persons, apart from [. . .] his barley, his emmer, [his] asses, his pigs, and [his flocks,] and Djehutinakhte's [house was given to the] peasant, [together with] all his [goods].[33]

Djehutinakhte suffers a reversal. He had unjustly captured the goods of the peasant, who is finally vindicated by the high steward. Upon his vindication the peasant is awarded Djehutinakhte's goods and household. The ironic reversal may recall the fate of the schemers who had Daniel put into the lions' den. Upon his vindication they themselves were cast to the lions—along with their households (see below). A sense of irony in the assigning of judgment is not unique to the Hebrew Scriptures, nor is the idea of punishment for the whole household of a rebellious vassal or criminal, as Egyptian sources well attest.

Hatti

We have noted two forms of household curse: a corporate solidarity form, in which the head of the household and the whole household with him are subject to slavery or destruction; and an internecine warfare form, in which household members wage war against each other. Both forms appear among the Hittites.

---

32. Ibid., 4–5.
33. Ibid., 49.

Corporate Solidarity Form

The corporate solidarity form of judgment appears in several treaties, both suzerain-vassal and parity. Among the suzerain-vassal treaties, an agreement between Šuppiluliuma (ca. 1358–1323 B.C.) and Tette, king of Nuḫašši, articulates the household consequences of covenant breaking: "If Tette does not retain these words of the treaty and oath, and transgresses the oath [made by] these gods: may they [i.e., the gods] annihilate Tette along with . . . his wives, his sons, his grandsons, his house, his city, his land, along with his possessions."[34] The oath is made, "by" the treaty gods, in the sense that the kings swear by those gods. The identical formula appears in a treaty between Šuppiluliuma and Aziru of Amurru.[35] Similar curses appear in treaties between Šuppiluliuma and Mattiwaza, king of Mitanni.[36] The same ideology may appear in a parity treaty between the Hittite emperor Hattušiliš and his Egyptian counterpart Ramses II, although the context is broken.[37]

Internecine Warfare Form

An early case of the internecine warfare form appears in Hatti in the fourteenth century B.C. in the annals of the emperor Muršiliš. Muršiliš has ascended the throne at a young age upon the death of his father and older brother. The new emperor learns that a number of his vassals have taken the opportunity afforded by the transition of power in Hatti to break free of the Hittite yoke.[38] The Hittite suzerain marches against one such rebellious vassal. He surrounds the vassal's city and lays siege. When the vassal pleads for mercy, the emperor replies sternly: "Because they had transgressed the covenant, I said to them: 'The covenant gods [lit., "gods of the oath"] must work their vengeance. The son must kill his father, brother must kill

---

34. Weidner, *Politische Dokumente aus Kleinasien*, 68–69, Rs. IV.48–52.
35. Ibid., 74–75, Rs. 12–16.
36. Ibid., 32–35, Rs. 59–69; 50–51, Rs. 25–27; cf. 50–55, Rs. 28–34.
37. Ibid., 122–33, Rs. 25–26, 30–31.
38. See Götze, *Die Annalen des Mursilis*, 14–23. The pattern is not uncommon in the ancient Near East. Compare the rebellion of Mesha after Ahab's death: "Now Mesha king of Moab raised sheep, and he had to supply the king of Israel with a hundred thousand lambs and with the wool of a hundred thousand rams. But after Ahab died, the king of Moab rebelled against the king of Israel" (2 Kings 3:4–5). We read subsequently how King Joram of Israel, with allies, marched against the rebellious Moabite king.

brother, and they must lay low their own flesh and blood.'"[39] The family destruction and internecine warfare occur "because they had transgressed the covenant." The covenant ethos in Hatti condemns both the rebel king and his household. It even extends, apparently, to the households of his people. The fact that the people must suffer for the covenant disobedience of their king is theologically important and will be discussed below.

Assyria

The same ethos apparent in Egypt and Hatti can be documented abundantly in Assyria. Death was often the penalty for disobedience to a covenant, and entire households of the enemy were annihilated.[40] In the most extreme form of household punishment, Tukulti-Ninurta I (1244–1208 B.C.) boasts that he burned alive a whole city of rebellious vassals.[41]

The milder form of household punishment was the capture of rebellious families. Assyrian kings regularly attest the capture and exile of covenant-breaking vassal kings and their households.[42] Tiglath-pileser I, for example, sets out on a campaign against the land Kadmuhu. That land was in revolt and had "withheld tribute and impost from the god Aššur, my Lord," according to the suzerain.[43] The king conquers them and punitively destroys their cities. But he declares in particular of their king, Kili-Teshub,

> I carried off his wives, his natural sons, his clan, 180 copper kettles. Five bronze bathtubs, together with their gods, gold and silver, the best of their property.[44]

39.　Ibid., 112–15.

40.　For whatever reason, the corporate solidarity form of household punishment appears to the virtual exclusion of the internecine warfare form in Assyria. Perhaps it suited Assyrian propaganda best to portray the king as one who held the lives of foes and rebels entirely in his hand and could exterminate them, extirpating seed and sire at his wish.

41.　Grayson, *Assyrian Rulers of the Third and Second Millennia B.C.*, 236 (A.0.78.1 Col. iii.44).

42.　Evidence appears before Tiglath-pileser I (1115–1077 B.C.), e.g., Adad-nirari I (1307–1275 B.C.); cf. Weidner, *Die Kämpfe Adadniraris I. gegen Ḫanigalbat*," 90 (Text A.48–52). If there is more evidence of such punishment from Assyria than from Hatti, it may well be because we have more Assyrian records, especially annals, than Hittite.

43.　Grayson, *Assyrian Rulers of the Early First Millennium B.C. I*, 14 (A.0.87.1 Col. i.90–91).

44.　Ibid., 15 (A.0.87.1, Col. Ii.28–32); cf. 15 (Col. ii.47–48), 22 (Col. v.17–18).

There are some remarkable parallels between this passage and Jesus' parable in Matthew 18. Both deal with relations between a king and a servant (the servant in the Assyrian case is a vassal to the Assyrian king).[45] In both cases there is debt. The servant in the parable owes money to the king. Tiglath-pileser's vassal/servant also owes money to his great king. Theologically expressed, it is tribute money due to Ashur. Practically expressed, it is money due to Tiglath-pileser, Ashur's vice-regent on earth.

Assyrian kings after Tiglath-pileser I attest the same ethos. Tukulti-Ninurta II (890–884 B.C.) declares of a Nairi king, "His sons, his daughters, his wives, the property of his palace, I carried away."[46] Tiglath-pileser III (744–727 B.C.) says of one Ursanika, "Himself, his wife, his sons and daughters, his gods I carried away."[47] Similar treatment of rebellious kings is attested by Sargon II (721–705 B.C.),[48] Sennacherib (704–681 B.C.),[49] Esarhaddon (680–669 B.C.),[50] and Ashurbanipal (668–627 B.C.), the last great Assyrian emperor, who declares of a rebel Dunanu,

> His wife, his sons, his daughters, his concubines, his singers, male and female—I led forth and counted as spoil. Silver, gold, the treasure of his palace—I brought forth and counted as spoil. The officials who stood before him, (his) smiths, his quartermasters—[I led forth] and counted as spoil.[51]

The same rationale applies in all of these cases. The conquered kings whose households, goods, and sometimes gods are taken were vassals, bound by covenant to the Assyrian suzerain. Because the Assyrian yoke was

---

45. In fact, the Akkadian term for "vassal" is *wardu* ("servant"). Cf. W. von Soden, *Akkadisches Handwörterbuch* (Wiesbaden: Harrassowitz, 1965–1981), 3:1464–66 (*[w]ardu[m]*, *[w]ardutu[m]*); *CAD*, vol. 1, pt. 2 (*ardu, ardutu*), 243–53.

46. Schramm, "Die Annalen des Assyrischen Königs Tukulti-Ninurta II," 148 (Vs.3); cf. more recently Grayson, *Assyrian Rulers of the Early First Millennium B.C. I*, 171 (A.0.100.5.3). This inscription of the king's annals contains a pervasive shifting between first- and third-person singular, which is brought out more effectively in Schramm's translation. The shift can hardly be explained except as a stylistic phenomenon. Cf. J. Sperber, "Der Personenwechsel in der Bibel," 23–33.

47. Rost, *Die Keilschrifttexte Tiglat-Pilesers III*, 8 (40–41).

48. Thureau-Dangin, *Une Relation de la Huitième Campagne de Sargon*, 52 (348).

49. Luckenbill, *Annals of Sennacherib*, 34 (46–48).

50. Borger, *Die Inschriften Asarhaddons Königs von Assyrien*, 48 (§ 27 Ep. 5.74–77).

51. Piepkorn, *Historical Prism Inscriptions of Ashurbanipal I*, 70 (vi.27–32).

onerous, the vassals strove to throw it off. They withdrew both fealty and tribute from the Assyrian emperor. In Assyrian parlance they "withheld tax and tribute from Ashur my Lord." As a result, the Assyrian suzerain was authorized to treat those covenant vassals as spoil—as plunder taken in payment for the debt of covenant breaking. We find a parallel ethos in the Old Testament, operative not only among God's people but also in the Babylonian cases they report.

Old Testament

Household Destruction

As we have noted, the most severe form of punishment for a covenant breaker in the ancient Near East was the destruction of himself and his household. This form also appears throughout Israelite history as a consequence of covenantal disobedience.

Wilderness and Conquest

Covenant breaking was a serious offense in the Old Testament. It was especially important to emphasize this point at the outset of the Lord's redemptive covenantal dealings with his people, Israel. So we find, during the wilderness wanderings and at the beginning of the conquest, cases of covenant disobedience and judgment that parallel the household punishment meted out by ancient Near Eastern kings to those who rebelled against their covenants. One is the rebellion of Korah, Dathan, and Abiram; another is the sin of Achan.

Korah, Dathan, and Abiram conspire to be priests equal with Moses. By doing so, they rebel against the covenantal arrangements of their Great King and thus withhold from God the honor due to him. Their punishment comes in a memorable form.

> Moses got up and went to Dathan and Abiram, and the elders of Israel followed him. He warned the assembly, "Move back from the tents of these wicked men! Do not touch anything belonging to them, or you will be swept away because of all their sins." So they moved away from the tents of Korah, Dathan and Abiram. Dathan and Abiram had come out and were standing with their wives, children and little ones at the entrances to their tents . . . and the earth opened its mouth and swallowed them, with

their households and all Korah's men and all their possessions. They went
down alive into the grave, with everything they owned; the earth closed
over them, and they perished and were gone from the community. (Num.
16:25–27, 32–33)

The list of covenant breakers—themselves, their wives, their sons and
little ones, and all their possessions—parallels those in the ancient Near
Eastern examples. As often occurs in extrabiblical cases of rebellion, the
gravity of the offense demands that the covenant breakers and their entire
households be destroyed.

Another Old Testament case in point occurs in Joshua 7. Achan, we recall, breaks the Lord's command by taking for himself some of the banned
goods of conquered Jericho. Once Achan's sin is uncovered by God, we read
how Joshua and all Israel take the covenant breaker to be stoned and burned
in the Valley of Achor: "Then Joshua, together with all Israel, took Achan
son of Zerah, the silver, the robe, the gold wedge, his sons and daughters,
his cattle, donkeys and sheep, his tent and all that he had, to the Valley of
Achor" (Josh. 7:24). Their punishment is stoning to death and burning, the
latter also a punishment to which covenant breakers in the Assyrian realm
were liable (as noted in the case of Tukulti-Ninurta I, above). A notable difference between the case of Joshua and Tukulti-Ninurta is that Joshua had
Achan and his family stoned to death and then burned, whereas the Assyrian suzerain burned alive a city full of covenant breakers. The difference
may not seem significant to some moderns, but it is still in keeping with
God's character that although he punished by death, his punishments never
showed the sort of deliberate cruelty, with the aim of inflicting maximum
pain, that appears in the pagan, and especially the Assyrian, accounts.

Monarchical Period

Household punishment for covenant breaking is not absent during the
monarchy. Jeroboam, Baasha, and Ahab are prime examples of covenant
breakers and their households treated as spoil because of their sin.

Jeroboam's legacy of covenant breaking would lead to the punishment
and exile of all Israel, as Ahijah had prophesied (1 Kings 14:14–16). But it
also led to divine punishment for the king and his household. Ahijah, the
seer, declares to Jeroboam's wife Yahweh's punishment for the king's covenant breaking idolatry:

> I am going to bring disaster on the house of Jeroboam. I will cut off from
> Jeroboam every last male in Israel—slave or free. I will burn up the house
> of Jeroboam as one burns dung, until it is all gone. *Dogs will eat those
> belonging to Jeroboam who die in the city, and the birds of the air will feed
> on those who die in the country. The* LORD *has spoken!* (1 Kings 14:10–11,
> emphasis added)

I put the curse in italics because it becomes a stock malediction in a
tradition that involves Jeroboam, Baasha, and Ahab. The curse here and
subsequently is part of a larger *Gattung*. Ahijah's prophetic address has the
form of an ancient Near Eastern covenant lawsuit (1 Kings 14:7–11).[52] The
Lord, who is both Prosecutor and Judge, is introduced first. A *historical
review* follows, which tells of the Lord's faithfulness to Jeroboam (vv. 7b–
8a). Then comes the *indictment*: although the Suzerain has been faithful,
the vassal has not. Jeroboam has been idolatrous and has instituted
idolatry nationally. He has broken and caused others to break the first
commandment—a major infraction of the Mosaic covenant (vv. 8b–9).
Judgment must follow (vv. 10–11).

Subsequent kings inherited both Jeroboam's legacy of idolatry and the
judgment that went with it. Jehu announces that judgment to Baasha of
Israel in much the same way that Ahijah cursed Jeroboam.

> Then the word of the LORD came to Jehu son of Hanani against Baasha:
> I lifted you up from the dust and made you leader of my people Israel,
> but you walked in the ways of Jeroboam and caused my people Israel to
> sin and to provoke me to anger because of their sins. So I am about to
> consume Baasha and his house, and I will make your house like that of
> Jeroboam son of Nebat. *Dogs will eat those belonging to Baasha who die
> in the city, and the birds of the air will feed on those who die in the country.*
> (1 Kings 16:1–4, emphasis added)

Shortly thereafter, it is reported how Zimri carried out this sentence
(1 Kings 16:11–13). Jehu uses the same covenant lawsuit form employed by

---

52.   For a brief discussion of this form in the ancient Near East and the Prophets, see
      Niehaus, "Amos," 318–21. For the form in the Prophets, see Huffmon, "Covenant
      Lawsuit in the Prophets," 285–95.

Ahijah and by ancient Near Eastern kings earlier. The Lord's address to the king *reviews* God's faithful behavior (v. 2a), *indicts* Baasha for his sins (v. 2b), and pronounces *judgment* in what now becomes traditional phraseology (vv. 3–4).

Ahab, who follows the path of those covenant breakers, receives the same doom, as the Lord declares through Elijah.

> I am going to bring disaster on you. I will consume your descendants and cut off from Ahab every last male in Israel—slave or free. I will make your house like that of Jeroboam son of Nebat and that of Baasha son of Ahijah, because you have provoked me to anger and have caused Israel to sin. . . . *Dogs will eat those belonging to Ahab who die in the city, and the birds of the air will feed on those who die in the country.* (1 Kings 21:21–24, emphasis added)

Elijah's use of traditional phraseology is not a phenomenon unique to Israel. Tradition was an important aspect of curses in the ancient Near East since the oldest curses, in the pagan world at least, were considered to be the most effective.[53]

The identical judgment of three royal households in the Old Testament comes because those households present identical cases of covenant breaking. In each case the monarch withholds tribute—namely, covenantal obedience—due to his Suzerain, the Great King. That entails a withholding of physical tribute, since resources that should have been put to godly use were diverted to idolatrous worship. So, in both a literal and a spiritual sense, the idolater withholds from God the tribute due to him. In a similar way, rebellious kings who were vassals of Assyria withheld both obedience and material tribute from the Assyrian great king (and by the same token from the Assyrian god, to whom they were bound by covenant).

Household Captivity

What we have called the corporate solidarity form of household punishment can involve either the destruction of an entire household or a milder

---

53. More generally, it is well established that standard phraseology could cover many centuries in ancient Near Eastern literary traditions. Cf., passim, Borger, *Einleitung in die assyrischen Königsinschriften*, and Schramm, *Einleitung in die assyrischen Königsinschriften*.

form of household punishment: the captivity of the rebellious household. We have been able to document the latter in the ancient Near East, and the Old Testament offers examples of the same.

Preexilic Cases

Preexilic examples of household punishment occur in the cases of Jehoram, Ahaz, Zedekiah, Jehoiachin, and in prophecies of Jeremiah. Elijah delivers one such prophecy of household doom to Jehoram.

> This is what the LORD, the God of your father David, says: "You have not walked in the ways of your father Jehoshaphat or of Asa king of Judah. But you have walked in the ways of the kings of Israel, and you have led Judah and the people of Jerusalem to prostitute themselves, just as the house of Ahab did. You have also murdered your own brothers, members of your father's house, men who were better than you. So now the LORD is about to strike your people, your sons, your wives and everything that is yours, with a heavy blow. You yourself will be very ill with a lingering disease of the bowels, until the disease causes your bowels to come out." (2 Chron. 21:12–15)

In this case death does come as a curse upon the king, but it comes upon him alone. His household is not killed but taken captive by the foe.

> The LORD aroused against Jehoram the hostility of the Philistines and of the Arabs who lived near the Cushites. They attacked Judah, invaded it and carried off all the goods found in the king's palace, together with his sons and wives. Not a son was left to him except Ahaziah, the youngest. (2 Chron. 21:16–17)

The judgment here may recall the case of Thutmose II (1495–1490 B.C.), who (for reasons that remain unclear) spared only one son of a rebellious vassal.[54] In this case, the Lord keeps one son, Ahaziah, alive so that Judah may still have a king upon the throne. God punishes the unfaithful royal

---

54. Breasted, *Ancient Records of Egypt*, 2:49 (§§ 121–22); the pharaoh kills the chief of Cush and his children and all of their males, except one of the chief's children, who was taken prisoner.

household but also displays undeserved mercy to the royal line of his unfaithful vassal.

Another example of household captivity comes from the reign of Ahaz.
We read that Ahaz was given by the Lord "into the hands of the king of
Israel, who inflicted heavy casualties on him. . . . The Israelites took cap-
tive from their kinsmen two hundred thousand wives, sons and daughters.
They also took a great deal of plunder, which they carried back to Samaria"
(2 Chron. 28:5, 8). Even though the Lord used the Israelites as a judgment
instrument against Judah, the prophet Obed later rebukes the Israelites because their rage was excessive and their killing and capturing went too far.
He warns them to return the captives, which they do (2 Chron. 28:9–15).
What concerns us here, however, is that their treatment of households is
typical of the ancient Near Eastern pattern.

As the litany of Israel's sins continues, Hezekiah reflects upon the his-
toric unfaithfulness of Judah and Jerusalem (2 Chron. 29:1–9). Because
their fathers did evil in the eyes of the Lord and forsook him, judgment fell
upon their households: "This is why our fathers have fallen by the sword
and why our sons and daughters and our wives are in captivity" (2 Chron.
29:9). To avoid such household calamity in the future, the king goes on
to make a new covenant with the Lord, involving the consecration of the
Levites and the purification of the temple, as well as renewed sacrifice and
worship (2 Chron. 29:10–36).

Judah regrettably did not remain faithful to Hezekiah's covenant any
more than they had remained faithful to the original, overarching Mosaic
covenant. Because of that unfaithfulness, the Lord would bring judgment.
Jeremiah in particular had the unhappy task of foretelling the punishment
to come. In several cases he couched that punishment in household terms.

Sometimes Jeremiah prophesied the extreme of household punishment—the extermination of the household. So he could say of the false
prophets and their hearers:

> Those same prophets will perish by the sword and famine. And the people
> they are prophesying to will be thrown out into the streets of Jerusalem
> because of the famine and sword. There will be no one to bury them or
> their wives, their sons or their daughters. I will pour out on them the
> calamity they deserve. (Jer. 14:15–16)

Such a calamity befell King Zedekiah. Jeremiah had warned him of the captivity of his household: "All your wives and children will be brought out to the Babylonians. You yourself will not escape from their hands but will be captured by the king of Babylon" (Jer. 38:23). After his capture, we read that "the king of Babylon slaughtered the sons of Zedekiah before his eyes and also killed all the nobles of Judah. Then he put out Zedekiah's eyes and bound him with bronze shackles to take him to Babylon" (Jer. 39:6–7; cf. 2 Kings 25:7).

The extreme form of household punishment did not always apply. The Lord carried out a milder judgment against King Jehoiachin: "Nebuchadnezzar took Jehoiachin captive to Babylon. He also took from Jerusalem to Babylon the king's mother, his wives, his officials and the leading men of the land" (2 Kings 24:15).[55] The captivity involved is just what we would expect against a background of covenantal justice in the ancient Near East.

Exilic Cases

All the cases we have considered have involved covenant breaking. In the Egyptian, Hittite, Assyrian, and Israelite realms, individuals bound by covenant to their suzerain have violated that bond and been condemned with their households.

Within a kingdom, however, as we saw in Egypt, rebellious people are subject to similar punishment. When a subject or subjects act in a way contrary to the king's wishes, or contrary to what he deems good for the country, a household judgment may ensue. There were theological reasons for this. A suzerain-vassal relation was thought to exist between the national god and both the king and his people. In such an arrangement, the people were the king's vassals.[56] It followed that subjects who disobeyed the king also disobeyed the god who had installed the king as his vassal.[57] Consequently, any judgment brought by the king was grounded in and justified by a nexus of divine-human covenantal relationships.

---

55. Related in spirit are those prophecies in which Jeremiah speaks of men's wives and fields being given to others, rather than being destroyed (Jer. 6:12; 8:10).

56. The people also could enter explicitly into a suzerain-vassal treaty with the king. As Wiseman, *Vassal Treaties of Esarhaddon*, 3–5, notes, the "people of Assyria, high and low" entered into such a treaty/covenant, and pledged loyalty to the crown prince, Ashurbanipal (3).

57. Cf. Niehaus, *God at Sinai*, 94–107, esp. 94–101, 103.

As Babylonian emperor, Darius would have been unique among ancient kings if he had not operated within such a theological-political framework. Evidence for a background of such covenant values appears in the case of Darius and Daniel. Darius regards Daniel so highly that he plans to set him over the whole kingdom, for Daniel is an able and trustworthy servant. But Daniel's fellow servants are jealous and seek a way to destroy Daniel. They get the king to issue an unalterable decree: for thirty days none may make a request of any other man or god. Requests may be made only of the king. Daniel, of course, prays to his God. His rivals report this infraction to Darius, who is obligated, much against his will, to cast Daniel into the lions' den. When Daniel is preserved, Darius is free to punish those who tricked him: "At the king's command, the men who had falsely accused Daniel were brought in and thrown into the lions' den, along with their wives and children. And before they reached the floor of the den, the lions overpowered them and crushed all their bones" (Dan. 6:24). The punishment is appropriate because Daniel's enemies have behaved in a treasonous manner. They have deceived their king in order to thwart his purposes, which in this case would have benefited both king and country. They are in essence rebellious vassals. The king treats them as such, and their fate is the same as that of other rebellious vassals in Mesopotamia and the ancient Near East.

Somewhat laconic, but related in spirit, is the edict of Darius providing for the building of the Lord's temple in Jerusalem. He declares, "Furthermore, I decree that if anyone changes this edict, a beam is to be pulled from his house and he is to be lifted up and impaled on it. And for this crime his house is to be made a pile of rubble" (Ezra 6:11). The intent of Darius's edict is clearly annihilation of the offender's household. That intent is made graphic by the destruction of the offender's house itself. Darius's warning is not a sign of his own devotion to the Lord but a deterrent to those who would behave rebelliously against him. Such punishment must come to those who break the royal laws, just as it comes to any rebellious vassal.

A final Old Testament case is that of Haman and Mordecai under King Xerxes. Haman conspires to destroy Mordecai (who would not bow down to him [Esther 3:2–5]). Outraged, he aims to have all of Mordecai's people—the Jews—destroyed. He counsels the king:

> There is a certain people dispersed and scattered among the peoples in all the provinces of your kingdom whose customs are different from those of

all other people and who do not obey the king's laws; it is not in the king's best interest to tolerate them. If it pleases the king, let a decree be issued to destroy them. (Esther 3:8–9)

Haman is able to counsel wholesale destruction on the (false) grounds that the Jews "do not obey the king's laws." They are rebellious vassals, who deserve to be eradicated. Their destruction, of course, also would mean Mordecai's death, and Haman has a gallows built by his own house for this very purpose. Esther's intercession for her people, however, turns the king against Haman. Ironically, Haman is sentenced to die on the very gallows he had erected for Mordecai's demise (Esther 7:10). Xerxes then gives Haman's house to Esther and Haman's signet ring to Mordecai, "And Esther set Mordecai over the house of Haman" (Esther 8:2 RSV). The king further undertakes to protect God's covenant people. The irony of Haman's death is now extended to any enemies of the Jews. The royal edict "granted the Jews in every city the right to assemble and protect themselves; to destroy, kill and annihilate any armed force of any nationality or province that might attack them and their women and children; and to plunder the property of their enemies" (Esther 8:11). This household punishment is carried out, and with particular reference to the household of Haman.

> The Jews struck down all their enemies with the sword, killing and destroying them, and they did what they pleased to those who hated them. In the citadel of Susa, the Jews killed and destroyed five hundred men. They also killed . . . the ten sons of Haman son of Hammedatha, the enemy of the Jews. But they did not lay their hands on the plunder. (Esther 9:5–10)

Because he conspired to destroy the queen's cousin (her only blood relation [cf. Esther 2:5–7]) and her people, Haman and his household are destroyed. No reason is given for the notable restraint, that the Jews "did not lay their hands on the plunder." But the pattern of the decree is the same as the pattern of the original Israelite conquest, which mandated that Israel leave no survivors (hence, certainly, no surviving households) among the inhabitants of the Promised Land (e.g., Deut. 7:16–26). God's people—his household—must annihilate the households of his enemies.[58]

---

58. With the notable exception of Rahab and her household, saved through her faith (cf. Josh. 2; Heb. 11:31).

Xerxes' injunction to the Jews is parallel to this. Such Old Testament types are realized in the eschaton, when the Lord and his saints (his household) annihilate his enemies and inherit the earth, that is, their possession.[59]

Household Salvation

The Lord also saves households in the Old Testament. Two examples will suffice to make this point. The first is the case of David after his victory over Absalom. The second is the case of Nehemiah and the defense of Jerusalem.

David

David's army fights victoriously for him against his own rebellious son, Absalom. David, however, had given instructions that Absalom himself, although defeated, should be kept alive. After the battle David is informed that Absalom has been killed. The king's inordinate grief discourages his army, and the army commander Joab rebukes the king.

> Today you have humiliated all your men, who have just saved your life and the lives of your sons and daughters and the lives of your wives and concubines. You love those who hate you and hate those who love you. You have made it clear today that the commanders and their men mean nothing to you. I see that you would be pleased if Absalom were alive today and all of us were dead. (2 Sam. 19:5–6)

David failed to understand how utterly his son was his foe, or, if he did understand it, he was conflicted by a father's love for his son. Absalom betrayed his king and his household and would likely have put them to death had he been able to usurp the kingship. He was an enemy of God's king and therefore of God. He was also thereby an enemy of the king's—and God's—household. In David's case, the king and his army fought to save the king's household and secure his kingdom. The eschatological parallel appears in Revelation 19, where the King of Kings and Lord of Lords leads his army as he wages war against his foe, who has persecuted his household and tried to rule the earth entirely as the "god of this age" (2 Cor. 4:4). But the Lord will establish his household and his kingdom forever.

---

59. It is their possession in prospect. Similarly, Abraham "possessed" the Promised Land, but only in prospect. Much later, Joshua would lead God's saints to conquer that which was already theirs through the Abrahamic covenant.

Nehemiah

Nehemiah also sees the salvation of households. In his case, the enemies of God would prevent the reconstruction of the temple. Sanballat, Tobiah, the Arabs, the Ammonites, and the men of Ashdod plot to attack Jerusalem and prevent the reconstruction. But Nehemiah and his people pray to God and Nehemiah counsels them:

> "Don't be afraid of them. Remember the Lord, who is great and awesome, and fight for your brothers, your sons and your daughters, your wives and your homes." When our enemies heard that we were aware of their plot and that God had frustrated it, we all returned to the wall, each to his own work. (Neh. 4:14–15)

In this case the men are urged to fight to save their own households. But this time, the salvation of those households is not accomplished by war. It is God who frustrates the foe as an answer to prayer. He comes in the midst of difficulty, just as at the eschaton he will come in answer to a prayer, "Even so, come, Lord Jesus" (Rev. 22:20 NKJV). He will come to deal in household terms: to destroy the household of Satan and to save the household of faith.

New Testament

The New Testament teaches the doctrine of opposed households. There is a household of faith and of God, but there is also a household of Satan and those bound to him. The latter appears from several texts.

When the Pharisees accuse Jesus of casting out demons by Beelzebub, the prince of demons, Jesus gives this remarkable reply:

> How can Satan drive out Satan? If a kingdom is divided against itself, that kingdom cannot stand. If a house is divided against itself, that house cannot stand. And if Satan opposes himself and is divided, he cannot stand; his end has come. In fact, no one can enter a strong man's house and carry off his possessions unless he first ties up the strong man. Then he can rob his house. (Mark 3:23–27)

A clear and appropriate parallel exists here between the kingdom and the house. For Satan is a king ("if Satan also is divided against himself, how will his kingdom stand?" [Luke 11:18 RSV]; cf. also Eph. 2:2, where he is "the prince of the power of the air" RSV). Satan is also the head of a household, for he has children, as Jesus makes clear when he informs the Jews, "You belong to your father, the devil, and you want to carry out your father's desire" (John 8:44).

In an ironic variant on the theme that we have been considering, Satan's household is plundered—and that in royal terms: "When a strong man, fully armed, guards his own house, his possessions are safe. But when someone stronger attacks and overpowers him, he takes away the armor in which the man trusted and divides up the spoils" (Luke 11:21–22). The strong man is Satan, and the spoil, in context, is a person or people whom the "strong man" has seized for himself. They are and remain part of his house (or "palace") until one stronger than he comes and snatches them away. Incidentally, the fact that the strong man trusted not in God but in his armor is reminiscent of Assyrian claims about covenant breakers, that they trusted "in their own strength," or the like, as opposed to the faithful Assyrian monarch, who trusted in Ashur his Lord. Here Satan, the rebel king par excellence, trusts in his armor against Christ, the King of Kings, who cannot be resisted.

Christ plunders Satan's kingdom, which is also Satan's house. The plunder is people—captive subjects. Christ populates his own kingdom, his own house, with these liberated captives. So he can say, in a warning to his disciples, "If the head of the house has been called Beelzebub, how much more the members of his household!" (Matt. 10:25). The disciples, of course, are "the members of his household." The apostle Paul states the same truth when he says, "Therefore, as we have opportunity, let us do good to all people, especially to those who belong to the family of believers" (Gal. 6:10). The whole church, the people of God's kingdom, are the "family of believers," or, more accurately translated, "the household of faith."

The same doctrine is made clear in Hebrews. Here we find that the New Testament house is a continuation of the Old Testament house of God.

He [i.e., Jesus] was faithful to the one who appointed him, just as Moses was faithful in all God's house. Jesus has been found worthy of greater honor than Moses, just as the builder of a house has greater honor than the house itself. For every house is built by someone, but God is the builder of everything. Moses was faithful as a servant in all God's house, testifying to what would be said in the future. But Christ is faithful as a son over God's house. And we are his house, if we hold on to our courage and the hope of which we boast. (Heb. 3:2–6)

Christ, as Son, has been set over the house that God built. So he is not only the king of God's kingdom but also the head of God's house. Satan in his distorted way imitates God's pattern—as king of his own kingdom and head of his own house. Augustine rightly noted that Satan never comes up with anything new but only distorts what God has done.

As head of God's household, Christ is also a priest. So we are exhorted to hold fast our confession, "since we have a great priest over the house of God" (Heb. 10:21). The typology of house and priest come together in Peter's exhortation, "You also, like living stones, are being built into a spiritual house to be a holy priesthood, offering spiritual sacrifices acceptable to God through Jesus Christ" (1 Peter 2:5; cf. 1 Cor. 3:16–17).

The doctrine of the household is also implicit in Ephesians 5:22–33, where Paul writes that "the husband is the head of the wife as Christ is the head of the church" (Eph. 5:23). To say that Christ is the head of the church is also to affirm that he is the head of God's house—"whose house we are" as the author of Hebrews stated (Heb. 3:6 NKJV).

Moreover, just as the head sets the tone for the household, so the household can be punished for the sin of the head, as was the case with Achan. Such is the case par excellence with Adam, the head of the household of all humanity. That we are his house is not in doubt, if only from the Hebrew term for human being, ben ʿadam, "son of Adam." All the individual sins of covenant breaking (or action against the king's will) that we have considered in the Old Testament find their human archetype in Adam, who sinned against the creation covenant of God, the Great King, acting against his will.[60]

The household of the first Adam was taken captive, absorbed into Satan's household, "sold under sin" (Rom. 7:14 NKJV; cf. Rom. 5:12–14, 18–19; 6:16–18). The familial outworking of punishment, in the first appearance of internecine warfare, came early in Adam's experience: "And while they were in the field, Cain attacked his brother Abel and killed him" (Gen. 4:8).

---

60. For the creation covenant, see Kline, *Images of the Spirit*, 19–20; Dumbrell, *Covenant and Creation*, 34–35; and Niehaus, *God at Sinai*, 143–50.

More broadly, the whole Adamic (human) family is subject to fratricide and death. But Christ, the stronger King, has come into Satan's palace and plundered his goods. He has incorporated those goods, namely, people, into his household—"the household of faith." So we are told: "To all who received him, to those who believed in his name, he gave the right to become children of God" (John 1:12). As Christ declared, "Here I am, and the children God has given me" (Heb. 2:13).

As head of the human household, Adam was "a pattern of the one to come" (Rom. 5:14). And the household model persisted, not only for all humanity, but also for nations. So we read of the "house of Israel" and the "house of Judah" (Heb. 8:8). So Jesus warns Jerusalem, which has rejected him, "Look, your house is left to you desolate" (Luke 13:35).[61] The same model appears in Old Testament cases of individual households, as we have seen. Nevertheless, just as whole households could be condemned, whole households also can be saved. God's angel tells Cornelius that Peter "will bring you a message through which you and all your household will be saved" (Acts 11:14). Paul and Silas promise the Philippian jailer, "Believe in the Lord Jesus, and you will be saved—you and your household" (Acts 16:31).[62]

Evidence from Egypt, Hatti, Assyria, and Babylon shows that the ancients had a strong concept of the significance of households, as either established by deity or taken as booty for covenant breaking and rebellion. These ideas, articulated in a fallen and darkened form in annals and other accounts, appear in a revealed and purer form in the Old Testament. The same truths appear more fully revealed in the New Testament. There the antipathy between Satan's "house" and "the household of God" is most evident. Those who belong to Christ are the "household of faith." They are children of a second Adam, whose blood speaks better things than the blood of Abel. They are vassals of a new and better covenant. And their Great King and Father is God.[63]

---

61. This may also be an allusion to the future abandonment of the temple—God's "house." Cf. Ezekiel 8–11 and the discussion in chapter 5, "City and Temple: Abandoned and Restored."

62. The point is not that the faith of the head automatically means that his household is saved. Rather, his lead provides an example for his household to follow, and God honors his faith in that way. Cf. the same principle at work in a somewhat diminished degree, even in a household where only one parent believes (1 Cor. 7:13–14).

63. Cf. Kline, *Treaty of the Great King.*

7

The Restoration of All Things

Our study has carried us through major themes that appear in both ancient Near Eastern and biblical theology: the divine or semidivine nature of the king who is also a savior, the divine source of law, the covenantal relationship between a king and his god and the conquest mandate that such a relationship entailed, the concept of an archetypal divine city, temple, and image, along with their earthly ectypes, as well as aspects of judgment, including abandonment of temple and city and judgment on the households of those who broke covenant. All of these themes were essential parts of covenantal relationships between gods and humans in the ancient world and find their true counterparts in biblical revelation. All of them also are caught up in a larger paradigm of divine-human activity, and a presentation of that paradigm will form an important part of this chapter.

Before we engage that paradigm, one final theme remains to be explored—that of restoration. The theme appears more clearly in Egypt than it does in any other ancient culture. Egyptian theology contains forms of restoration that are fundamentally biblical and yet not found (or scarcely found) to date in other ancient Near Eastern cultures. The restoration of which we speak takes two forms. The first is the restoration of the individual in the form of a personal, bodily resurrection and ascension to join the divine beings in heaven. The second is the restoration of all things on earth as they were at the beginning of time, when they were pristine and without fault. Both restorations resonate with biblical revelation, which sets forth the very same two themes as its major goals: the restoration of fallen individuals through their resurrection and ascension into heaven, and the restoration of all things as they were at the beginning through the creation of a new heavens and earth.

Hatti

Although the Egyptian data are more extensive and contain more explicit biblical parallels, there is relevant material from the Hittite realm that deserves attention. The themes of individual resurrection and national resurrection do not appear abundantly in the Hittite materials, but the concepts can be found there. For instance, it was understood that the Hittite emperor, upon his death, would ascend to heaven and join the gods. Hence, the Hittite phrase for the death of an emperor was that he had "become [a] god," as statements regarding more than one Hittite emperor attest.[1] Moreover, there is some mention in the Hittite treaties of a personal resurrection of the vassal king, although the expression in every context is clearly figurative. For instance, the vassal, Mattiwaza, king of Mitanni, anticipates the time when Šuppiluliuma becomes his suzerain, and he characterizes this as follows: "When you, my lord, awaken me to life."[2] Similarly, Bentesina, king of Amurru, says to Hattušiliš III, the Hittite who has become his suzerain, "You have awakened me to life."[3]

The second restoration concept, that of national resurrection, also appears in the Hittite realm in a suzerain-vassal treaty between Šuppiluliuma and Mattiwaza, king of Mitanni. Here again the context makes it clear that the usage is figurative. The suzerain gives his daughter in marriage to the vassal, and he declares, "So that the land of Mitanni, the great land, might not perish, the great king (i.e., suzerain), the king of the land of Ḫatti, awakened the land of Mitanni to life, for the sake of his daughter."[4] As in the cases of individual resurrection, the resurrection motif is used metaphorically. Still, a figurative usage implies a literal background—a concept of a factual truth. Just as the gods could make a Hittite king immortal, so the Hittite emperor, who styled himself the sun god, could awaken a vassal to life. Just as the sun shines upon fallow land and enables it to bring forth

---

1. Götze, *Die Annalen des Mursilis*, 14–15 (VsI.4), 16–17 (VsI.10–11).
2. Weidner, *Politische Dokumente aus Kleinasien*, 42–43 (Vs. 28).
3. Ibid., 128–29 (Vs. 24).
4. Ibid., 18–19 (Vs. 57–58).

life and bear fruit, so the Hittite suzerain, who styled himself "the sun," could awaken a vassal's land to life and fecundity.

Egypt

Individual Resurrection

The concept of individual resurrection appears elsewhere in the ancient Near East. The god Dumu-zi (Tammuz) in Mesopotamia (Sumeria), for example, supposedly came back from the dead. Baal likewise, according to Ugaritic lore, was rescued from the clutches of Mot (the god of death) and brought back to the surface by his sister/consort Anat. Both of these divine resurrections are at the core of vegetation myths: the god who brings rain and fruitfulness has died and the land suffers drought or winter; when he is resurrected, spring returns, the beneficent rains come, and plants begin to grow, bearing fruit for human sustenance. The situation in Egypt is both similar and different. There the god Osiris symbolized in his death the annual drought and in his rebirth the periodic flooding of the Nile and the growth of grain. Sustained by those Nile floods, which deposited rich silt and provided water for irrigation, Egypt had no need of sky or weather gods who must come back from death in order to ensure a bountiful harvest. For them it was the Nile god whose rebirth provided the needed bounty. Bur more important for our concerns is the fate of that incarnate god who ruled Egypt during so much of her recorded history, namely, the pharaoh. After his death, the king of Egypt experienced a bodily resurrection, and after that resurrection he would ascend into heaven to take his place with the panoply of gods, of whom he was one, as an incarnation of Ra, the sun god. The Pyramid Texts (ca. 2350–2175 B.C.) give us a good picture of this resurrection theology. The following schematic draws upon the Pyramid Texts and shows some biblical parallels.

Egypt	Bible
O King, there comes this time of . . . three-days; a stairway	Hos. 6:1–2;
to the sky is [set up] for you.[5]	Luke 24:46

---

5. Faulkner, *Ancient Egyptian Pyramid Texts*, 280 (Utterance 667 §1941); cf. 144 (Utterance 437 §794), 216 (Utterance 556 § 1384).

Raise yourself, O King; receive your head, collect your bones,	Ezek. 37:1–14
gather your limbs together, throw off the earth from your flesh.[6]	
The King has ascended on a cloud.[7]	Acts 1:9
The King ranks as first-born to the extent of eternity.[8]	Col. 1:15, 18
He . . . opens for you the doors of the sky . . .	Eph. 4:8–10
he makes a road for you that you may ascend by means of it	
into the company of the gods.[9]	Acts 2:30–36
The King will not decay . . . the King will not become corrupt.[10]	Ps. 16:8–11; Acts 2:25–36
The King receives his spirit form before the gods[11]	1 Cor. 15:35–49

The Pyramid Texts contain other outstanding parallels in addition to these. The sky goddess, Nut, declares that the dead and risen king is "my beloved, with whom I am well pleased."[12] Nut also says he is "my beloved, my first-born."[13] The king says, "I am the essence of a god, the son of a god, the messenger of a god."[14] He apparently split open the earth on the day of his resurrection.[15] He is told, "The tomb is opened for you, the doors of the

6. Ibid., 123 (Utterance 373 §§ 654–55); cf. 113 (Utterance 355 § 572), 115 (Utterance 375 § 584), 119 (Utterance 364 § 617), 121 (Utterance 367 § 635), 138 (Utterance 419 §§ 747–48), 150 (Utterance 450 § 840), 205 (Utterance 536 § 1292), 249 (Utterance 603 §1675), and passim.

7. Ibid., 260 (Utterance 627 § 1774), 76 (Utterance 267 § 365, cloud of incense; cf. 294, Utterance 684 § 2054); 109 (Utterance 337 § 549, to the sound of thunder), 187 (Utterance 511 §§ 1149–50, to the sound of an earthquake), 284 (Utterance 669 § 1961, in a great storm).

8. Ibid., 260 (Utterance 627 § 1781); cf. 1 (Utterance 3 § 2).

9. Ibid., 281 (Utterance 667 § 1943). "He" is Osiris, god of resurrection.

10. Ibid., 135 (Utterance 412 § 722); cf. 200 (Utterance 532 §§ 1257–58), 231 (Utterance 576 § 1501).

11. Ibid., 144 (Utterance 437 § 795).

12. Ibid., 1 (Utterance 1 § 1); cf. 207 (Utterance 539 § 1316); cf. Matthew 3:17.

13. Ibid., 1 (Utterance 3 § 2); cf. 271 (Utterance 660 § 1871); cf. Colossians 1:15; Hebrews 1:6.

14. Ibid., 160 (Utterance 471 § 720); cf. John 8:16; 9:4; 14:10.

15. Ibid., 63 (Utterance 254 § 281); cf. Matthew 27:51–53; 28:2.

tomb-chamber are thrown open for you."[16] The risen king declares, "I am the one who escaped from the coiled serpent. I have ascended in a blast of fire, having turned myself about."[17] He is triumphant over the serpent, and says that with "this foot of mine . . . I strike you [i.e., the serpent] on your face so that your venom may fail."[18] The king is Wisdom and is seated at the right hand of his father, Ra.[19] From his seat in glory he governs humans and judges the living.[20] He also judges the gods.[21] He will rule with an iron scepter.[22] But he will also have at least his own tears wiped away.[23] Like the king Melchizedek, a type of Christ according to the author of Hebrews, he has no (human) father or mother.[24] Although he ascends to heaven, he also descends to the realm of the dead: "Those who are in the Netherworld have recovered their wits, they have unstopped their ears at this King's voice, for he descends among them."[25] Finally, like Jesus, he is the faithful witness: "This King is this one, the lord of witness regarding the Just One."[26] And he may ascend "as the Morning Star."[27]

Egyptian records subsequent to the Pyramid Texts also attest to the resurrection and ascension of departed pharaohs. According to pharaonic annals, dead pharaohs ascend to join the gods in general, or they join and even mingle with the sun god, their father. Pharaohs from Amen-em-het I (1991–1961 B.C.) to Psammetichus II (595–589 B.C.) join or mingle with the sun god.[28] Pharaohs from Thutmose II (1495–1490 B.C.) to Ramses III (1195–1164 B.C.) join the gods in heaven or at the horizon.[29] Since, accord-

---

16.   Ibid., 276 (Utterance 665A § 1909); cf. Matthew 28:2; John 20:1.
17.   Ibid., 107 (Utterance 332 § 541); cf. Hebrews 2:14–15; 1 Corinthians 15:55; Acts 2:24.
18.   Ibid., 129 (Utterance 390 §§ 685–86); cf. Genesis 3:15; 1 Corinthians 15:55.
19.   Ibid., 61 (Utterance 250 §§ 267–68); cf. 1 Corinthians 1:24; Hebrews 1:3.
20.   Ibid., 62 (Utterance 252 § 273); cf. 133 (Utterance 407 § 713); cf. Acts 10:42.
21.   Ibid., 135 (Utterance 412 § 732); cf. 1 Corinthians 6:3; 2 Peter 2:4.
22.   Ibid., 276 (Utterance 665C § 1915); cf. Revelation 2:27; 12:5; 19:15.
23.   Ibid., 286 (Utterance 670 §§ 1983–84); cf. Revelation 7:17; 21:4.
24.   Ibid., 289 (Utterance 675 §§ 2002–3); cf. Hebrews 7:1–3.
25.   Ibid., 297 (Utterance 688 §§ 2084–85); cf. 1 Peter 3:19–20.
26.   Ibid., 318 (Utterance 758 § 2288); cf. Revelation 1:5.
27.   Ibid., 154 (Utterance 461 § 871); cf. 2 Peter 1:19; Revelation 22:16.
28.   Breasted, *Ancient Records of Egypt*, 1:235 § 491; 2:20 § 46 (Amen-hotep I), 234 § 592 (Thutmose III); 4:112 § 187 (Ramses III; cf. 163 § 390; 205 § 411), 505 § 988E (Psammetichus II). And cf. 4:505 § 988G (Nitocris), from the end of the Sixth Dynasty (2350–2200 B.C.).
29.   Ibid., 2:44 § 108 (Thutmose I), 48 § 118 (Thutmose III); 3:107 § 263 (Seti I; cf. 114 § 278; 220 § 517); 4:200 § 400 n.a (Ramses III).

ing to one adage, absence of evidence is not evidence of absence, we might suggest that all pharaohs assumed the same, even if each one has not left us an explicit claim to an Acts 1 type experience.

The truly remarkable parallelism of themes between the Pyramid Texts and the Bible naturally raises the question of whether Egyptian tradition influenced the biblical material in any way. To date, no such influence can be demonstrated. The tentative conclusion that we draw, then, is that such doctrine in Egypt had a spiritual source (cf. 1 Tim 4:1), and thus is a good example of a spiritual counterfeit, much like the temple pattern revelation to Gudea of Lagash. In any case, the parallels are remarkable in their detail and make it clear that the Egyptians claimed for pharaohs a heavenly destiny in which, for the most part, others could not hope to participate.

The biblical data present a very different picture, for in this matter, as in others that we have observed, the prerogatives of ancient kings become democratized: now any believer can look forward to a bodily resurrection and heavenly glory.

"As at the Beginning"

Pharaoh might look forward to a heavenly residence in a glorified body, but on earth he had work to do. His job, as son of Ra, was to restore all things as they were at the beginning so that the rule of ma'at was completely reestablished. To do so, he would require and receive the help of his father, Ra, who worked so powerfully in and through him.

The correlation between a god and his image and the belief that a god, as a metaphysical being or essence, would inhabit a physical idol made in his image were well established in Egypt. We recall that Ptah was the creator of the heavenly city, Anu, and also of that city's heavenly temples (palaces) and the gods who inhabited them. But Ptah was also the creator of the earthly Anu and of its earthly temples and idols. Pharaohs who ruled Egypt after Ptah, and under him, likewise were expected to build temples and make idols after the heavenly archetypes. So Ptah could say to Ramses II: "Men and gods acclaim thy name like mine. . . . Thou fashionest the statues [i.e., idols], thou buildest their holy places as I did at the beginning."[30] Ramses can make the gods and build the temples just as Ptah did at the beginning, because those functions are part of his being like Ptah. Put more largely, because Pharaoh is Ptah's image, he does what Ptah has done.

---

30. Ibid., 3:179 (§ 406).

A biblical parallel exists. Primordially God made a temple, Eden, inhabited by his images, Adam and Eve. Through sin those images and that temple passed away. But God will restore both his images and his temple "according to the beginning."[31] As a stage in achieving those goals, God has his Son build an earthly temple, the church, inhabited by God's images, his people. God's work of restoration will appear in its final form when his people inhabit that ultimate Eden: "To him who overcomes, I will give the right to eat from the tree of life, which is in the paradise of God" (Rev. 2:7).[32] Just as Pharaoh did what Ptah had done before, so the Son does what his Father had done. Moreover, God's images on earth are inhabited by his Spirit, just as Pharaoh was inhabited by Ra and as divine images in Egypt's temples were inhabited by the gods. And just as Pharaoh did the works of his father, it is enough for believers to be like their Lord and Master and do the same works that he has done (Matt. 10:25; John 14:12).

A Major Paradigm

What we have said about the advance of Pharaoh's kingdom (which involves the extension of the rule of *ma'at* and the restoration of things as at the beginning) and the advance of God's kingdom (which involves a parallel extension of God's truth and ultimate restoration of all things) implies a paradigm of divine activity that deserves investigation and statement. We have noted how Egyptian theology alone offers clear and consistent parallels to the biblical concepts of restoration, both of the individual, through resurrection, and of the world, by divine action through an incarnate son. Likewise, Egypt alone offers a clear and consistent parallel to the dynamic of divine activity portrayed in the Bible.

What we have said about Ra and his activity through his incarnate son may be demonstrated in a brief paradigm as follows:

Amon Ra

↓

Pharaoh

son of Ra

"Ra in his limbs"

↓

---

31.   Ibid., 1:335 (§ 760).
32.   Cf. Luke 23:43; 2 Corinthians 12:3–4.

warfare
↓
covenant with conquered
↓
temple service

It is immediately apparent that the paradigm offered above incorporates the major themes that we have already considered. The god Ra works through his incarnate son, by means of warfare, to conquer those who resist his authority and bring them into his kingdom by covenant. When he brings them into his kingdom, he also brings them into his service so that they live under the protection of his son and pay tribute to him, tribute that is used by his son to sustain and further advance his kingdom and also to support the ministry of his temple. We even saw how foreign vassals were sometimes made servants in the temples of Egypt.

The structure of thought that we see in this *precis* of Egyptian theology presents a dynamic of divine activity and kingdom advance that is also fundamental to the Bible, as the following paradigm shows.

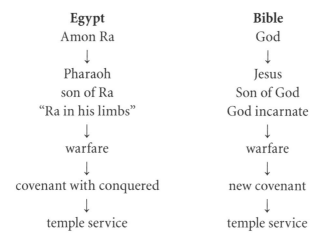

Egypt	**Bible**
Amon Ra	God
↓	↓
Pharaoh	Jesus
son of Ra	Son of God
"Ra in his limbs"	God incarnate
↓	↓
warfare	warfare
↓	↓
covenant with conquered	new covenant
↓	↓
temple service	temple service

We place the biblical paradigm next to the Egyptian in order to illustrate the degree of parallelism between them. As Ra worked through Pharaoh, so God works through his incarnate Son to advance his kingdom by warfare, establish a covenant with his former enemies (sinners), and establish a temple, which is both the church and the individual believers in it, for divine service.

But how does the Son wage war? He declared that his kingdom was advancing forcefully (Matt. 11:12), and indeed the kingdom of God does advance with power. It must do so because there is no neutral ground, no "demilitarized zone" in the world. Either one is darkness or one is light. In order for the kingdom of light to advance, it must push back the kingdom of darkness. When Jesus talked of binding the strong man and plundering his house, he gave a figure for all of God's kingdom advance under the new covenant (Luke 11:21–22). Whenever the kingdom of God gains ground, the kingdom of his opponent, the "god of this world," loses ground, and the enemy does not give up ground willingly. If we understand that Satan became the god of this world when God's vassals, Adam and Eve, chose to follow him, thus giving him legal entrée into the world and dominion over it (under God's sovereignty and permission, of course), we understand the context in which the Son wages war to advance God's kingdom. The Son combats and defeats the god of this world every time someone comes to faith in Christ. That is, the Son brings the person out of vassalage to Satan so that that person now becomes a vassal to God—a "slave of God" (cf. Rom. 6:22)—in which he or she actually finds perfect freedom. And we must remember that the warfare the Son wages in order to defeat the foe is not waged with the sword. The use of physical warfare to advance God's kingdom passed away when the old covenant, with the Old Testament form of God's kingdom, the nation state of Israel, passed away.[33] God now advances his kingdom not by the drawn sword, but by the sword of the Spirit, who does the job of conviction regarding sin, righteousness, and judgment (John 16:8). So in a sense, whenever one does a work of the Spirit—whether it be counseling, preaching, scholarship, healing, or casting out demons—one commits an act of war against the kingdom of darkness, advancing the kingdom of light.[34]

So what the Egyptians claimed for Pharaoh and what the Bible says of

---

33. This reflects a more general principle, that the form of God's kingdom determines the form of certain divine activities, including warfare and judgment. E.g., false prophets are put to death in the old covenant form of the kingdom (Deut. 13:5) but excluded from the church—anathematized (hence, "eternally condemned," NIV)—in the new covenant form of the kingdom (Gal. 1:8–9). The church does not (or should not!) advance God's kingdom by the sword and does not execute false prophets.

34. For a fuller discussion of the issues raised in this paragraph, see Jeffrey J. Niehaus, *Biblical Theology*, forthcoming.

the Son now also can be true for all believers. Although there has been only one incarnate Son, there are many children, and since Pentecost the Spirit has been working through those children to advance God's kingdom. It is true that no new covenants are being made as part of that kingdom advance because the new covenant is final and complete. On the other hand, a new covenant relationship is created every time someone comes to faith in Christ, for that individual now becomes a vassal to his Lord in a personal relationship that had not yet come into existence for that individual before that act of faith. However, the parallelism between the work of the Spirit through the Son and the work of that same Spirit through believers does not stand in isolation. The Spirit has worked in a parallel way through the prophets of the Old Testament, through the incarnate Word, and through the church, as the following schema demonstrates:

KINGDOM DYNAMIC PARADIGM

Old Testament	*Jesus*	*Church*
Father and Son	Father	Father and Son
↓	↓	↓
Holy Spirit	Holy Spirit	Holy Spirit
↓	↓	↓
Prophet/Seer	Incarnate Word	Church
↓	↓	↓
Kingdom Work	Kingdom Work	Kingdom Work

The Word's incarnate ministry gives us a model for understanding the way of God's kingdom advance, which ultimately leads to restoration, both of the individual and eschatologically "of all things." All the cases that the Bible offers are parallel. Just as the Spirit worked through the Son to advance God's kingdom, so he worked through the prophets of old, and so he works today. When God affirmed the Davidic covenant, the prophet David could declare, "The Spirit of the LORD spoke through me; his word was on my tongue" (2 Sam. 23:2). The Spirit produced God's words, which reconfirmed the Davidic covenant and kingdom. In a similar way the prophet Agabus could say, "The Holy Spirit says . . ." (Acts 21:11). The Spirit through that prophet produced words of covenant administration, a prophecy that warned Paul of a future challenge to his own kingdom work. What was true for Agabus also has been true for all of God's people in the church age. God's Spirit is at work *within* God's people to advance God's kingdom. That is the work of sanctification. But he is also at work *through* God's people to advance God's kingdom. That is the manifold work of the Spirit through the church in evangelization, healing, and prophetic manifestation of God's truth and love. And that work, like all of God's kingdom advance, is a matter of warfare. I assume here but argue elsewhere that from the Fall onward, God's Spirit has worked through prophet figures to wage war in order to establish and advance God's kingdom in the world.[35]

Our understanding of God's mode of kingdom establishment/advance now enables us to produce a more nuanced version of our major paradigm. We saw the paradigm as a parallel to the structure of Egyptian theology, in which Amon-Ra worked through his incarnate son to do the work that advanced his kingdom and aimed at restoration. In the biblical parallel, it is the Spirit who works through the incarnate Son to do the same. But the same dynamic was at work through the prophets of old, and is at work today in and through the church. The final form of the paradigm thus illustrates God's way of kingdom advance in any age.

The Major Paradigm (Final Form)

1   God works
2   by his Spirit
3   through the Word/a prophet figure
4   to war against and defeat his foe(s).
5   God establishes a covenant with a people.
6   God's covenant establishes that people as God's people.
7   God establishes a temple among his people,
      because he will reside among them.

God conducts warfare through a prophet figure on the analogy of the Son. Why? Because all prophets through whom the Father worked before the Incarnation were modeled on the Son. Although they came before him, in truth he was before them (cf. John 1:30). And all who have the Spirit of Christ after Pentecost are modeled also on the Son, for God's Spirit works within us to remake us into the Lord's likeness (cf. 2 Cor. 3:18) and through us to do the works that our Father is doing.

---

35. Ibid.

Conclusion

A Symphony of Parallels

At the outset of this work, we noted three possible sources of parallels between the Old Testament (and Bible as a whole) and the ancient Near East: the mutual recollection of major events that actually did occur (e.g., Creation, the Flood), the use by biblical writers of literary and legal forms already current in the ancient Near East (e.g., poetic parallelism with its stock word pairs, the second millennium B.C. international treaty/covenant form), and, finally, the activity of deceiving, demonic spirits (producing parallels between supposed acts of pagan gods and the acts of God as they appear in the Bible). Primarily we have explored the third of these grounds of parallelism. Our exploration not only has shown that the pagan cultures of the ancient Near East had certain fundamentally important concepts in common with the biblical authors, but it also has shown that those pagan cultures shared a theological structure of thought with that of the biblical writers. We have endeavored to summarize and outline that structure.

It may be a modern irony that theology often is practiced more as an academic discipline than as a spiritual one. But the spiritual dimension of theology is paramount, whether or not it receives paramount attention at the hands of many theologians. In the cases of parallelism that we have considered in this book, there are almost always two ways of looking at the data. The first way is to consider them to be part of an ancient Near Eastern worldview. In that case, the biblical authors are just couching things in terms familiar to them from their contemporary thought world. The second way is to consider the parallels as rooted in truth: revealed truth in the Old Testament and the Bible, and distorted truth in the ancient Near East. We prefer the second approach because it is consistent with the claims made by the biblical writers and speakers themselves.

For example, we are told that David gave Solomon "the plans of all that the Spirit had put in his mind for the courts of the temple of the LORD and all the surrounding rooms, for the treasuries of the temple of God and for the treasuries for the dedicated things" (1 Chron. 28:12). Those plans included the weight of gold and silver for the lamp stands and their lamps and for the tables and the weight of gold for the forks, sprinkling bowls, pitchers, and dishes, as well as for the altar of incense (1 Chron. 28:14–18). "'All this,' David said, 'I have in writing from the hand of the LORD upon me, and he gave me understanding in all the details of the plan'" (1 Chron. 28:19).

Thutmose III (1490–1436 B.C.) erected a holy of holies for Amon and received divine guidance, not only for the temple construction, but also for fashioning the temple's liturgical equipment:

> . . . a great vase of electrum . . . [. . .] silver, gold, bronze, and copper . . . the Two Lands were flooded with their brightness, like the stars in the body of Nut [i.e., the sky goddess], while my statue followed. Offering tables of electrum . . . I made it for him out of the conceptions of my heart, by the guidance of the god himself.[1]

When a pagan king makes the same claim that a biblical king does, and when that claim is a spiritual one and involves divine guidance, an evaluation that says the biblical king is just understanding these things the way any ancient Near Eastern monarch would understand them does not do justice to the data. David either got guidance from God by "the hand of the LORD" upon him, or he did not. If he did not, then his statement to the contrary makes him either a liar or a deceived, and perhaps a self-deceived man. Since nothing elsewhere in the Bible gives us any reason to think that David's statement was in error, we can only conclude that it was true. If it was true, then David's experience of inspiration, or divine guidance, was a genuine experience that produced the results

---

1. Breasted, *Ancient Records of Egypt*, 2:68 (§ 164).

that God wanted. But how are we then to understand the similar claims of divine guidance made by Thutmose III? It would be most bizarre if an Egyptian who predated David by centuries made an almost identical claim to divine guidance for making temple furnishings for his god and made that claim by coincidence. Or, to put it another way, the true God just happened to do to David what Thutmose claimed his god did for him a few centuries earlier.

The parallels we have explored in this book are of this sort. We have concluded that they cannot be explained as cases of biblical dependence on ancient Near Eastern theology. We also conclude that they cannot be explained as coincidences, if only because the accumulation of such coincidences sooner or later strains credibility. Our belief need not be strained, however, because the Bible itself gives us the reason for such parallels. Passages such as Deuteronomy 32:16–19; 1 Corinthians 10:20; and 1 Timothy 4:1 tell us clearly enough that demonic powers and intelligences are behind false religion, and even behind false theology in the church. The activities of Satan and demons are not given much press between the covers of Scripture and deservedly so, since the Bible is primarily about God and his acts and his kingdom and not about the other side. On the other hand, Paul can write that he and the early church were not ignorant of the Devil's schemes (2 Cor. 2:11). God in his wisdom has not left his people ignorant of those matters. At least, he has given his church the wherewithal, in the Bible and by his Spirit, to understand certain fundamental things about the Enemy and his ways. Demonic inspiration of false religion (which produces the sort of parallels we have considered, including the major paradigm in its pagan articulations) is one of the things that the Bible teaches quite clearly in the passages noted. Of course the church can, unfortunately and in spite of what Paul wrote, be ignorant of such matters, just as believers can be ignorant of any biblical truths that they may choose to ignore or happen not to know.

We said earlier in this work that the topic of the ancient Near Eastern divine assembly would not form a major topic of discussion for us, and it will not. It needs to be noted at this point, however, that in light of what Moses and Paul wrote about false religions, a proper understanding of the pagan pantheons is in order. A broad understanding is presented in the following schema.

Mesopotamia
An (supreme god)
Enlil (storm god)
Divine assembly
Humans

Canaan
El (supreme god)
Baal (storm god)
Divine assembly
Humans

Greece
Chronos (supreme god)
Zeus (storm god)
Divine assembly
Humans

Rome
Saturn (supreme god)
Jupiter (storm god)
Divine assembly
Humans

Biblical View
The Father (supreme God)
The Son (also God, of course, appearing in storm theophany)
Angelic assembly (e.g., Job 1–2)
Humans

The biblical view of reality presented above is paralleled by the pagan worldviews, which both predate and postdate the Bible. The ancient world understood that there was a supreme God, with whom all things originated and who held all authority and yet was relatively inactive in human affairs. But they also understood that there was another god, the storm god, who was indeed active among both divine and human affairs. A constitutional monarchy may present an analogy, in which the monarch theoretically holds authority and instructs the prime minister to form a government, but it is the prime minister who is truly active, who "gets things done." So it was in the ancient world with Enlil, Baal, Zeus, and Jupiter. To carry the analogy further, it may be that the Son is the one who is the more "active" person of the Trinity, the one who "gets things done" by the power of the Spirit working through him and who is associated with storm theophanies (e.g., Matt. 26:64).[2] In any case, the parallel that concerns us now is that which obtains between the pagan divine assemblies and the biblical assembly of angels, or "sons of God" (Job 1–2 RSV). Holy angels refuse human

---

2. Cf. Niehaus, *God at Sinai*, 333–84. To the extent that this analogy is true, of course, the Father does not hold a merely theoretical authority!

worship (cf. Rev. 19:10), but fallen angels clearly do not, as Moses and Paul have indicated. It seems reasonable to agree with these biblical writers, and such agreement leads us to understand that the common pagan theological structure presented above is a theological counterfeit not only endorsed by all ancient pagan thought, but imposed upon the ancients by the misleading inspiration of fallen angels (or, to use Paul's words to Timothy, "doctrines of demons," 1 Tim. 4:1 RSV).[3]

The Bible devotes the lion's share of its attention not to Satan and his works but to God and his works, and that is where our attention belongs as well. He is the one who, in his providential care for humanity, has allowed such theological parallels as we have explored to become manifest over many centuries in the ancient world so that truth would appear, even in darkened and polytheistic forms. Truth in such forms could have no saving power. But it did prepare a matrix of thought, a background of theological understanding, so that when God truly appeared and did such things as the pagans had claimed for their gods—instituting covenant, giving laws, commanding conquest and extending his kingdom, even by signs and wonders—his revelation would come to a people who had some theological preparation for it. In this way God was glorified even by the distortions of pagan religion, for even in their darkness the pagans had retained or obtained common grace reflections of his truth. It is the fuller revelation of that truth that now makes true life possible, and also makes possible all works of Christian theology. And the fuller revelation of that truth also encourages us to wait patiently until the God of truth does finally, on a day and hour that he knows, come back once and for all to restore all things.

---

3. Cf. the misleading guidance provided by a "lying spirit," or "spirit of deception," through the mouths of false prophets in 1 Kings 22.

Bibliography

Beale, G. K. *The Temple and the Church's Mission: A Biblical Theology of the Dwelling Place of God.* Downers Grove, IL: InterVarsity Press, 2004.

Block, D. I. *The Gods of the Nations: Studies in Ancient Near Eastern National Theology.* Evangelical Theological Society Monograph Series 2. Jackson, MS: Evangelical Theological Society, 1988.

Borger, Riekele. *Die Inschriften Asarhaddons Königs von Assyrien.* Archiv für Orientforschung: Beiheft 9. Graz, Austria: E. Weidner, 1957.

————. *Einleitung in die assyrischen Königsinschriften.* Erster Theil. Leiden, Netherlands: Brill, 1961.

Breasted, James H., ed. and trans. *Ancient Records of Egypt: History Documents from the Earliest Times to the Persian Conquest.* 5 vols. Chicago: University of Chicago Press, 1906.

————. *Development of Religion and Thought in Ancient Egypt.* Philadelphia: University of Pennsylvania Press, 1972.

Budge, E. A. Wallis. *The Book of the Dead.* New York: Random House, 1996.

Budge, E. A. Wallis, and L. W. King. *Annals of the Kings of Assyria.* Vol. 1. London: Harrison & Sons, 1902.

Calvin, John. *The Epistle of Paul the Apostle to the Hebrews and the First and Second Epistles of St. Peter.* Translated by William B. Johnston. Grand Rapids: Eerdmans, 1974.

Cassuto, Umberto. *Biblical and Oriental Studies.* Vol. 2. Jerusalem: Magnes, 1973.

Clifford, Richard J. *Creation Accounts in the Ancient Near East and in the Bible.* Catholic Biblical Quarterly Monograph Series 26. Washington, DC: Catholic Biblical Association of America, 1994.

Cogan, Morton. *Imperialism and Religion: Assyria, Judah and Israel in the Eighth and Seventh Centuries B.C.E.* Missoula, MT: Scholars Press, 1974.

Cooper, Jerrold S. *Sumerian and Akkadian Royal Inscriptions, I, Presargonic.* New Haven, CT: American Oriental Society, 1986.

Delitzsch, Friedrich. *Babel and Bible.* Edited by C. H. W. Johns. New York: B. P. Putnam's Sons, 1903.

Dickason, C. Fred. *Angels Elect and Evil.* Chicago: Moody, 1975.

Driver, G. R., and John C. Miles. *The Babylonian Laws.* Oxford: Clarendon, 1955.

Dumbrell, W. I. *Covenant and Creation.* Nashville: Thomas Nelson, 1984.

Eliot, George. *Middlemarch.* New York: New American Library, 1964.

Engnell, Ivan. *Studies in Divine Kingship in the Ancient Near East.* Oxford: Basil Blackwell, 1967.

Faulkner, R. O. *The Ancient Egyptian Pyramid Texts.* Oxford: Clarendon, 1969.

Fischer, Loren. *Ras Shamra Parallels.* Rome: Pontificum Institutum Biblicum, 1972.

Frankfort, Henri. *Kingship and the Gods.* Chicago: University of Chicago Press, 1948.

———. *The Problem of Similarity in Ancient Near Eastern Religions.* Oxford: Clarendon, 1951.

Frayne, Douglas R. *Old Babylonian Period.* The Royal Inscriptions of Mesopotamia, Early Periods 4. Toronto: University of Toronto Press, 1990.

Frazer, Sir James George. *Folk-lore in the Old Testament.* 3 vols. London: Macmillan, 1918.

———. *The Golden Bough.* Part 7: *Balder the Beautiful.* 2 vols. 1913. Reprint, New York: St. Martin's, 1990.

Gelb, Ignace J., et al., eds. *The Assyrian Dictionary of the Oriental Institute of the University of Chicago.* Chicago: Oriental Institute, 1958–2005.

Götze, Albrecht. *Die Annalen des Mursilis.* Darmstadt: Wissenschaftliche Buchgesellschaft, 1967.

Grayson, Albert Kirk. *Assyrian Rulers of the Early First Millennium B.C. I (1114–859 B.C.).* The Royal Inscriptions of Mesopotamia Assyrian Periods. Vol. 2. Toronto: University of Toronto Press, 1991.

————. *Assyrian Rulers of the Third and Second Millennia B.C. (to 1115 B.C.)*. The Royal Inscriptions of Mesopotamia Assyrian Periods. Vol. 1. Toronto: University of Toronto Press, 1987.

Green, Joel B., Scot McKnight, and I. Howard Marshall. *Dictionary of Jesus and the Gospels*. Downers Grove, IL: InterVarsity Press, 1991.

Green, W. M. "The Eridu Lament." *Journal of Cuneiform Studies* 30 (July 1978): 127–61.

————. "The Uruk Lament." *Journal of the American Oriental Society* 104, no. 2 (April–June 1984): 253–79.

Gunkel, Hermann. *Schöpfung und Chaos in Urzeit und Endzeit*. Göttingen: Vandenhoeck und Ruprecht, 1895.

Hall, Calvin S., and Gardner Lindzey. *Theories of Personality*. New York: John Wiley & Sons, 1957.

Harrison, R. K. *Introduction to the Old Testament*. Grand Rapids: Eerdmans, 1969.

Heidel, Alexander. *The Babylonian Genesis*. Chicago: University of Chicago Press, 1942.

————. *The Gilgamesh Epic and Old Testament Parallels*. Chicago: University of Chicago Press, 1946.

Huffmon, Herbert B. "The Covenant Lawsuit in the Prophets." *Journal of Biblical Literature* 78 (1959): 285–95.

Jacobsen, Thorkild. *The Treasures of Darkness*. New Haven, CT: Yale University Press, 1976.

Keil, C. F., and F. Delitzsch. *Jeremiah*. Vol. 8 of *Commentary on the Old Testament*. Grand Rapids: Eerdmans, 1977.

Kitchen, K. A. *Ancient Orient and Old Testament*. Downers Grove, IL: InterVarsity Press, 1973.

————. *The Bible in Its World*. Downers Grove, IL: InterVarsity Press, 1978.

Kline, Meredith G. *Images of the Spirit*. Grand Rapids: Baker, 1980.

————. *Treaty of the Great King*. Grand Rapids: Eerdmans, 1963.

Köhler, Joachim. *Wagner's Hitler: The Prophet and His Disciple*. Oxford: Blackwell, 2000.

Kramer, S. N. "Lamentation over the Destruction of Nippur: A Preliminary Report." *Eretz-Israel* 9 (1969): 89–93.

Kutscher, Raphael. *Oh Angry Sea*. New Haven, CT: Yale University Press, 1975.

Lambert, W. G. *Three Unpublished Fragments of the Tukulti-Ninurta Epic*.

Archiv für Orientforschung: Beiheft 18. Graz, Austria: E. Weidner, 1957–1958.

Liddell, Henry George, and Robert Scott. *A Greek-English Lexicon*. Oxford: Clarendon, 1974.

Longman, Tremper, III. *Fictional Akkadian Biography*. Winona Lake, IN: Eisenbrauns, 1991.

Luckenbill, Daniel David. *The Annals of Sennacherib*. The University of Chicago Oriental Institute Publications 2. Chicago: University of Chicago Press, 1924.

Michalowski, Piotr. *The Lamentation over the Destruction of Sumer and Ur*. Winona Lake, IN: Eisenbrauns, 1989.

Moran, William L. "A Note on the Treaty Terminology of the Sefire Stelas." *Journal of Near Eastern Studies* 22, no. 3 (July 1963): 174.

Mosse, George L. *The Crisis of German Ideology: Intellectual Origins of the Third Reich*. New York: Grosset and Dunlap, 1964.

Niehaus, Jeffrey J. "Amos." In *The Minor Prophets: An Exegetical and Expository Commentary*. Edited by Thomas Edward McComiskey. Grand Rapids: Baker, 1992.

———. *God at Sinai*. Grand Rapids: Zondervan, 1995.

———. "Joshua and Ancient Near Eastern Warfare." *Journal of the Evangelical Theological Society* 31, no. 1 (March 1988): 37–50.

———. "*Pa am Ehat* and the Israelite Conquest." *Vetus Testamentum* 30 (April 1980): 236–39.

Oppenheim, A. Leo. *Ancient Mesopotamia: Portrait of a Dead Civilization*. Chicago: University of Chicago Press, 1964.

Piepkorn, Arthur Carl. *Historical Prism Inscriptions of Ashurbanipal I*. Chicago: University of Chicago Press, 1933.

Polzin, Robert. *Moses and the Deuteronomist*. New York: Seabury, 1980.

Price, Ira M. *The Monuments and the Old Testament*. Philadelphia: Judson, 1925.

Pritchard, J. B., ed. *Ancient Near Eastern Texts Relating to the Old Testament*. 3rd ed. Princeton, NJ: Princeton University Press, 1969.

Rost, Paul. *Die Keilschrifttexte Tiglat-Pilesers III*. Bd. 1. Leipzig, Germany: Verlag von Eduard Pfeiffer, 1893.

Schramm, Wolfgang. "Die Annalen des Assyrischen Königs Tukulti-Ninurta II." *Bibliotheka Orientalis* 27, no. 3/4 (May–July 1970): 147–60.

———. *Einleitung in die assyrischen Königsinschriften*. Zweiter Theil. Leiden, Netherlands: Brill, 1973.

Seux, M. J. *Èpithètes Royales Akkadiennes et Sumériennes*. Paris: Letouzey et Ané, 1967.

Simpson, D. P. *Cassell's New Latin Dictionary*. New York: Funk & Wagnalls, 1960.

Simpson, William Kelley, ed. *The Literature of Ancient Egypt*. New Haven, CT: Yale University Press, 1972.

Sperber, J. "Der Personenwechsel in der Bibel." *Zeitschrift für Assyriologie* 21 (1918–1919): 23–33.

Tallqvist, Knut. *Akkadische Götterepitheta*. Leipzig, Germany: Harrassowitz, 1938.

Thompson, R. Campbell, and M. E. L. Mallowen. "The British Museum Excavations at Nineveh, 1931–1932." *University of Liverpool Annals of Archaeology and Anthropology* 20 (1933): 71–127.

Thureau-Dangin, François. *Die Sumerischen und Akkadischen Königsinschriften*. Leipzig, Germany: J. C. Hinrichs, 1907.

———. *Une Relation de la Huitième Campagne de Sargon*. Paris: Librarie Paul Geuthner, 1912.

Van Dijk, J. "Le motif cosmique dans la pensée sumeriénne." *Acta Orientalia* 28, no. 1–2 (1964): 1–59.

Walton, John H. *Ancient Near Eastern Thought and the Old Testament*. Grand Rapids: Baker, 2006.

Weidner, Ernst F. *Das Alter der mittelassyrischen Gesetzestexte*. Archiv für Orientforschung: Beiheft 12. Graz, Austria: E. Weidner, 1937–1939.

———. *Die Kämpfe Adadniraris I. gegen Hanigalbat*. Archiv für Orientforschung: Beiheft 5. Graz, Austria, 1928–1929.

———. *Politische Dokumente aus Kleinasien, die Staatsverträge in akkadischer Sprache aus dem Archiv von Boghazköi*. Leipzig, Germany: J. C. Hinrichs'sche Buchhandlung, 1923.

Whitehead, A. N. *Science and the Modern World*. New York: Free Press, 1967.

Wilson, John A. *The Burden of Egypt*. Chicago: University of Chicago Press, 1951.

Wiseman, D. J. "A New Stela of Assur-nasir-pal II." *Iraq* 14, no. 1 (1952): 24–44.

———. *The Vassal Treaties of Esarhaddon*. London: British School of Archaeology in Iraq, 1958.

Scripture Index

Subject Index